T0328561

Ten States, Five Dynasties, One Great Emperor

TEN STATES, FIVE DYNASTIES, ONE GREAT EMPEROR

HOW EMPEROR TAIZU UNIFIED CHINA IN THE SONG DYNASTY

HUNG HING MING

Algora Publishing
New York

Library of Congress Cataloging-in-Publication Data —

Hung, Hing Ming.
    Ten states, five dynasties, one great emperor : how Emperor Taizu unified China in
the Song Dynasty / Hung Hing Ming.
        pages cm
    Includes bibliographical references and index.
        ISBN 978-1-62894-072-5 (soft cover : alkaline paper) -- ISBN 978-1-62894-073-2
(hard cover : alkaliner) -- ISBN 781628940749 (ebook) 1. Song Taizu, Emperor of China,
927-976. 2. China--Kings and rulers--Biography. 3. China--History--Song dynasty, 960-
1279. I. Title.
    DS751.6.S98H86 2014
    951'.024092--dc23
    [B]
                                    2014025400

Table of Contents

INTRODUCTION

This book is about one of the greatest emperors in Chinese history, Zhao Kuang Yin (927–976), Emperor Taizu of the Song Dynasty (960–1279). Chinese historians have highly praised him because he unified China in the extremely chaotic period of "Five Dynasties and Ten States" (907–960). He brought peace and tranquility to the realm and saved the people from great sufferings.

By the end of the Tang Dynasty (Tang Dynasty: 618–907), the emperor was very weak and could not rule the country. Power was in the hands of the regional military governors, and popular uprisings were common. A famine in 875 devastated the eastern part of China. A man named Huang Chao led the hungry people in a revolt. In December of 880, Huang Chao seized control in Chang'an, the capital of the Tang Dynasty. The Emperor had to escape to Chengdu (now Chengdu, Sichuan Province). The regional military governors tried to defeat Huang Chao's army, but they could not.

However, one of Huang Chao's own generals, Zhu Wen, betrayed him and went over to the side of the Emperor. The Emperor granted him the name of Zhu Quan Zhong, "loyal to the court." Zhu Quan Zhong was instrumental in defeating Huang Chao's insurrectionists and became a powerful man. By the time Huang Chao's army was destroyed and he was killed, Zhu Quan Zhong already controlled a vast area in Central China. He gained so much power that he was able to force the Emperor of the Tang Dynasty to step down in 907. Zhu Quan Zhong took the throne himself and established the (Later) Liang Dynasty. He made his capital in Daliang (now Kaifeng, Henan Province). From then on, China entered into a period known as "Five Dynasties and Ten States" (907–960).

China was hopelessly divided and the wars were never-ending. In March 923, Li Cun Xu declared himself emperor of the (Later) Tang Dynasty. In October 923 he took Daliang and destroyed Zhu Quan Zhong's (Later) Liang Dynasty.

Emboldened, he then set his sights on Taiyuan.

In response, in May 936, Shi Jing Tang, the Regional Military Governor of Hedong (the area of Taiyuan, Shanxi Province), sought an alliance with the Emperor of the State of Khitan. He promised to cede to him sixteen prefectures including Youzhou (now the area around Beijing) and Yunzhou (now the area around Datong, Shanxi Province), so as to get the help from the State of Khitan to defeat the army of the (Later) Tang Dynasty. With the help of the State of Khitan, Shi Jing Tang defeated Li Cun Xu and his (Later) Tang army, and the Emperor of the State of Khitan named him Emperor of the (Later) Jin Dynasty. Now the tables were turned. Shi Jing Tang commanded his army and the Khitan army in a march south to Luoyang, the capital of the (Later) Tang Dynasty, and took it.

In June 942 the victorious Emperor Shi Jing Tang died. His eldest son Shi Cong Gui succeeded to the throne of the (Later) Jin Dynasty. However, he decided not to submit to the Emperor of the State of Khitan anymore. Rash decision. The Emperor of the State of Khitan commanded a great army to march south to Daliang, the capital of the (Later) Jin Dynasty. Shi Cong Gui realized his error, and he surrendered.

The Emperor of the State of Khitan changed the name of his state from the "State of Khitan" into the "State of Liao." The Emperor of the State of Liao did not enjoy the hot weather in Central China, so he went back to the north. Liu Zhi Yuan, the Regional Military Governor of Hedong, seized the chance to march his army to Daliang in June 947 and established himself as emperor of the (Later) Han Dynasty. But the next January Liu Zhi Yuan died. His son Liu Cheng You succeeded to the throne. In December 948, General Guo Wei forced Liu Cheng You to step down from the throne and promptly took his place. He established the (Later) Zhou Dynasty.

In this period, apart from the five dynasties in Central China, there were ten states in China. These ten states were: the State of Wu in the southeast part of China — later replaced by the State of Southern Tang; the State of Former Shu (in what is now Sichuan Province) — later replaced by the State of Later Shu; the State of Wuyue in what is now Zhejiang Province; the State of Chu in what is now Hunan Province; the State of Min in what is now Fujian Province; the State of Northern Han in what is now the area around Taiyuan, Shanxi Province; the State of Southern Han in what is now Guangdong Province; and the State of Nanping in what is now the southern part of Hubei Province.

Zhao Kuang Yin enters our story as an astute man who joined the army under General Guo Wei. When Guo Wei ascended the throne and established the (Later) Zhou Dynasty, Zhao Kuang Yin was promoted to the rank of commander under Guo Rong, the Emperor's adopted son. Emperor Guo Wei died in January 954. Guo Rong assumed the throne of the (Later) Zhou Dynasty in the same month. The valiant Zhao Kuang Yin took part in many great battles and expeditions commanded by Emperor Guo Rong, such as the great battle of Gaoping against the State of Northern Han, three expeditions against the State of Southern Tang, and the northern expedition against the State of Liao. In these battles and expeditions, Zhao Kuang Yin fought bravely and showed that he was a man of great ability. He was promoted to the highest military rank, that is, the Commander-in-chief of the Royal Guard Army.

In June 959 Emperor Guo Rong died. His seven-year-old son Guo Zong Xun inherited the throne of the (Later) Zhou Dynasty. Assuming this left the (Later) Zhou Dynasty in a weak position, in January 960 the army of the State of Liao invaded the northern border area. The young emperor ordered Zhao Kuang Yin to command a great army to march to the north to repel the attack. The army under Zhao Kuang Yin crossed the Yellow River and reached a place named Chenqiao, about twenty kilometers north of Daliang (now Kaifeng, Henan Province). Zhao Kuang Yin ordered the troops to camp in Chenqiao and he himself stayed in the Courier Station of Chenqiao. That night, the generals and officers decided to make Zhao Kuang Yin emperor because the present emperor was too young. At dawn the generals and officers entered the house where Zhao Kuang Yin was sleeping. They draped him with a yellow robe and forced him to accept the emperorship. When the army went back to Daliang, the capital, the generals and officers forced the young Guo Zong Xun to step down. Zhao Kuang Yin established the Song Dynasty, which lasted over 300 years and introduced important innovations to the world.

Emperor Zhao Kuang Yin knew very well the reason for the chaos in the period of the Five Dynasties: the regional military governors held too much military power. So Emperor Zhao Kuang Yin invited these powerful generals to a wine party. He allured them with the pleasures of a life of luxury, and succeeded in persuading them to reduce their own burdens by distributing the military power. In this way Emperor Zhao Kuang Yin tempered their power and removed their incentives to cause chaos. Tranquility settled over the realm.

Emperor Zhao Kuang Yin was determined to unify China. His policy was to try peaceful means before resorting to force. In this way he took control of the State of Nanping, the State of Chu, the State of Shu, the State of Southern Han, and the State of Jiangnan (originally the State of Southern Tang), one by one.

Emperor Zhao Kuang Yin was on the throne for seventeen years. He established the Song Dynasty which lasted for more than three hundred years. Historians commented that the Song Dynasty was as great as the Han Dynasty (Former Han Dynasty: 206 BC–AD 9; Later Han Dynasty: 25–220) and the Tang Dynasty (618–907).

Historians summed up his great contributions in the following words: He was draped with a yellow robe in the Courier Station of Chenqiao; this great man pacified the whole realm; this great Emperor sat on the throne in the golden palace in the Eastern Capital and he used his great power to unify China; he had done all he could to make the country prosperous.

Before his mother died, Emperor Zhao Kuang Yin made a vow to pass the throne to his younger brother Zhao Guang Yi. So when he died, he did not pass the throne to his son but he passed the throne to his younger brother Zhao Guang Yi.

After Zhao Guang Yi ascended the throne, he conquered the State of Northern Han. So the great cause of unification of China was completed. The following chapters will tell how this was all accomplished.

Statue of Zhao Kuang Yin, Emperor Taizu of the Song Dynasty, (927–976)

Map of China

Chapter One: Background: The Chaotic Period of Five Dynasties and Ten States (907–960)

1. The Five Dynasties

Late in the Tang Dynasty, during the reign of Emperor Li Xuan (862–888), the Tang Dynasty was very weak and the political and economic situation was getting out of control. The power that the Emperor should have wielded was in the hands of the regional military governors. A particularly harsh famine hit the east part of China in 875, leading a man named Huang Chao, an illegal salt dealer, to call for an uprising in the area of Caozhou (now Caoxian, in the west part of Shandong Province) in May. Tens of thousands of the hungry people joined his revolt. A man named Zhu Wen left his home in the area of Songzhou (now Shangqiu, in the east part of Henan Province) and joined in the uprising led by Huang Chao. He fought bravely and very soon was promoted to the commander of a detachment. In December 880, Huang Chao stormed Chang'an (now Chang'an, Shaanxi Province), the capital of the Tang Dynasty, and the city fell. The Emperor of the Tang Dynasty ran away to Chengdu (now Chengdu, Sichuan Province), and after entering Chang'an, Huang Chao declared himself Emperor of Qi.

Huang Chao thought highly of Zhu Wen's ability. He sent Zhu Wen to station his army near the bridge over the Weishui River (now Wei He River, Shaanxi Province) to the north of Chang'an. Zhuge Shuang, a general of the Tang Dynasty, stationed his army in Yueyang (now Yueyang, Shaanxi Province). Huang Chao gave Zhu Wen the task of persuading Zhuge Shuang to change sides. Zhu Wen went to Yueyang to talk with him, and he succeeded in persuading Zhuge Shuang to come over.

The next year, Huang Chao, Emperor of Qi, ordered Zhu Wen to lead an army to capture Nanyang (now Nanyang, in the west part of Henan Province). From then on, Huang Chao granted him the authority to attack any city he wanted. Zhu Wen attacked Zuopingyi (now Dali, Shaanxi Province) and took it. Wang Chong Rong, the Regional Military Governor of Hezhong area of the Tang Dynasty, decided to put an end to this. He commanded a great army to attack Zhu Wen, and Zhu Wen was defeated several times. Zhu Wen wrote several letters to Emperor Huang Chao, asking him to send reinforcements. But all the letters were detained by Meng Kai, the officer sent by Huang Chao to supervise Zhu Wen's army. Zhu Wen was informed that Huang Chao's power had been weakened and there was discord between Huang Chao and his generals. Then Zhu Wen knew that Huang Chao could not last long. So in September 883, Zhu Wen surrendered to Wang Chong Rong.

Wang Chong Rong immediately sent an envoy to Chengdu to report to Emperor Li Xuan of the Tang Dynasty that Zhu Wen had surrendered. When the Emperor got the report, he was very glad and said, "Heaven has sent him to me!" He immediately gave Zhu Wen the title of Grand General and granted him the name "Quan Zhong" (meaning "complete devotion"). From then on, Zhu Wen was Zhu Quan Zhong. The Emperor also appointed him Deputy Commander of Hezhong Command of the Tang Army for Suppressing the Rebellion. Now, Zhu Quan Zhong commanded his army together with the Tang army under Wang Chong Rong, the Regional Military Governor of Hezhong, in battles against Huang Chao's army and won many victories. In March 884, the Emperor of the Tang Dynasty appointed Zhu Quan Zhong Regional Military Governor of Xuanwu (governing Bianzhou area, the area which is now Kaifeng area, Henan Province) and told him that when the Bianzhou area was recovered, he could take his office in Daliang (now Kaifeng, Henan Province).

Li Ke Yong, a young man from the Shatuo Tribe (a sub tribe of the Western Turks), had an army in the area of Yanmen (now the area of Yanmen Guan, in the north part of Shanxi Province). The Emperor of the Tang Dynasty made him Military Governor of Yanmen and ordered him to lead his army to Chang'an to attack Huang Chao. Therefore, in December 882, Li Ke Yong commanded his army of forty thousand men to march from Yanmen to Hezhong Prefecture (now an area including Puzhou, Yong Ji, Hejin, Linyi, Wenxi and Yuncheng, in the southwest part of Shanxi Province). Then he commanded his army to cross the Yellow River to Xiayang (now Xiayang village, Heyang County, Shaanxi Province). By February 883, Li Ke Yong was able to march his army to Gankeng (in the southwest of Shayuan in the south of Dali, Shaanxi Province).

Shang Rang, a general under Huang Chao, stationed his army of one hundred fifty thousand men in Liangtianpo, which was not far from Gankeng. The next day, a great battle was fought, a battle that raged from noon to sunset. Li Ke Yong won a resounding victory. More than thirty thousand soldiers under Shang Rang were killed or captured. Then Li Ke Yong marched his army to attack Huazhou (now Huaxian, Shaanxi Province). In March Shang Rang commanded an army to rescue Huazhou, and a battle was fought, but Shang Rang was defeated again.

Then Li Ke Yong marched his army to the bridge over the Weishui River which was situated to the north of Chang'an. On April 4, Li Ke Yong commanded his army to fight Huang Chao's army in Weinan (now Weinan, Shaanxi Province). Three battles were fought in one day. Huang Chao's army was defeated and collapsed. On April 8, Li Ke Yong commanded his army to enter Chang'an through Guangtai Gate (the east gate of Chang'an). Huang Chao put up a strong resistance in the face of Li Ke Yong's army but failed. Then Huang Chao ordered his soldiers to set fire to the palaces, and the palaces were burned down to the ground. Huang Chao commanded his army to retreat to Lantian (now Lantian, Shaanxi Province) then into Shangshan Mountain (located in Shangluozhen, in the southeast of Shaanxi Province).

At that time, Li Ke Yong was only twenty-eight years old. He was the youngest among the generals, but he had played the greatest role in defeating Huang Chao and recovering the capital. In July the Emperor of the Tang Dynasty appointed him Regional Military Governor of Hedong (now the area around Taiyuan, Shanxi Province). In that same month, he went to Hedong to take up his appointment as regional military governor.

Zhu Quan Zhong (Huang Chao's former champion) and other generals also entered Chang'an. Then he commanded his army to march eastward. In July 883 he took Daliang (now Kaifeng, Henan Province). At that time Huang Chao's armies were still strong and controlled many areas. The Emperor of the Tang Dynasty appointed Zhu Quan Zhong the Commander of the Army of the Northeast Front.

The armies under Huang Chao were still strong. The Emperor of the Tang Dynasty ordered Li Ke Yong to reinforce the army to the south of the Yellow River. In February 884, Li Ke Yong commanded an army of fifty thousand men to cross the Yellow River to the south. Huang Chao had laid siege to Chenzhou (now Huaiyang, Henan Province) for a long time. Now, Zhu Quan Zhong and other generals marched south to rescue the city. On April 3, the armies under Zhu Quan Zhong took Taikang (now Taikang, Henan Province). When Huang Chao got the news that a great army was coming, he was afraid. He lifted his siege of Chenzhou and retreated to Guyangli, to the north.

Zhu Quan Zhong knew that Huang Chao was retreating northward and Daliang would be threatened, so he commanded his army to return to Daliang. Huang Chao heard that Li Ke Yong was coming. On May 3 Huang Chao commanded his army to march towards Bianzhou (now the area around Kaifeng, Henan Province). Shang Rang, the general under Huang Chao, commanded five thousand cavalrymen to march to Daliang. Zhu Quan Zhong sent an envoy to Li Ke Yong to ask him urgently to rescue Daliang. On May 6 Li Ke Yong caught up with Huang Chao in Wangmandu, where there was a ford on the Bianhe River, in Zhongmou (now Zhongmou, Henan

Province). Huang Chao's army was defeated. Shang Rang surrendered.

Huang Chao fled northward. Li Ke Yong gave hot pursuit and caught up with him in Fengqiu (now Fengqiu, Henan Province). On May 9, a battle was fought and Huang Chao was defeated again. Huang Chao with about a thousand men retreated to Yanzhou (now Yanzhou, Shandong Province). Li Ke Yong pursued them to Yuanju (in the northwest of Caoxian, Shandong Province), but only several hundred cavalrymen were following him. They were very tired and they ran out of food. Thus they had to give up their chase and turn back.

On May 14 Li Ke Yong made it back to Bianzhou and camped outside the city of Daliang. Zhu Quan Zhong invited Li Ke Yong to enter into the city, and Li Ke Yong and his followers stayed in Shangyuan Guesthouse. Zhu Quan Zhong gave a grand banquet to entertain Li Ke Yong. During the banquet, when Li Ke Yong was warm with the wine, he said to his host Zhu Quan Zhong, "What do you think you are? You were only a rebel under Huang Chao!" Needless to say, this made Zhu Quan Zhong very angry.

When the banquet was over late in the evening, nearly everyone was drunk. Li Ke Yong was helped back to the guesthouse by his guards. It was a night of heavy rain, with thunder and lightning. At midnight Zhu Quan Zhong commanded his army to attack the guesthouse. The war cries of Zhu Quan Zhong's soldiers shook the sky. But Li Ke Yong was too drunk to hear. His guards fought very furiously. One of his servants hid Li Ke Yong under the bed and splashed cold water in his face. Li Ke Yong opened his eyes and grabbed his sword and bow. Several soldiers under Zhu Quan Zhong were killed by Li Ke Yong's guards. Then fire and smoke rose everywhere in the guesthouse. Li Ke Yong and his guards broke through the encirclement. Some of his guards were killed. They clambered up the city wall and got down, outside the wall, using baskets and ropes.

When Li Ke Yong got back to his own camp, he wanted to launch an attack on Zhu Quan Zhong. His wife cautioned him, saying, "You have come here to suppress the rebels and rescue the generals in the east area. Now, Zhu Quan Zhong is not observing proper ethics and he's trying to kill you. You should lodge a complaint with the Emperor. If you decide by yourself to attack him, the people will not be able to tell who is right and who is wrong. And this will provide an excuse to Zhu Quan Zhong to attack you." Li Ke Yong took his wife's advice and led his army back to Jinyang (now Taiyuan, Shanxi Province) where the headquarters of his office as Regional Military Governor of Hedong were situated. From then, on Li Ke Yong and Zhu Quan Zhong became diehard enemies.

The year 994 was not over yet. In June General Li Shi Yue and Shang Rang pursued Huang Chao to Xiaqiu (in the northeast of Yanzhou, Shandong Province), and a battle was fought. Huang Chao was defeated; all his men were killed or had deserted. Huang Chao reached a valley named Langhugu. He told his nephew Lin Yan, "My head is worth a fortune. If you kill me and take my head to the emperor, you will be rewarded with wealth and high rank." But Lin Yan was not cold-hearted enough to kill his own heroic uncle. So Huang Chao killed himself with his own sword. Seeing this, Lin Yan went ahead and killed Huang Chao's brothers and wife and cut their heads from their bodies. He intended to go to General Shi Pu. But on his way, he ran into an army of Shatuo Tribe. They killed Lin Yan and took all the heads to present to General Shi Pu. Then General Shi Pu sent the heads of Huang Chao, his brothers, his wife and Lin Yan to Chengdu, to the Emperor of the Tang Dynasty. The Emperor held a grand ceremony on the Daxuan Tower of the city wall of Chengdu to receive these heads.

Although Huang Chao had died, Qin Zong Quan, the Regional Military Governor of Caizhou (now Runan, Henan Province), who had an army of over thirty thousand men, began to invade the neighboring prefectures. His army looted and killed the people cruelly. In spring 886, Qin Zong Quan occupied Ruzhou (now Linru, Henan Province), Luoyang (now Luoyang, Henan Province), Huaizhou (now Qinyang, Henan Province), Mengzhou (now Mengxian, Henan Province), Tangzhou (now Biyang, Henan Province), Dengzhou (now Dengxian, Henan Province), Xuzhou (now Xuchang, Henan Province), and Zhengzhou (now Zhengzhou, Henan Province). He had amassed a vast territory in central China. The regional military governors began to attack each other and China was still in great chaos.

In January 885, Emperor Li Xuan of the Tang Dynasty returned from Chengdu to Chang'an, the capital of the Tang Dynasty, but on 2 March 888, he fell ill. Three days later Emperor Li Xuan appointed his younger brother Li Jie as successor to the throne, and on 6 March, Emperor Li Xuan died at the age of twenty-seven. He left an imperial order that his brother Li Jie should change his name to Li Min, showing that a new era was beginning, and take his place. Li Min ascended the throne of the Tang Dynasty that very day.

In August 888, Zhu Quan Zhong defeated the rapacious Qin Zong Quan. Qin Zong Quan gave up all the sites he had occupied and fled for his life. Zhu Quan Zhong, who had tried to kill Li Ke Yong after getting him drunk at the banquet, took all these places and sent generals to defend them. The unfortunate Qin Zong Quan was captured in December 888 by one of his subordinate generals, who turned him in to Zhu Quan Zhong. Zhu Quan Zhong in turn presented Qin Zong Quan to Emperor Li Min of the Tang Dynasty in February 889. Qin Zong Quan was executed. The Emperor made Zhu Quan Zhong King of Dongping (meaning the king who pacified the east part of China) in recognition of his contributions in defeating Qin Zong Quan.

In May 889 Li Ke Yong raised a great army and ordered Generals Li Kan Zhi and Li Cun Xiao to command this great army in an attack on Meng Fang Li, the Governor of Mingzhou (now Yongnian, Hebei Province). In June they took Cizhou (now Cixian, Hebei Province) and Mingzhou. Meng Fang Li sent two generals commanding over thirty thousand men to fight against Li Ke Yong's army, but they were defeated. Exploiting this victory, Li Ke Yong attacked Xingzhou (now Xingtai, Hebei Province). Meng Fang Li felt so ashamed that he killed himself by taking poison. His younger brother Meng Qian sent an envoy to Zhu Quan Zhong to ask for help.

Zhu Quan Zhong asked Luo Hong Xin, the Regional Military Governor of Weizhou (now Daming, Hebei Province) and Bozhou (now Liaocheng, Shandong Province), for permission to let his army to pass Weizhou to rescue Xingzhou. Luo Hong Xin refused to give such permission. Zhu Quan Zhong had to send a general and several hundred elite troops by back roads to Xingzhou. Li Ke Yong attacked Xingzhou fiercely in January 890. Meng Qian could not withstand the attack and had to surrender to Li Ke Yong, even handing over the general and all the soldiers sent by Zhu Quan Zhong. In February the heady Li Ke Yong attacked Yunzhou (now Datong, Shanxi Province) and took the eastern part of the city.

He Lian Duo, the commander of the army defending Yunzhou, filed a memorandum to the Emperor asking him to launch a punitive expedition against Li Ke Yong. Zhu Quan Zhong also filed a memorandum to the Emperor stating that Li Ke Yong would cause great trouble to the Tang Dynasty, and he asked permission to unite with Li Kuang Wei, Regional Military Governor of Lulong (in the north part of Hebei Province), Wang Rong, Regional Military Governor of Chengde (in the northwest part of Hebei Province) and Luo Hong Xin, Regional Military Governor of Weizhou and Bozhou (in the south of Hebei Province and northwest of Shandong Province) to attack Li Ke Yong. In May, the Emperor issued an imperial order to deprive Li Ke Yong of all the titles granted to him and deployed forces to attack Li Ke Yong. In October, Zhu Quan Zhong sent an envoy to Luo Hong Xin, Regional Military Governor of Weizhou and Bozhou, to ask once again for permission to take his army past Weizhou to attack Li Ke Yong. Again Luo Hong Xin refused. This time, Zhu Quan Zhong commanded an army to cross the Yellow River from Liyang (now Xunxian, Henan Province) to attack Weizhou. Five battles were fought in January 891 between the army under Luo Hong Xin and the army under Zhu Quan Zhong. Zhu Quan Zhong won every time. Luo Hong Xin finally read the tea leaves and submitted to Zhu Quan Zhong. From then on Weizhou and Bozhou were under Zhu Quan Zhong's jurisdiction.

Li Ke Yong sent an envoy to Chang'an to lodge a memorandum to the Emperor, stating: "Everyone knows that there is a deep-seated hatred between Zhu Quan Zhong and me. Now I have been deprived of all my titles. I am regarded as a criminal. I dare not go back the place where I was made regional military governor. I have no place to go. I will stay for now in the area of Hezhong, awaiting further instructions from Your Majesty." After reading the memorandum, the Emperor had pity on him and issued an imperial order to grant him all his titles again, and allowed Li Ke Yong to go back to Jinyang to be the Regional Military Governor of Hedong.

On 5 May 895, Li Mao Zhen, Regional Military Governor of Fengxiang (now the area around Fengxiang, Shaanxi Province), Wang Xing Yu, Regional Military Governor of Binning (now the area around Binxian, Shaanxi

Province), and Han Jian, Regional Military Governor of Zhenguo (Huazhou, now the area around Huaxian, Shaanxi Province), each commanding several thousand cavalrymen, converged on Chang'an, the capital of the Tang Dynasty, and arrayed their impressive army under the city wall. The Emperor of the Tang Dynasty ascended the city wall to address them and said, "You have not sent me any request, and you have commanded armies to the capital without my permission. What are you seeking?" Han Jian replied, "Wang Xing Yu wanted to be named Premier, but he was refused the position. Liangyuan Town is near Binzhou. Wang Xing Yu wanted to put this town under his jurisdiction. I wanted Heyang to be put under my jurisdiction. But our requests have been turned down by the eunuchs around Your Majesty." Hearing this, the Emperor let them into the city and held a banquet to entertain them. But apparently they did not drink enough.

On that day Wang Xing Yu killed many officials and eunuchs. Further, he joined Li Mao Zhen and Han Jian in conspiring to depose Emperor Li Min and put Li Bao, King of Ji, on the throne of the Tang Dynasty.

Li Ke Yong, once again Regional Military Governor of Hedong, commanded a great army to march southward. Of the three conspirators, Li Mao Shen turned back to Fengxiang, Wang Xing Yu turned back to Binzhou, and Han Jian turned back to Huazhou, each leaving two thousand men to defend the capital. Wang Xing Yue, Wang Xing Yu's younger brother, was the Regional Military Governor of Kuangguo. He tried to hold off Li Ke Yong's army. A battle was fought in Zhaoyi (now Zhaoyi, Shaanxi Province). Wang Xing Yue was defeated and on 4 July he reached Chang'an, the capital. Wang Xing Shi, Wang Xin Yue's younger brother, was the commander of the Left Army of the Royal Guards. Wang Xing Shi reported to the Emperor that Li Ke Yong's army was coming and recommended that Emperor Li Min go to Binzhou. But Li Ji Peng, Li Mao Zhen's adopted son, was the commander of the Right Army of the Royal Guards. He conspired to kidnap the Emperor and take him to Li Mao Zhen, who had now reached Fengxiang. Then Wang Xing Shi commanded the Left Army of the Royal Guards to attack the Right Army of the Royal Guards. The beating of the drums and war cries shook the sky. When the Emperor understood that two armies were fighting, he went up the Chengtian Tower of the palace wall and tried his best to stop the fighting. Li Jun, the head of the Bodyguards of the Emperor, commanded the soldiers under him to defend the Emperor. Li Ji Peng commanded the army of Fengxiang to attack the soldiers under Li Jun. Meanwhile the officials helped the Emperor down from the tower. Li Ji Peng ordered his soldiers to set fire to the gates of the palace. The fire and smoke billowed high overhead.

At that time, an army of Yanzhou was stationed in the capital. Emperor Li Min ordered this army to come to his rescue. When they arrived, Li Ji Peng commanded his army back to Fengxiang and Wang Xing Shi commanded his army back to Binzhou. There was mayhem in the city. The Emperor and his relatives escaped to the camp of Li Jun's army. Then came news that Wang Xing Yu and Li Mao Zhen were on their way to meet the Emperor.

The Emperor was afraid that he would be kidnapped by them, so on 6 July, protected by the bodyguards under Li Jun, the Emperor and his relatives left Chang'an by the south gate and went into the Nanshan Mountains ("Southern Mountains"), now Zhongnan Shan Mountain, Shaanxi Province. That night they stayed in Shacheng Town in the mountains. Li Ke Yong reached Tongzhou (now Dali, Shaanxi Province) on 7 July. Two days later the Emperor moved to Shimen Town in the Nanshan Mountains.

On 12 July the Emperor sent an envoy to Li Ke Yong to ask him to go to Xinping so as to stop Wang Xing Yu's army from coming to the capital from Binzhou. The Emperor also ordered Zhang Dang, the Regional Military Governor of Zhangyi, to lead his army in Jingyuan (now Jingyang, Shaanxi Province) to stop Li Mao Zhen's army from coming to the capital from Fengxiang. On 6 August, Li Ke Yong marched his army to the Bridge over the Weishui River (north of Chang'an). On 8 August Li Ke Yong sent General Shi Yan to command three thousand cavalrymen to Shimen Town to protect the Emperor.

Li Mao Zhen had had enough. He killed Li Ji Peng and sent an envoy to present Li Ji Peng's head to Emperor Li Min. He begged the Emperor to pardon him and asked to make peace with Li Ke Yong. The Emperor sent an envoy to Li Ke Yong to ask him to spare Li Mao Zhen and concentrate his army to attack Wang Xing Yu. Then Li Ke Yong wrote a memorandum to the Emperor inviting the Emperor to go back to Chang'an, the capital. Li Ke Yong stationed three thousand cavalrymen along the Weishui River (now Wei He River, Shaanxi Province) to prevent a sudden attack from the north. On 28 August the Emperor returned to the capital. Mopping up, in September Li Ke Yong commanded his army to attack Binzhou. Wang Xing Yu gave up the city and fled. When Wang Xing Yu entered the area of Qingzhou (now Qingyang, Gansu Province), he was killed by his own men. His head was presented to the Emperor in Chang'an. In December, in order to reward Li Ke Yong for his great deeds, the Emperor made him King of Jin.

On 6 November 898, Liu Ji Shu (a eunuch), the commander of the Left Army of the Royal Guards, and Wang Zhong Xian (also a eunuch), commander of the Right Army of the Royal Guards, conspired with each other and kidnapped Emperor Li Min and put him under house arrest in the Eastern Palace. They made Li Yu, the Emperor's son, the emperor of the Tang Dynasty with a sham imperial order from Emperor Li Min.

Liu Ji Shu sent his adopted son Liu Xi Du to Daliang to see Zhu Quan Zhong. In exchange for Zhu Quan Zhong's support, he promised to offer the Jade Seal of the Tang Dynasty; the bronze Tripod of the Tang Dynasty. (Usually kept in the ancestral temple of the royal clan, the tripod was a token representing the dynasty itself. As long as the tripod existed, the dynasty existed. If the tripod was lost, it augured the end of the dynasty.) He even offered the throne of the Tang Dynasty to Zhu Quan Zhong. Then Liu Ji Shu sent Li Feng Ben to Daliang to show Zhu Quan Zhong the sham imperial order. Zhu Quan Zhong hesitated. He was very much tempted to accept the offers. He called in his subordinates to discuss this matter. One of them, Li Zhen noted, "Now the eunuchs have started a rebellion against the Emperor and have put him under house arrest. If you can't put down their rebellion, you will not be able to control the local kings who have grown in power." This observation helped Zhu Quan Zhong realize that he should resolutely refuse Liu Ji Shu's offers, and he sent Li Zhen to Chang'an to secretly discuss with Cui Yun, the Prime Minister, arrangements to kill Liu Ji Shu and Wang Zhong Xian.

Accordingly, on January 1 in 899, Prime Minister Cui Yun secretly ordered General Sun De Zhao, the commander of the Emperor's bodyguards, to kill Liu Ji Shu and Wang Zhong Xian. General Sun De Zhao succeeded in killing them both, and he escorted Emperor Li Min back to the throne. In order to reward Zhu Quan Zhong for loyalty and his invaluable work in crushing the rebellion, the Emperor made him King of Liang.

Now, in returning Emperor Li Min to the throne, Zhu Quan Zhong intended to put the head of the Tang Dynasty under his strict control. He presented several memorandums to the Emperor suggesting that he should move the capital to Luoyang, which was not far from Kaifeng. He sent some officials to Luoyang to repair the palaces. In April 904, Zhu Quan Zhong presented a memorandum to the Emperor stating that the palaces in Luoyang had been beautifully restored and urging the Emperor to start his journey to Luoyang. The Emperor knew that Zhu Quan Zhong did not mean well by suggesting such a move, but he had no means to counter the pressures brought to bear by Zhu Quan Zhong. So with a heavy heart, the Emperor had to go to Luoyang, with the Empress and the whole royal clan.

Zhu Quan Zhong of course had an ambition to take over the Tang Dynasty from Emperor Li Min. He knew that the Emperor would not simply abdicate and hand over the throne; so he decided to get rid of him and put a young and inexperienced emperor in place so that he could get the throne more easily. Zhu Quan Zhong sent Li Zhen to Louyang to arrange the assassination of Emperor Li Min. Indeed, in August 904 Emperor Li Min was assassinated in the bed chamber in the palace in Luoyang. Emperor Li Min's ninth son Li Zuo was ordered to change his name to Li Zhu, and he was put on the throne at the age of thirteen.

1.1 The (Later) Liang Dynasty

Before three years had passed, the young Emperor Li Zhu sent a minister to see Zhu Quan Zhong. He told him that he intended to abdicate and hand the throne to Zhu Quan Zhong. Zhu Quan Zhong coyly demurred. The minister went back to report to the Emperor. A month later, in February, the Emperor again offered to abdicate and hand over the throne to Zhu Quan Zhong. This time, all the ministers went to Daliang to talk to Zhu Quan Zhong about it. Again he gracefully declined the offer. In March the Emperor of the Tang Dynasty sent the same minister, Xue Yi Ju, to persuade Zhu Quan Zhong to accept the offer. This time Zhu Quan Zhong acceded to the wishes of the Emperor and his ministers and at last accepted the offer. Then Li Zhu, Emperor of the Tang Dynasty, issued an imperial edict stating in effect that he would abdicate in favor of Zhu Quan Zhong.

On 14 April 907, wearing the dragon robe of an emperor, Zhu Quan Zhong ascended the throne in Jinxiang Hall of the palace in Daliang. He changed the name of the dynasty to the Great Liang Dynasty. (Historians call this the "Later Liang Dynasty" so as to distinguish it from the Liang Dynasty established by Xiao Yan and which lasted from 502 to 557.) The Emperor of the Liang Dynasty then gave Li Zhu the kingship of Jiyin. The new Emperor moved quickly; that same month he issued an imperial order to deprive Li Ke Yong of all the titles the Emperor of the Tang Dynasty had granted him.

Portrait of Zhu Quan Zhong, Emperor Taizu of the (Later) Liang Dynasty

In the northeast part of China, along the upper reaches of the Liaohe River (now in Liaoning Province of China), there lived a tribe called the Khitan. The Tribe of the Khitans was divided into eight sub tribes. In 907 Yelu Abaoji, the King of the Khitans, defeated the other seven sub tribes and unified the whole Khitan Tribe. He then took over the area where the Jurchen Tribe lived. Next he occupied the area where the Turks lived. He established a vast State of Khitan covering the area of what are now Liaoning Province, Jilin Province, Heilongjian Province, the Inner Mongolia Autonomous Region of China and the eastern part of Mongolia. He declared himself Emperor of the

State of Khitan. In May, Yelu Abaoji sent an envoy to Daliang to establish a friendly relationship with the Later Liang Dynasty.

On 1 January 908, Li Ke Yong fell seriously ill. Feeling that death was near, he appointed his eldest son Li Cun Xu as his successor to the throne as the King of Jin. He said to the ministers around him, "This young man has great ambition. I am sure he will achieve the goal I am fighting for. I hope you will assist him to achieve my goal." On 4 January Li Ke Yong died in Jinyang at the age of fifty-three, and Li Cun Xu became King of Jin in Jinyang at the age of twenty-four.

On 26 April 908 Li Cun Xu, the new King of Jin, led an army to Huangnian, which was twenty-two kilometers away from Luzhou (now Changzhi, Shanxi Province). A great army of the Later Liang Dynasty was stationed there. On 1 May Li Cun Xu launched a surprise attack and the Later Liang army was defeated. More than ten thousand of its soldiers were killed.

In January 909, the Emperor of the Later Liang Dynasty moved his capital from Daliang (now Kaifeng, Henan Province) to Luoyang (now Luoyang, Henan Province). He made Daliang the Eastern Capital. He appointed his adopted son Zhu You Wen, King of Bo, as the commander-in-chief of the army stationed in the Eastern Capital.

In May 912, the Emperor of the Later Liang Dynasty fell ill himself, in Luoyang. He had four sons: the eldest son, Zhu You Yu, had died early; the second was his adopted son Zhu You Wen, and the Emperor of the Later Liang Dynasty loved him best; the third son was Zhu You Gui and the fourth son was Zhu You Zhen. Aware that the Emperor intended to pass the throne to his adopted son, the third son, Zhu You Gui, and some soldiers under him broke into the Emperor's bed chamber at midnight on 2 June and murdered him. They kept the death of the Emperor secret; and Zhu You Gui fabricated an imperial order commanding Zhu You Zhen to kill Zhu You Wen in the Eastern Capital. Once he received word that Zhu You Wen had been killed, on 5 June Zhu You Gui announced the death of his father and ascended the throne of the Later Liang Dynasty. Zhu Quan Zhong's temple title was Taizu (meaning Supreme Ancestor, in other words, the founder) of the Liang Dynasty.

In February 913 Zhu You Zhen, the fourth son of the late Emperor, secretly planned with General Yuan Xiang Xian, who was a nephew of the late Emperor, to kill Zhu You Gui. On 17 February the General commanded several thousand soldiers to break into the palace in Luoyang, and Zhu You Gui was duly assassinated. General Yuan Xiang Xian brought the imperial jade seal of the Liang Dynasty back to Daliang. He and other ministers and generals planned to escort Zhu You Zhen to Luoyang to take the throne there, but Zhu You Zhen said, "Daliang is the place where the Great Liang Dynasty was established. There is no need to go to Luoyang." And he ascended the throne of the Later Liang Dynasty in Daliang.

Weizhou was a rich and strong prefecture, and Yang Shi Hou, the regional military governor of Weizhou and Bozhou became bold and ambitious. In March 915, he met an untimely death. The Emperor of the Later Liang Dynasty took this chance to reduce the power of that position by dividing the generals and soldiers and the contents of the treasury of Weizhou in two. One part would be sent to Xiangzhou (now Anyang, Henan Province), and one part would stay in Weizhou. The generals and soldiers were shocked by the court's decision. The soldiers of Weizhou began to riot, looting and robbing people in the streets. They kidnapped He De Lun, the newly appointed Regional Military Governor of Weizhou and Bozhou. The Emperor sent General Liu Xun with an army to suppress the riots.

The soldiers of Weizhou forced He De Lun to send a letter to Li Cun Xu, King of Jin, to ask for help. When Li Cun Xu got the letter, he sent an army to Weizhou. On 1 June He De Lun and the generals and soldiers of Weizhou opened the city gate and invited Li Cun Xu in. Then He De Lun presented the seal of the regional military governor to Li Cun Xu. He accepted the seal, and from then on, Weizhou and Bozhou were under the control of Li Cun Xu.

1.2 The (Later) Tang Dynasty

In March 923 Li Cun Xu, King of Jin, ordered that an altar be built to the south of the city of Weizhou (now Daming, Hebei Province). On 25 April, he went up to the altar. In a grand ceremony, sacrifices were offered to Heavens. Then Li Cun Xu ascended the throne and declared himself emperor. The name of the dynasty Li Cun Xu established was the Great Tang Dynasty. Historians called this dynasty the "Later Tang Dynasty" so as to distinguish it from the Tang Dynasty established by Li Yuan, which lasted from 618 to 907. He made Weizhou the Eastern Capital and Taiyuan the Western Capital.

Li Cun Xu was on a winning streak. On 2 October 923, now the Emperor of the Later Tang Dynasty, he commanded a great army to cross the Yellow River from Yangliu (now Dong'e, Shandong Province). He reached Yùnzhou (now Yuncheng, Shandong Province) the next day. He sent Li Si Yuan, an adopted son of Li Ke Yong, to command an army as the vanguards. The great army of the Later Tang Dynasty marched towards Daliang, the capital of the Later Liang Dynasty, defeating all the Later Liang armies on its way. The Emperor of the Later Liang Dynasty did not have enough military strength to stop the advancing army; there was nothing he could do about it. He wept all day long.

Emperor Zhu You Zhen kept the imperial seal in his bed chamber. But one day he saw that it was missing. Some minister had stolen it, to hand it over to the Emperor of the Later Tang Dynasty. The enemy army was very close to Daliang. The Emperor said to Huang Pu Lin, the commander of his bodyguards, "The family of Zhu and the family of Li are die-hard enemies. I cannot surrender to Li Cun Xu. And I will not be killed by him. Now, you may kill me with your sword." Huang Pu Lin hesitated for some time. The Emperor urged him to act. Thus the very man who was devoted to protecting the Emperor of the Later Liang Dynasty had to kill him; and then he killed himself with his own sword. On the morning of 9 October, the Later Tang army under Li Si Yuan reached Daliang and attacked Fengqiu Gate of the city wall. The general defending Daliang opened the gate and let Li Si Yuan and his army in. On the same day Li Cun Xu, Emperor of the Later Tang Dynasty, entered the city of Daliang.

Portrait of Li Cun Xu, Emperor Zhuangzong of the (Later) Tang Dynasty

On 12 November 923, the Emperor of the Later Tang Dynasty issued an imperial order stating that he had decided to move to Luoyang; he would start his journey to Luoyang on 24 November. On that day, the imperial carriages carrying Emperor Li Cun Xu and the royal clan started out from Daliang. On 1 December, the Emperor of the Later Tang Dynasty reached Luoyang. A grand ceremony was held to welcome the Emperor into the palaces.

On 1 February 926, the soldiers of Weizhou who were stationed in Beizhou (now Qinghe, Hebei Province) rioted. They forced Zhao Zai Li to be their leader. Then this rioting army looted the city of Beizhou and set fire to it. They marched southward to Linqing (now Linqing, Hebei Province), then to Guantao (now Guantao, Hebei Province), looting on their way. On 5 February, the rioting army entered Weizhou (Now Daming, Hebei Province), which Emperor Li Cun Xu of the Later Tang Dynasty had renamed as Yedu. On 8 February the Emperor sent Li Shao Rong, the Regional Military Governor of Guide, to command three thousand cavalrymen to Yedu to put down the rioting army. Li Shao Rong started to attack Yedu on 13 February but he could not capture it. On 26 February the Emperor sent Li Si Yuan to attack Yedu. He reached the outskirts on 6 March. The army under Li Si Yuan pitched their camps to the southwest of the city. On 8 February, Li Si Yuan issued an order to attack the city the next morning. But that night Zhang Po Bai, a sergeant, ordered the soldiers under him to rebel. They killed their generals and set fire to the camps. Li Si Yuan went to persuade the rebelling soldiers to calm down, but he was pushed by the rebelling soldiers into the city of Yedu. Zhao Zai Li, the commander of the rioting army in Yedu, welcomed Li Si Yuan. Li Si Yuan said to him, "The success of a cause depends on the number of troops. I will go out to gather all the soldiers under me and place them under you." Zhao Zai Li agreed and let him go out of the city of Yedu.

That night Li Si Yuan stayed in Weixian (now Weixian, Hebei Province). The soldiers under Li Si Yuan gradually gathered together again. Li Shao Rong retreated to Weizhou (now Weihui, in the northeast part of Henan Province). He sent a report to the Emperor that Li Si Yuan had been defected and joined the rebellion. Li Si Yuan sent envoys to the Emperor to explain the situation, but they could not reach the Emperor because Li Shao Rong intercepted every one of them.

Li Si Yuan was trapped. General Shi Jing Tang, his son-in-law, said to him, "You have entered the city of the rebels. The Emperor suspects that you have joined in the rebellion. You will be punished for it. Hesitation is harmful to a military commander. If you decide to take action, you should act resolutely. Daliang is a great city. I am willing to command three hundred cavalrymen to take Daliang. Then you may enter Daliang as soon as possible."

Li Si Yuan quickly assigned three hundred cavalrymen to Shi Jing Tang. With Shi Jing Tang in command, the three hundred cavalrymen crossed the Yellow River from Liyang (now Xunxian, Henan Province), and then marched to Daliang. They attacked Daliang from the west gate and broke into the city and took it. On 26 March Li Si Yuan entered Daliang. At that time the Emperor of the Later Tang Dynasty, commanding an army of twenty five thousand men had reached Rongze, a place just five kilometers from Daliang. When he learned that Li Si Yuan had entered Daliang, he sent a general to lead an army to attack Daliang. But this general betrayed the Emperor and sided with Li Si Yuan. Li Cun Xu, the Emperor of the Later Tang Dynasty, had to go back to Luoyang.

On 1 April 926, the Emperor of the Later Tang Dynasty prepared to march from Luoyang to the east. The cavalry had lined up outside Xuanjiao Gate (the east gate of Luoyang Palace) and the foot soldiers had lined up outside Wufeng Gate (one of the south gates of Luoyang Palace), waiting for the Emperor. Guo Cong Qian, a commander of the cavalry, ordered the cavalry under him to rush out from their camp and attack Xingjiao Gate (one of the south gates of Luoyang Palace). At that time the Emperor was dining in the palace. When he heard of the attack, he commanded his guards to resist the attackers. But the rebelling soldiers set fire to Xingjiao Gate. Then they climbed up the palace wall and entered the palace itself. The Emperor was shot by an arrow and was killed. The rebelling soldiers looted the city and set fire to the city. Luoyang was in great chaos.

When Li Si Yuan heard that Li Cun Xu had been murdered, he cried bitterly. On 3 April 936, he commanded an army to march to Luoyang. He stopped the looting, and peace and order was resumed. The ministers of the Later Tang Dynasty presented letters to ask Li Si Yuan to be the Protector. On 8 April, Li Si Yuan accepted the position. On 12 April, the Protector appointed Shi Jing Tang the Commander-in-chief of the army in Shanzhou (now Shanxian, in the west part of Henan Province). On 20 April, Li Si Yuan claimed the throne of the Later Tang Dynasty at the age of sixty. Li Cun Xu, the late emperor, was given the temple title of Zhuangzong (meaning Solemn Ancestor) of the (Later) Tang Dynasty.

In July 926, Yelu Abaoji, Emperor of the Khitans, died in Fuyu City during an expedition against the Koguryo, and this left his power in the hands of his wife Empress Shulu. In September, Empress Shulu made her second son Yelu Deguang Emperor of the Khitans.

In November 933, the northern tribes moved to the northern borders of the Later Tang Dynasty. In order to prevent their invasion, the Emperor of the Later Tang Dynasty appointed Shi Jing Tang as the Commander-in-chief of the army in Northern Capital (Taiyuan), Regional Military Governor of Hedong, and the Commander-in-chief of the armies in Datong (now Datong, Shanxi Province), Zhenwu (now the area around Hohhot and Horinger of Inner Mongolia Autonomous Region) and Zhangguo (now around Yunyuan, in the north part of Shanxi Province). Shi Jing Tang went to Jinyang (now Taiyuan, Shanxi Province) to take the office of the Regional Military Governor of Hedong. Liu Zhi Yuan, a general under Shi Jing Tang, was entrusted to take care of all the important matters in the office of the Regional Military Governor of Hedong.

The Emperor of the Later Tang Dynasty had several sons: the first son was Li Cong Rong, who was made King of Qin and was appointed a high ranking position in charge of confidential affairs in the court; the third son was Li Cong Hou, who was made King of Song and was appointed Regional Military Governor of Ye, so he stayed in Yedu (now Daming, Hebei Province). Li Cong Rong was a proud, hot headed and unruly man, but Li Cong Hou was a quiet and staid man, so the ministers in the court spoke highly of Li Cong Hou. Li Cong Rong felt that Li Cong Hou was a threat to him and was always on guard against him.

On 17 November 933, the Emperor of the Later Tang Dynasty was gravely ill. Li Cong Rong went to see his father. The Emperor could not even raise his head. When Li Cong Rong left the bed chamber, he heard the weeping of the maids attending the Emperor. Li Cong Rong thought that his father had died. But that night the Emperor felt better and asked the maids to serve him food. Li Cong Rong did not know this. His only worry was that he could not succeed to the throne because the ministers in the court disliked him. So on 20 November he commanded an army of a thousand men to line up in battle formation outside the palace. The general of the soldiers guarding the palace reported to the Emperor that Li Cong Rong had organized troops outside the palace and was ready to attack. The Emperor was both sad and angry, and he entrusted the commander of the royal guards to suppress Li Cong Rong's rebellion. The commander sent six hundred cavalrymen to attack the rebel troops; and Li Cong Rong was killed. On 21 November the Emperor sent an envoy to Yedu (now Daming, Hebei Province) to summon Li Cong Hou to Luoyang. On 26 November, Emperor Li Si Yuan died at the age of sixty-seven. Li Cong Hou arrived in Luoyang three days later. On 1 December he ascended the throne of the Later Tang Dynasty.

Li Cong Ke was an adopted son of Li Si Yuan. He had fought very fearlessly for the establishment of the Later Tang Dynasty and done many great deeds. During the reign of Emperor Li Si Yuan, Li Cong Ke served as Regional Military Governor of Fengxiang (now Fengxiang, Shaanxi Province) in 928 and was made King of Lu in 929. His eldest son Li Zhong Ji was the commander-in-chief of the Royal Guards of Emperor Li Si Yuan. But after Li Cong Hou ascended the throne, he sent Li Zhong Ji out of the capital and appointed him Commander-in-chief of the army in Bozhou (now Bozhou, Anhui Province). From this Li Cong Ke knew that Emperor Li Cong Hou was suspicious of him because he, too, had many achievements to his name. In February 934, the Emperor appointed Li Cong Ke Regional Military Governor of Hedong and ordered him to leave Fengxiang. Li Cong Ke understood that the Emperor was planning to reduce his power, and so he refused to go. The Emperor sent a great army to attack Fengxiang. On 15 March the army sent by Emperor Li Cong Hou began to attack Fengxiang, but on 16 March most of the Emperor's troops switched over to Li Cong Ke. On 17 March, Li Cong Ke marched with his army eastward, so that by 28 March, Emperor Li Cong Hou had to flee from Luoyang to Weizhou (now Daming, Hebei Province). Li Cong Ke entered Luoyang on 3 April and two days later the throne of the Later Tang Dynasty was his. On 9 April, Li Cong Hou was killed.

1.3 The (Later) Jin Dynasty

Shi Jing Tang was Emperor Li Si Yuan's son-in-law and he, too, had played an important part in their successes. Emperor Li Cong Ke suspected that Shi Jing Tang would rebel against him, so he was always on guard against Shi Jing Tang and tried his best to reduce his power. On 5 May 936 Emperor Li Cong Ke issued an order to make Shi Jing Tang Regional Military Governor of Yùnzhou (now Yuncheng, Shandong Province) and send him away. Shi Jing Tang refused to accept the imperial order.

On 12 May, Shi Jing Tang presented a memorandum to Emperor Li Cong Ke. The memorandum read, "You are the adopted son of Emperor Mingzong. You have no right to succeed to the throne of the Tang Dynasty. You should pass the throne to the King of Xu who is the true son of Emperor Mingzong." When Emperor Li Cong Ke read the memorandum, he was furious. On 16 May he issued an imperial order stripping Shi Jing Tang of all official titles. On 20 May he sent a great army to lay siege to Taiyuan where the office of the Regional Military Governor of Hedong was situated. Meanwhile, Shi Jing Tang sent an envoy to Khitan to ask Yelu Deguang, the Emperor of Khitan, for help. His letter essentially said that Shi Jing Tang would be willing to submit himself as a vassal to the Emperor of Khitan, that he would treat the Emperor of Khitan as his own father, and that he would cede the sixteen prefectures north to Yanmen Guan Pass including Youzhou (now the area around Beijing) and Yunzhou (now the area around Datong, Shanxi Province) to Khitan. When Yelu Deguang, the Emperor of Khitan, got the letter, he was overjoyed.

In September he personally commanded a great army of over fifty thousand Khitan cavalrymen to march southward to relieve Shi Jing Tang. The Khitan army passed through Yanmen Guan Pass and on 14 September reached Taiyuan. Shi Jing Tang sent out Liu Zhi Yuan in command of an army to fight alongside the Khitan army. On 15 September a great battle between the Khitan army and the Later Tang army was fought outside the city of Taiyuan. The Later Tang army was defeated and lost more than ten thousand soldiers.

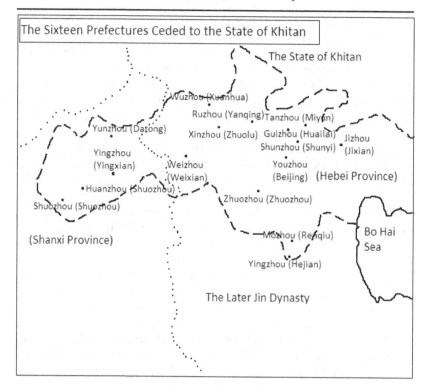

The Sixteen Prefectures Ceded to the State of Khitan

That night Shi Jing Tang went out of the city to meet the Emperor of Khitan. On 16 September the army under Shi Jing Tang came out of the city and joined forcess with the Khitan army. They surrounded the main force of the Later Tang army camped in Jin'an (to the southwest of Taiyuan, Shanxi Province). From then on, all communication was cut off between the Later Tang army and Emperor Li Cong Ke. The Emperor was shocked. After several months, his Later Tang Army surrendered to the Khitan.

On 12 November 936 Yelu Deguang, the Emperor of Khitan, made Shi Jing Tang Emperor of the Great Jin Dynasty, and Shi Jing Tang took the throne. Historians called this the Later Jin Dynasty so as to distinguish it from the Jin Dynasty established by Sima Yi (266–420). In return, Shi Jing Tang ceded the following sixteen prefectures to Khitan: Youzhou (now the area around Beijing), Jizhou (now the area around Jixian, Hebei Province), Yingzhou (now the area around Hejian, Hebei Province), Mozhou (now the area around Renqiu, Hebei Province), Zhuozhou (now the area around Zhuozhou, Hebei Province), Tanzhou (now the around Miyun, Beijing), Shunzhou (now the area around Shunyi, Beijing), Xinzhou (now the area around Zhuolu, Hebei Province), Guizhou (now the area around Huailai, Hebei Province), Ruzhou (now the area around Yanqing, Beijing), Wuzhou (now the area around Xuanhua, Hebei Province), Yunzhou (now the area around Datong, Shanxi Province), Yingzhou (now the area around Yingxian, Shanxi Province), Huanzhou (now the area to the east of Shuozhou, Shanxi Province), Shuozhou (now the area around Shuozhou, Shanxi Province), and Weizhou (now the area around Weixian, Hebei Province). And Shi Jing Tang promised to contribute three hundred thousand bolts of woven silk to Khitan every year.

On 11 of the second November (that's right — 936 was a leap year and so it had two Novembers) Yelu Deguang, the Emperor of Khitan, said farewell to Shi Jing Tang and heaed back north to Khitan. The Emperor of Khitan had a general, commanding a great Khitan army, accompany Shi Jing Tang on his march to Luoyang. On 25 November Shi Jing Tang reached a place north to Heyang (now Mengxian, Henan Province) which was situated to the north of the Yellow River. Chang Cong Jian, the Regional Military Governor of Heyang of the Later Tang Dynasty, surrendered. There were ships and boats on the north bank of the Yellow River. On that day the Later Jin army and the Khitan army crossed the Yellow River. On 27 November Shi Jing Tang reached the outskirts of Luoyang. Seeing this, Li Cong Ke, the Emperor of the Later Tang Dynasty, set himself on fire and burned to death. He was later given the temple title of Modi (which means "the last emperor of the dynasty"). That night Shi Jing Tang entered the city of Luoyang. It was indeed the end of the Tang Dynasty.

Portrait of Shi Jing Tang, Emperor Gaozu of the (Later) Jin Dynasty

In March 937, Shi Jing Tang decided to move the capital of the Later Jin Dynasty from Luoyang to Daliang (now Kaifeng, Henan Province). On 4 April he reached Daliang. Shi Jing Tang was grateful to Yelu Deguang, the Emperor of Khitan, for making all this possible. In his letters, Shi Jing Tang called him "Father Emperor" and called himself "Son Emperor." But the ministers and generals of the Jin Dynasty felt ashamed to be subjugated to the Khitan.

In July 941 Emperor Shi Jing Tang appointed Liu Zhi Yuan as commander-in-chief of the armies in Taiyuan (now Taiyuan, Shanxi Province), the Northern Capital of the Later Jin Dynasty, and also appointed him Regional Military Governor of Hedong (now the area of the northeast part of Shanxi Province).

On 13 June 942 Emperor Shi Jing Tang died at the age of fifty-one. He was given the temple title of Gaozu of the (Later) Jin Dynasty. Shi Cong Gui, Shi Jing Tang's elder brother's son, succeeded to the throne on the same day. In July, Shi Cong Gui, the new Emperor, sent a letter to Emperor Yelu Deguang of Khitan. His letter was somewhat more nuanced. Shi Cong Gui called himself a "Grandson" of the Emperor of Khitan but did not call himself his "vassal." The Emperor of Khitan was very angry and sent an envoy to ask about this apparent slight. Jing Yan Guang, a minister of the Later Jin Dynasty, diplomatically explained that while Emperor Shi Jing Tang had been made Emperor by the Emperor of Khitan, and was therefore his vassal, now Shi Cong Gui was made Emperor by the Later Jin Dynasty, not by the Emperor of Khitan. By this reasoning Shi Cong Gui was no more a vassal of the Emperor of Khitan. When the envoy reported the explanation to the Emperor of Khitan, Yelu Deguang was furious and made up his mind to attack the Later Jin Dynasty.

In January 944 the Emperor of Khitan started an extensive invasion from the north. The Emperor of the Later Jin Dynasty sent armies to resist the onslaught. The war lasted for more than two years. In December 946 Du Wei, the Regional Military Governor of Tianxiong (commanding the armies in Weizhou (now Daming, Hebei Province) and Bozhou (now Liaocheng, Shandong Province)), Li Shou Zhen, Regional Military Governor of Tianping (commanding the armies in Yùnzhou (now Yuncheng, Shandong Province) and Zhang Yan Ze, Regional Military Governor of Xiangzhou (now Anyang, Henan Province) surrendered to Khitan.

Next. the Emperor of Khitan sent Zhang Yan Ze to command two thousand cavalrymen to attack Daliang, the capital of the Later Jin Dynasty. On 17 December, Zhang Yan Ze and his army broke into Daliang. Now Shi Cong Gui, the proud Emperor of the Later Jin Dynasty, set fire to the palace and was planning to self-immolate. But Zhang Yan Ze arrived in time to show him a letter written by the Emperor of Khitan to allay Shi Cong Gui's worst fears. So he gave up the idea of burning himself to death.

On 1 January 947 the Emperor of Khitan entered Daliang. Shi Cong Gui surrendered to him.

On January 17 the Emperor of Khitan sent six hundred cavalrymen to escort the deposed Emperor of the Later Jin Dynasty north, to Jianzhou of Khitan, a very cold place. He stayed there till he died. He was given the temple title of Shaodi.

On 1 February 947 the Emperor of Khitan held court in the palace of Daliang. He issued an imperial order to change the name of the state from Great Khitan to Great Liao.

1.4 The (Later) Han Dynasty

Liu Zhi Yuan, Regional Military Governor of Hedong, had recruited many new soldiers to prepare to fend off the invasion by Khitan. When the Khitan army invaded the Later Jin Dynasty, he sent troops to defend the area of Hedong (now the area of the northeast part of Shanxi Province). Guo Wei, a general under Liu Zhi Yuan, advised him, "The Emperor of Khitan is after you. He is very greedy and the people do not have faith in him. He will not be able to occupy the area of Central China for long."

On 13 February 947 some ministers and generals presented a letter to Liu Zhi Yuan suggesting that he should take the throne. Liu Zhi Yuan hesitated. Guo Wei, Yang Bin and Shi Hong Zhao persuaded him, saying, "Now all the people have the same idea, that you should ascend the throne. This is the will of Heaven. You should seize this Chance; otherwise the opportunity will slip from you figures. In time, the people will turn to other men." Liu Zhi Yuan thought this view had some merit, and on 15 February 947 he ascended the throne in the palace in Taiyuan.

As for Yelu Deguang, the Emperor of Liao, he could not stand the hot weather in Central China. So he decided to go back to the north. On 17 March the Emperor of Liao started his journey from Daliang back north. By 21 February when the Emperor of Liao reached Zhaozhou (now Zhaoxian, Hebei Province), he wasn't feeling well. The next day he reached Luancheng (now Luancheng, Hebei province), but he was seriously ill and died. His nephew Yelu Yuan ascended the throne of the State of Liao.

When Liu Zhi Yuan heard that the Emperor of Liao had left Daliang, he started his march from Taiyuan to Daliang on 12 May. On 3 June Liu Zhi Yuan entered Luoyang without any resistance. On 11 June he entered Daliang. On 15 June Liu Zhi Yuan issued an imperial order to change the name of the dynasty from Jin to Han, and it was decided that the capital of the Han Dynasty was Daliang. Historians called this the "Later Han Dynasty" (the first Han Dynasty was established by Liu Bang and lasted from 206 BC to AD 9).

後漢高祖像

Portrait of Liu Zhi Yuan, Emperor Gaozu of the (Later) Han Dynasty

The Emperor of the Later Han Dynasty appointed Guo Wei as the minister in charge of military affairs. On 14 January 948 Emperor Liu Zhi Yuan of the Later Han Dynasty took to his bed. He summoned Guo Wei, Yang Bin and Shi Hong Zhao to the bed chamber in the palace and entrusted them with assisting his young son Liu Cheng You in managing the important political and military affairs. On 27 January, Emperor Liu Zhi Yuan died at the age of fifty-four. He was given the temple title of Gaozu.

On 1 February 948 Liu Cheng You ascended the throne of the Later Han Dynasty at the age of seventeen. At that time, Yang Bin was in charge of all the political affairs of the court; Guo Wei was in charge of all the military affairs; Shi Hong Zhao was in charge of the defense of the palace; Wang Zhang was in charge of the financial affairs. In March 948 Li Shou Zhen, the Military Governor of Huguo, rebelled in Hezhong (now the area around Yuncheng, Shanxi Province). In August 948 Guo Wei commanded a massive army to suppress the rebellion. In July 949 Guo Wei attacked the city of Hezhong and took it. Li Shou Zhen burned himself to death.

As Emperor Liu Cheng You began to mature, he hated being under the control of all those the ministers and generals. He planned to get rid of them. On 13 November, while Yang Bin and Shi Hong Zhao were en route to the court, they were assassinated by soldiers who ambushed him by the gate of the palace. Then Emperor Liu Cheng You sent a secret envoy to Yedu with an imperial order ordering Commanders Guo Chong and Cao Ying to kill Guo Wei. On 14 November Guo Wei somehow got wind of this secret order and on the next day he took a great army from Yedu to Daliang. On 19 November the young Emperor sent armies to counter the army commanded by Guo Wei. On 22 November Emperor Liu Cheng You was killed by one of his subordinates at the age of twenty. He was later given the temple title of Yindi. Guo Wei entered Daliang that day.

1.5 The (Later) Zhou Dynasty

Portrait of Guo Wei, Emperor Gaozu of the (Later) Zhou Dynasty

Guo Wei and the ministers went to see the Empress Dowager of the Later Han Dynasty and asked her to hold court and serve as head of state. On 27 November, 950, reports from Zhenzhou (now Zhengding, Hebei Province) and Dingzhou (now Dingxian, Hebei Province) showed that the Emperor of Liao had commanded more than thirty thousand cavalrymen to attack the prefectures in the area north of the Yellow River. The Empress Dowager of the Later Han Dynasty sent Guo Wei to command a great army to fight the Liao Army. On 1 December Guo Wei set out from Daliang. On 19 December Guo Wei and the army crossed the Yellow River from Huazhou (now Huaxian, in the northeast part of Henan Province); then they reached Chanzhou (now Puyang, in the northeast part of Henan Province) and stayed there for the night. On the morning of 20 December when the army was about to march forward, several thousand officers and men suddenly started shouting and making noise. Guo Wei ordered the door to be closed so he could think. The soldiers climbed up the outer wall and came into the house. They said to Guo Wei, "You should be our emperor. We don't want any emperor from the Liu family."

Then a soldier tore a big piece of cloth from a yellow banner and put it on Guo Wei. The soldiers held Guo Wei up and shouted, "Long live!" The soldiers carried Guo Wei to go back to the south. On 25 December Guo Wei reached Qilidian, a village just outside the city of Daliang. The ministers and generals in the court all came out of the city to welcome Guo Wei. The Empress Dowager of the Later Han Dynasty was wise enough. On 27 December she appointed Guo Wei as Protector. On 5 January 951 she passed the imperial seal of the Emperor to Guo Wei. On the same day Guo Wei ascended the throne. He changed the name of the dynasty into Zhou (the "Later Zhou Dynasty," not to be confused with the Zhou Dynasty established by Ji Fa, 1122 BC–256 BC).

After Guo Wei had ascended the throne of the Later Zhou Dynasty, in January 951 he sent an envoy to the State of Liao to tell Yelu Yuan, the Emperor of Liao, the news. Emperor Yelu Yuan responded by sending an envoy to Liu Chong, the commander-in-chief of the armies in the Taiyuan area appointed by Liu Zhi Yuan, to make Liu Chong King of the State of (Northern) Han. However, in June Yelu Yuan, the Emperor of Liao, was assassinated. Yelu Jing, Emperor Yelu Deguang's eldest son, ascended the throne as Emperor of Liao.

2. The Ten States

2.1 & 2.2. The State of Wu and the State of Southern Tang

Since the trajectories of these two states are compeletely intertwined, we have to count two states in one section here. How much can we force history into a structure? In 895 General Yang Xing Mi occupied the vast area south to the Huai River (an area including the northern part of Jiangsu Province, Anhui Province, part of Jiangxi Province and part of Hubei Province). In March 902 Emperor Li Min of the Tang Dynasty appointed Yang Xing Mi Regional Military Governor of Huainan and made him King of Wu. In November 905 Yang Xing Mi died of illness at the age of fifty-four. His eldest son Yang Wo succeeded as King of Wu. But at that time the power of the State of Wu was in the hands of Zhang Hao, the commander-in-chief of the left army of Huainan, and Xu Wen, the commander-in-chief of the right army of Huainan.

Yang Wo wanted to kill them. But on 5 May 908 Zhang Hao dispatched a team of assassins who murdered Yang Wo in his bed chamber. On 17 May, Zhang Hao was himself killed by persons sent by Xu Wen. Xu Wen put Yang Wei, Yang Xing Mi's second son, in the position of Master of the State of Wu, but retained all the real power of the State of Wu. In March 919, Xu Wen suggested that Yang Wei go ahead and declare himself Emperor of Wu. But Yang Wei turned down the suggestion. On 1 April, Yang Wei did ascend the throne of King of the State of Wu. The ceremony of ascending the throne of King of Wu was just as grand as that of an emperor ascending the throne. The King of Wu appointed Xu Wen as Grand Premier in charge of all the political and military affairs of the state; he also appointed Xu Zhi Gao, Xu Wen's adopted son, as one of the premiers. In April 920, Yang Wei, King of Wu, died at the age of twenty-four. Yang Pu, Yang Xing Mi's fourth son, ascended the throne of King of Wu. In October 927, Xu Wen died. The King of Wu posthumously granted him the title of King of Qi. Xu Wen's adopted son Xu Zhi Gao succeeded his adopted father as both the Grand Premier and the titular King of Qi.

Now, in September 927, Yan Pu, the King of Wu, declared himself to be Emperor. In August 937 Yang Pu, Emperor of Wu, stepped down from the throne and offered the throne to Xu Zhi Gao. In October 937 Xu Zhi Gao ascended the throne in Jinling (now Nanjing, Jiangsu Province). He changed his name from Xu Zhi Gao back to Li Sheng, his original name. He changed the name of the state from Wu to Tang. Historians called this State of Tang "Southern Tang." He stayed on the throne for seven years. In 944 he died. His son Li Jing succeeded to the throne of Southern Tang.

2.3. & 2.4. The State of Former Shu and the State of Later Shu

By the end of the Tang Dynasty, in the war to suppress Huang Chao's rebellion, Wang Jian played a significant role. He also contributed greatly in protecting Emperor Li Xuan of the Tang Dynasty. So he was promoted to the Governor of Bizhou (now Tongjiang, Sichuan Province) in 886. By 890, Wang Jian occupied most of the areas of Chuandong (now the east part of Sichuan Province) and Chuanxi (now the west part of Sichuan Province). In October, Wang Jian took a large army to attack Chengdu (now Chengdu, Sichuan Province). In July 891, the defenders of Chengdu opened the city gate of Chengdu and welcomed Wang Jian into the city. In April 907, Zhu Quan Zhong declared himself Emperor and established the Later Liang Dynasty, but that same November Wang Jian also declared himself Emperor, of the State of Shu, and he made Chengdu his capital. Historians call this State of Shu the "Former State of Shu." He enjoyed it for ten years. In June 917 Wang Jian died at the age of seventy-two. His son Wang Yan succeeded to the throne of the State of Shu.

On 10 September, 925, Emperor Li Cun Xu of the Later Tang Dynasty issued an imperial order to send an expeditionary force against the State of Shu. He appointed Li Ji Ji, the King of Wei, as commander-in-chief of an army of sixty thousand men. The expedition army marched from Luoyang on 18 September. On 21 November Li Ji Ji reached Deyang (now Deyang, Sichuan Province). Wang Yan, Emperor of Shu, sent him an envoy with a letter stating that he would surrender to the Later Tang Dynasty. On 27 November, Li Ji Ji reached the outskirts of Chengdu and held a ceremony to accept Wang Yan's surrender. Not one to rest on his laurels, the next day Li Ji Ji commanded the army of Later Tang Dynasty to march into the city of

Chengdu. From the day when the Later Tang army started from Luoyang to the day when the Later Tang army entered Chengdu only seventy-five days had passed.

Meng Zhi Xiang, the commander-in-chief of the Later Tang army in Taiyuan (now Taiyuan, Shanxi Province), was appointed Regional Military Governor of Chuanxi (now the west part of Sichuan Province) in December 925. In January 926, Meng Zhi Xiang arrived at Chengdu.

At that time Dong Zhang was the Regional Military Governor of Chuandong (now the east part of Sichuan Province). By 932 Meng Zhi Xiang had defeated him and he took the area of Chuandong. In February the Emperor of the Later Tang Dynasty appointed Meng Zhi Xiang Regional Military Governor of both Chuanxi (the west part of Sichuan Province) and Chuandong (the east part of Sichuan Province), and made him King of Shu. In January 934 Meng Zhi Xiang declared himself Emperor of the State of Shu in Chengdu. Historians called this State of Shu "the State of Later Shu." In July 934, Meng Zhi Xiang died at the age of sixty-one. His son Meng Chang succeeded the throne of the State of Later Shu at the age of sixteen.

2.5. The State of Wuyue

Qian Liu had been heroic in the war against Huang Chao's rebellion. In 893 Emperor Li Min of the Tang Dynasty appointed him Regional Military Governor of Zhenhai (now the area around Hangzhou, Zhejiang Province). In 907 Zhu Quan Zhong, Emperor of the Later Liang Dynasty, made Qian Liu King of Wuyue. Qian Liu owned the areas of Zhedong (now the east part of Zhejiang Province) and Zhexi (now the west part of Zhejiang Province). The capital of the State of Wuyue was Hangzhou (now Hangzhou, Zhejiang Province). Qian Liu died in March 932 at the age of eighty-one. His fifth son Qian Yuan Guan succeeded to the throne of the State of Wuyue and ruled for nine years. Qian Yuan Guan died in August 941 at the age of fifty-five. His son Qian Zuo succeeded him. Qian Zuo stayed in the throne for seven years and died in 947. His brother Qian Zong succeeded to the throne of the State of Wuyue. Then in December 947 General Hu Jin provoked a rebellion and captured Qian Zong. He deposed Qian Zong and put his younger brother, Qian Ti, on the throne of the State of Wuyue in January 948.

2.6. The State of Chu

By the end of the Tang Dynasty Ma Yin occupied Hongzhou (now the area around Nanchang, Jiangxi Province), Ezhou (now the area around Wuhan, Hubei Province), Tanzhou (now the area around Changsha, Hunan Province), and Guizhou (now the northern part of Guangxi Zhuang Autonomous Region). In September 896, Emperor Li Min of the Tang Dynasty put Ma Yin in charge of the military affairs in Hunan (now the area of Hunan Province). In April 907 Emperor Zhu Quan Zhong made him King of Chu, and he ruled for many years. In November 930, Ma Yin died at the age of seventy-nine. His son Ma Xi Sheng succeeded him as King of Chu. In 932 he, too, died. His younger brother Ma Xi Fan succeeded to the throne. That lasted fifteen years, and in 947 Ma Xi Fan died. His younger brother Ma Xi Guang took the throne as King of Chu. What about his elder brother, Ma Xi E? He was very angry. In December 950 Ma Xi E commanded a great army to attack Changsha (now Changsha, Hunan Province) and won. Ma Xi E captured his brother Ma Xi Guang and ordered him to kill himself. Then Ma Xi E declared himself King of the State of Chu.

In September 951 General Xu Wei of the State of Chu commanded some troops to attack the palace of Chu and they captured Ma Xi E. Xu Wei sent Ma Xi E into exile in Hengshan County (now Hengshan, Hunan Province). Xu Wei put Ma Xi Chong, a younger brother of Ma Xi E, on the throne of the King of the State of Chu. The generals escorting Ma Xi E to Hengshan County made Ma Xi E King of Hengshan when they reached there. Xu Wei was afraid and wanted to kill Ma Xi Chong. Ma Xi Chong sent a secret envoy to see Li Jing, the Emperor of the State of Southern Tang, to ask for help. Li Jing sent General Bian Gao at the head of a great army to the State of Chu. In October 950 General Bian Gao entered Changsha. Ma Xi Chong surrendered to General Bian Gao. In November 951 General Bian Gao sent the whole royal clan of King Ma Xi Chong of the State of Chu to the State of Southern Tang. Then General Bian Gao sent a general with an army to Hengshan to escort Ma Xi E to the State of Southern Tang.

In September 952 Liu Yan, a general in Langzhou (now Changde, Hunan Province), assisted by General Wang Kui and General Zhou Xing Feng, commanded a great army to march to Changsha. In October General Bian Gao of the State of Southern Tang gave up the city of Changsha and led his army back to the State of Southern Tang. Then Liu Yan entered Changsha. He sent an envoy to see Emperor Guo Wei of the Later Zhou Dynasty. The Emperor of the Later Zhou Dynasty appointed him Grand Commander-in-chief of Langzhou and Regional Military Governor of Wuping, appointed Wang Kui Regional Military Governor of Wu'an and appointed Zhou Xing Feng Chief of Staff of the army in Wu'an. In August 953, Wang Kui killed Liu Yan. Emperor Guo Wei of the Later Zhou Dynasty made Wang Kui Regional Military Governor of Wuping. In February 956 Wang Kui was killed by Pan Shu Si, one of his own generals, in Langzhou. In turn Zhou Xing Feng killed Pan Shu Si. Then Emperor Guo Wei of the Later Zhou Dynasty appointed Zhou Xing Feng as Grand Commander-in-chief of Langzhou and Regional Military Governor of Wuping.

2.7. The State of Min

By the end of the Tang Dynasty Wang Chao and his younger brother Wang Shen Zhi occupied the area of Min (now the area of Fujian Province). In October 894 Emperor Li Min of the Tang Dynasty appointed Wang Chao Governor of Fujian (now Fujian Province). Wang Chao made Wang Shen Zhi Deputy Governor of Fujian. In 897, Wang Chao Died. Wang Shen Zhi succeeded his brother's title of Governor of Fujian. In 909 Emperor Zhu

Quan Zhong of the Later Liang Dynasty made Wang Shen Zhi King of the State of Min. In December 925, Wang Shen Zhi died at the age of sixty-four. His eldest son Wang Han succeeded to the throne of King of the State of Min. In December 926 Wang Yan Jun, Wang Han's younger brother, led an army to attack Fuzhou (now Fuzhou, Fujian Province), and Wang Han was killed.

Wang Yan Jun ascended the throne of King of the State of Min. Then Wang Yan Jun changed his name to Wang Lin. In October 934, Wang Lin was killed by his son Wang Ji Peng. Wang Ji Peng ascended the throne of King of the State of Min and changed his name to Wang Chang. In summer 938, Wang Yan Yi, Wang Shen Zhi's son, killed Wang Chang and declared himself King of the State of Min. He changed his name to Wang Xi. He stayed on the throne for six years. In February 944 Wang Xi was killed by his subordinates. Wang Yan Zheng, another son of Wang Shen Zhi, ascended the throne of the State of Min. In 946 Li Jing, Emperor of the State of Southern Tang, sent an army to attack the State of Min and captured the king, Wang Yan Zheng. The State of Min was destroyed.

2.8. The State of Northern Han

In May 947, before Emperor Liu Zhi Yuan of the Later Han Dynasty started his march to Luoyang and Daliang from Taiyuan (now Taiyuan, Shanxi Province), he appointed Liu Chong, his cousin, commander-in-chief of the armies in the Taiyuan area. Emperor Liu Zhi Yuan died in January 948. His son Liu Cheng You succeeded to the throne. In January 951 Guo Wei took power from the Later Han Dynasty and established the Later Zhou Dynasty. Then Liu Chong declared himself Emperor of the Han Dynasty. The area east to the Yellow River was his (now the area of Shanxi Province). The capital of this Han Dynasty was Taiyuan. Historians called this Han Dynasty "the State of Northern Han."

2.9. The State of Southern Han

By the end of the Tang Dynasty, Liu Qian, a general in Guangzhou (now Guangzhou, Guangdong Province), had made a name for himself in suppressing the rebellion led by Huang Chao. In 882 Liu Qian was appointed Governor of Fengzhou (now Fengxian, Guangdong Province). After he died, his son Liu Yin succeeded as Governor. In 905 Liu Yin was promoted to Regional Military Governor of Qinghai (now the area of the east part of Guangdong Province) and Jinghai (now the area of the north part of Vietnam). In 911 Emperor Zhu Quan Zhong of the Later Liang Dynasty made him King of Hainan.

In March 911 Liu Yin died. His younger brother Liu Zhi inherited all his titles. In August 917 Liu Zhi declared himself Emperor in Guangzhou (now Guangzhou, Guangdong Province). The state he established was "Great Han." Historians called this State of Han the "State of Southern Han." Liu Zhi stayed on the throne for twenty-six years. In April 942 he died at the age of fifty-four. His eldest son Liu Fen succeeded to the throne. Liu Cheng, Liu

Zhi's second son, conspired with Liu Chāng, Liu Zhi's third son, to murder Liu Fen, and in 944 Liu Fen was killed by an assassin. Liu Cheng ascended the throne of the State of Southern Han. In 951 there was a chaos in the royal family of Ma of the State of Chu. Liu Cheng took this opportunity to send armies to seize Chenzhou (now Chenzhou, Hunan Province), Guizhou (now Guilin, Guangxi Zhuang Autonomous Region), and Hezhou (now Hexian, Guangxi Zhuang Autonomous Region) which were situated in the south area of the State of Chu. In the second July of 958 (958 was an intercalary year which had two months of July) Liu Cheng died at the age of thirty-nine. His eldest son Liu Chang ascended the throne at the age of seventeen.

2.10. The State of Nanping

In May 907 Emperor Zhu Quan Zhong of the Later Liang Dynasty appointed Gao Ji Xing as Regional Military Governor of Jingnan (now the area around Jiangling and Gong'an, Hubei Province). In March 924 Emperor Li Cun Xu of the Later Tang Dynasty made Gao Ji Xing King of Nanping. The capital of the State of Nanping was Jiangling (now Jiangling County in Jingzhou, Hubei Province). In December 928, Gao Ji Xing died at the age of seventy-one. His eldest son Gao Cong Hui succeeded to the throne of King of Nanping. Gao Cong Hui died in October 948 at the age of fifty-eight. His third son Gao Bao Rong succeeded to the throne of King of Nanping

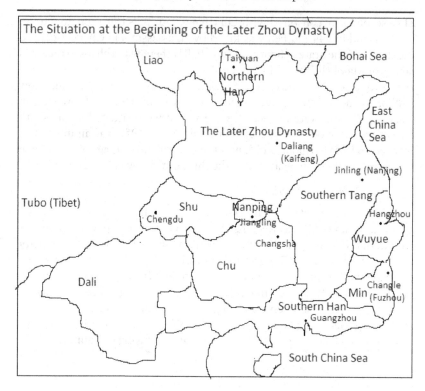

The Situation at the Beginnning of the Later Zhou Dynasty

CHAPTER TWO: IN THE PERIOD OF THE (LATER) ZHOU DYNASTY

1. The Birth of Zhao Huang Yin

Zhao Kuang Yin was born in the army camp of Jiamaying in Luoyang in 927 in the period of the Later Tang Dynasty. When he was born there was a red light around the house and a special fragrance filled the house for several days. The color of gold shone in his body. This color lasted for three days. Zhao Kuang Yin's father was Zhao Hong Yin, a general in the army of the Later Tang Dynasty. Zhao Kuang Yin's mother was Lady Du.

Zhao Kuang Yin grew to become a tall and strong young man with a gracious appearance. He was clearly remarkable. When he learned horse riding and archery together with other young men, he excelled. Once he rode a wild horse without reins. The horse galloped up the slope leading to the top of the city wall. Zhao Kuang Yin smacked his head on the lintel of the gate and fell to the ground. The on-lookers thought that his skull must have been crushed. But shortly, Zhao Kuang Yin got up from the ground, and ran so fast that he caught up with the horse and jumped up again! Once, he was gambling with Han Ling Kun in a clay-walled house. Suddenly many birds started fighting outside the house, making a very loud noise. Zhao Kuang Yin and Han Ling Kun went out of the house to drive the birds away. As soon as they stepped out of the house, the house collapsed.

Zhao Kuang Yin had a younger brother named Zhao Kuang Yi. Zhao Kuang Yi was twelve years younger than Zhao Kuang Yin. In the early period of the Later Han Dynasty, Zhao Kuang Yin started a journey. He roamed around the country, but he found nothing. Then one night he stayed in a temple. An old monk who was good at fortune-telling said to Zhao Kuang Yin, "I can see that you will have a very bright future. Go northward and you will find your fortune." Zhao Kuang

Yin followed his advice. It happened that Guo Wei, the minster of the Later Han Dynasty in charge of military affairs, was about to lead an army to attack Li Shou Zhen. The army was recruiting new soldiers. Zhao Kuang Yin joined the army under the command of Guo Wei.

2. Under the Reign of Emperor Guo Wei of the (Later) Zhou Dynasty

In January 951 Guo Wei ascended the throne of the Later Zhou Dynasty. Zhao Kuang Yin was promoted to the rank of commander and was appointed deputy commander of the army in Huazhou (now Huaxian, Henan Province). In March 953 Guo Rong, the adopted son of Guo Wei, was made King of Jin and was appointed Commander-in-chief of the army stationed in Kaifeng, the capital of the Later Zhou Dynasty. Guo Rong transferred Zhao Kuang Yin to Kaifeng to be commander of the army stationed in Kaifeng.

In December 953, Emperor Guo Wei felt death approaching. On 11 January 954 Emperor Guo Wei entrusted all the state affairs to the care of Guo Rong, King of Jin. On 15 January he died at the age of fifty-one. He left an imperial order that Guo Rong should take the throne of the Later Zhou Dynasty in front of Emperor Guo Wei's own coffin. So Guo Rong ascended the throne of the Later Zhou Dynasty on 21 January 954.

3. Under the Reign of Emperor Guo Rong of the (Later) Zhou Dynasty

Portrait of Guo Rong, Emperor Shizong of the (Later) Zhou Dynasty

3.1. The Great Battle of Gaoping

When Liu Chong, Emperor of the State of Northern Han, got news that Emperor Guo Wei of the Later Zhou Dynasty had died, he was overjoyed. He made up his mind to carry out a large scale invasion. He sent an envoy to the State of Liao to ask Yelu Jing, the Emperor of Liao, to send an army to assist him. The Emperor of Liao sent General Yang Gun, in command of over ten thousand cavalrymen, to Jinyang (now Taiyuan, Shanxi Province) to join forces with Liu Chong. In February 954 Liu Chong, the Emperor of the State of Northern Han, personally led thirty thousand men to march from Jinyang southward towards Luzhou (now the area around Changzhi, Shanxi Province) together with the Liao cavalrymen. On 12 February the Northern Han army camped in Lianghouyi, which was fifty kilometers northwest to Luzhou.

Li Jun, the Regional Military Governor of Zhaoyi of the Later Zhou Dynasty, sent General Mu Ling Jun to lead two thousand cavalrymen to fight head-on against the Northern Han army. Li Jun commanded the main force to station themselves in Taipingyi, forty kilometers northwest to Luzhou. When the Northern Han army under the command of Zhang Yuan Hui and the Later Zhou army under the command of Mu Ling Jun met, Zhang Yuan Hui pretended to be defeated and he retreated. Mu Ling Jun commanded his cavalrymen to give hot pursuit but fell into an ambush and was killed. Over a thousand Later Zhou soldiers were killed. Li Jun fled back to Shangdang (now Changzhi, Shanxi Province), which was the main city of the Luzhou area.

When Emperor Guo Rong heard that Liu Chong had commanded a great army to invade the territory of the Later Zhou Dynasty, he decided to personally lead the army to fight against the Northern Han. On 1 March 954, borne along by the momentum of the victory in Lianghouyi Liu Chong commanded his army to march southward to threaten Luzhou. Emperor Guo Rong issued an imperial order to send Fu Yan Qing, the Regional Military Governor of Tianxiong, to command an army to march from Guzhen Town of Cizhou (now Cixian, Hebei Province) to the rear of the Northern Han army; Emperor Guo Rong appointed Guo Chong, Regional Military Governor of Zhenning, as deputy commander of this army. Emperor Guo Rong named Wang Yan Chao, Regional Military Governor of Hezhong, to command an army to march from Jinzhou (now Linfen, Shanxi Province) to march northeastward to attack the Northern Han army. He appointed Han Tong, Regional Military Governor of Baoyi, as deputy commander of this army. Then Emperor Guo Rong order Fan Ai Neng, Regional Military Governor of Ningjiang, He Hui, Regional Military Governor of Qinghuai, Bai Chong Jin, Regional Military Governor of Yicheng, Shi Yan Chao, Commander-in-chief of the army in Zhengzhou (now Zhengzhou, Henan Province), and Fu Yan Neng, the former Commander-in-chief of the army in Yaozhou, to lead their armies in a march towards Zezhou (now the area around Jincheng, Shanxi Province).

On 11 March, 954, Emperor Guo Rong started from Daliang (now Kaifeng). On 16 March he reached Huaizhou (now Qinyang, Henan Province). Two days later he passed Zezhou. Liu Chong, Emperor of the State of Northern Han, did not know that Emperor Guo Rong of the Later Zhou Dynasty was coming. He commanded his army to go past Luzhou and leave it unattacked. That night he ordered his army to pitch camps to the south of Gaoping (now Gaoping, Shanxi Province), which was thirty-two kilometers northeast of Zezhou. On 19 March the vanguards of the Later Zhou army met the Northern Han army. After a battle, the Northern Han army retreated. Emperor Guo Rong was afraid that the Northern Han army would retreat, so he urged the army to march quickly. Liu Chong, Emperor of the State of Northern Han, arranged his army in battle formation on Bagongyan (now Bagong, Shanxi Province) which was situated to the north to Zezhou (now Jincheng, Shanxi Province). General Zhang Yuan Hui commanded his army on the east wing of the battle formation; Yang Gun, the commander of the Liao army, commanded his cavalrymen on the west wing of the battle formation. At that time the rear army of the Later Zhou Dynasty commanded by Liu Ci, Regional Military Governor of Heyang, had not yet arrived. The Northern Han army outnumbered the Later Zhou army. So the soldiers of the Later Zhou Dynasty were afraid. But Emperor Guo Rong of the Later Zhou Dynasty was determined. He ordered Bai Chong Jin, Regional Military Governor of Yicheng, and Li Chong Jin, the Commander of the Royal Guards, to command the Left Army on the west wing of the battle formation. He ordered Fan Ai Neng and He Hui to command the Right Army on the east wing of the battle formation. He ordered Shi Yan Chao to command the elite troops of cavalrymen at the center of the battle formation. Emperor Guo Rong personally supervised the whole army. Zhang Yong De, who was the son-in-law of the late Emperor Guo Wei, commanded the royal guards defending Emperor Guo Rong.

Liu Chong, the Emperor of the State of Northern Han, saw that his army greatly outnumbered that of the Later Zhou Dynasty. He regretted inviting the Liao army to come; he would be indebted for assistance he'd never need. He said to the generals around him, "I will defeat the Zhou army with my own army. It is not necessary to ask the Liao army to fight in the battle. Today I will conquer the Zhou army. And I will show to the Liao generals that I can do it by myself." All his generals agreed with him.

Yang Gun, the commander of the Liao army, rode forward and studied the battle formation of the Later Zhou Dynasty. Then he rode back to Liu Chong and said, "The Zhou army is a strong enemy. We should not take them lightly and attack." Liu Chong said, excitedly, "I must seize this chance. Say no more. You may just stay aside and watch me fight." Yang Gun was very uncomfortable. The northeast wind was blowing hard. But suddenly the direction of the wind changed, and a south wind was blowing hard. General Li Yi said to Liu Chong, "It is time to start the battle." Liu Chong agreed with him. But Wang De Zhong, a learned man, held the reins of Liu Chong's horse and said, "Li Yi should be killed for suggesting starting the battle in such unfavorable conditions. The wind is against us." Liu Chong shouted, "You pedantic old scholar! Say no more. Otherwise I will kill you."

Then Liu Chong ordered the army of the east wing to attack the enemy first. General Zhang Yuan Hui commanded two thousand cavalrymen to attack. When the two armies met and the battle began, Fan Ai Neng and He Hui led the cavalry under them to run away. The Right Army of the later Zhou Dynasty collapsed. More than a thousand foot soldiers of the Right Army laid down their weapons and surrendered to the Northern Han army. Emperor Guo Rong of the Later Zhou Dynasty saw that the situation was very unfavorable to the Later Zhou army. Then he personally rode forward to supervise the battle against the rain of arrows and stones. At that time Zhao Kuang Yin was the general of the Royal Guards. He said to his fellow generals, "Our Emperor is in such a dangerous situation. We must fight to death to defend our Emperor." Then he said to Zhang Yong De, "Now, our enemies are very proud and self-conceited. If we fight hard we will defeat them. I suggest that you will command the soldiers under you to attack the left wing of the enemy battle formation and I will command the soldiers under me to attack the right wing of the enemy battle formation. The safety of our Emperor and the State depends on this battle." Zhang Yong De agreed and they moved into action. Each of them commanded two thousand men to attack the enemy battle formation. Zhao Kuang Yin rode ahead of the soldiers under him and attacked. The soldiers under Zhao Kuang Yin fought very bravely and each man took on ten enemy soldiers. The Northern Han army collapsed. Ma Quan Yi, the commander of the bodyguards of Emperor Guo Rong, said to the Emperor, "Now the enemy is at the end of its resources. I hope Your Majesty will stay here and watch the generals fight and defeat the enemy." Then Ma Quan Yi commanded five hundred cavalrymen to attack the remaining enemy battle formation.

Liu Chong, the Emperor of the State of Northern Han, found out that Guo Wei, the Emperor of the Later Zhou Dynasty, was in the battle formation of the Later Zhou army. He ordered Zhang Yuan Hui to attack the Later Zhou army, offering him a very handsome reward if he could defeat the enemy. Zhang Yuan Hui commanded his soldiers to attack the battle formation. But when he reached the front of the battle formation, his horse slipped and he fell from the horse. The Later Zhou soldiers rushed forward and killed Zhang Yuan Hui. Zhang Yuan Hui was the fiercest general of the State of Northern Han. When he was killed, the morale of the Northern Han army plummeted. And the southern wind was blowing hard. The soldiers of the Later Zhou army fought very bravely. The Northern Han army was routed and dispersed. The Emperor of the Northern Han upheld the red banner, trying to rally the scattered soldiers, but in vain. Yang Gun, the commander of the Liao army, was afraid of the strong army of the Later Zhou Dynasty. He was also angry about the words Liu Chong had said before the battle. So he did not command his army to rescue the defeated Northern Han army. He just commanded the cavalrymen under him to retreat.

Fan Ai Neng and He Hui led several thousand cavalrymen to retreat southward. Emperor Guo Wei of the Later Zhou Dynasty sent envoys to run after them and ordered them to come back. But they would not accept the order of the Emperor. Some of the envoys were killed by the retreating soldiers. Liu Ci, commanding the rear army, arrived. He met Fan Ai Neng and He Hui. Fan Ai Neng and He Hui advised him not to go forward because the Later Zhou army had been defeated by the Northern Han army and the Liao army.

Liu Ci ignored their advice and commanded the rear army to go ahead. At that time Liu Chong, the Emperor of the State of Northern Han, still had more than ten thousand men. Liu Chong arranged his forces along a stream. In late afternoon, Liu Ci arrived with the rear army. Guo Rong ordered the army of the Later Zhou Dynasty to cross the stream and attack the Northern Han. The Northern Han army was defeated again. Wang Yin Si, a general of the Northern Han army, was killed. The Later Zhou army pursued the enemy to Gaoping. So many Northern Han soldiers were killed that their dead bodies were spread all across the valley.

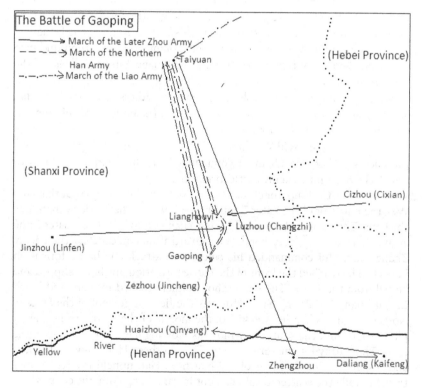

Map of the Battle of Gaoping

Guo Rong of the Later Zhou Dynasty spent that night in the wild. Fan Ai Neng and He Hui got word that the Later Zhou army had won a resounding victory; then they led their troops back. On 20 March Emperor Guo Rong commanded the Later Zhou army to Gaoping and let the soldiers have a rest. Liu Chong, the Emperor of the State of Northern Han, was fleeing on horseback day and night. He was already old and weak. With great difficulty he at last made it back to Jinyang.

Emperor Guo Rong of the Later Zhou Dynasty wanted to kill Fan Ai Neng and He Hui so as to discipline the generals and soldiers of his army. Yet he hesitated and could not make up his mind. On 25 March he fell into deep thought while lying on his bed in his tent in the daytime. Zhang Yong De was standing by the side of the bed. The Emperor asked Zhang Yong De, "I intend to kill Fan Ai Neng and those who ran away from the battlefield so as to discipline the generals and men of the army. What do you think?" Zhang Yong De said, "Fan Ai Neng has not made any remarkable contribution to your success. Now he ran away from the battlefield when he saw the enemy. He deserves to be executed. Now, Your Majesty is working hard to pacify the whole country. If military law is not observed by the generals and men of the army, then the army cannot help Your Majesty to accomplish your goals, even if there are million men in the army." Emperor Guo Rong jumped up from the bed and threw the pillow to the ground and said, "Good advice!" Then he ordered the arrest of Fan Ai Neng and seventy officers under him. All of them were brought before the Emperor. The Emperor scolded them, saying, "You have served as generals and officers for the Zhou Dynasty for a long time. You are not unable to fight. Now you ran away when you saw the enemy. Your sole aim was to sell me to Liu Chong. All of you deserve the punishment of being executed!" And all of them were brought to execution ground and executed. Emperor Guo Rong wanted to spare He Hui because he had done great military deeds before. But military law must be observed, so he also ordered his arrest, and He Hui was put to death.

On 26 March Emperor Guo Rong rewarded those who had made extraordinary contributions in the battle of Gaoping. He appointed Li Chong Jin, the Commander of the Royal Guards, concurrently as Regional Military Governor of Zhongwu. He appointed Zhang Yong De concurrently as Regional Military Governor of Wuxin. He appointed Shi Yan Chao as Regional Military Governor of Zhenguo. Zhang Yong De highly praised Zhao Kuang Yin's bravery and wits in front of Emperor Guo Rong. The Emperor promoted Zhao Kuang Yin to the position of High Ranking Commander of the Royal Guards.

On 3 May, 954, Emperor Guo Rong of the Later Zhou Dynasty marched his army to the city of Jinyang (now Taiyuan, Shanxi Province), the capital city of the State of Northern Han. At that time a Liao army of four thousand cavalry was stationed in the area between Xinzhou (now Xinzhou, Shanxi

Province) and Daizhou (now Daixian, Shanxi Province). Emperor Guo Rong sent Li Jun and Zhang Yong De to command an army to go north to attack the Liao cavalry. On 23 March the Later Zhou army met with the Liao army. They fought in the area of Xinzhou. The Later Zhou army was defeated, and many soldiers were killed or wounded. Li Jun and Zhang Yong De had to command their army to turn back to Jinyang. They put up a prolonged attack on the city of Jinyang but could not take it. It rained for days. The Later Zhou Dynasty soldiers were tired and many of them were ill. Emperor Guo Rong of the Later Zhou Dynasty decided to retreat, and on 2 June Emperor Guo Rong commanded his army to retreat. A lot of food of the Later Zhou army stored under the city of Jinyang had to be burned to ashes. The cities taken by the Later Zhou army had to be given up and were taken back by the army of the State of Northern Han. On 21 June Emperor Guo Rong reached Zhengzhou (now Zhengzhou, Henan Province). On 27 June Emperor Guo Rong came back to Daliang, the capital of the Later Zhou Dynasty.

3.2. Emperor Guo Rong of the (Later) Zhou Dynasty Reorganizes the Royal Guard Army

In the former dynasties the royal guards were treated very well. They stayed in the army for as long as tey could and would not be sent away. Thus, many soldiers in the royal guard army were old and weak. When they faced strong enemies, many of them would run away or surrender to the enemies. From the Battle of Gaoping Emperor Guo Rong saw this clearly.

One day in October 954, Emperor Guo Rong said to the ministers and generals around him, "What constitutes the essence of an army is not the number of soldiers but that the quality of the troops. Now, a hundred peasants work very hard in the fields to grow crops to provide for one soldier in the army. If they work so hard to provide for a weak, old soldier who cannot fight in a battle, they have worked hard in vein. If an army is made up of cowards, this army is useless." So he ordered a reorganization of the Royal Guard armies and the cavalry and infantry. Brave warriors were selected and promoted. Weaker soldiers were asked to leave. There were many brave warriors in different military regions, so the Emperor ordered that the regional military governors should send the brave and young warriors in their regions to the capital. He ordered Zhao Kuang Yin to reorganize the Royal Guards. Zhao Kuang Yin selected the bravest and most skillful warriors to be Royal Guards. Emperor Guo Rong ordered the generals of the cavalry and infantry to reorganize their army. From then on the armies of the Later Zhou Dynasty were constituted of elite troops and became invincible.

3.3. The Death of Liu Chong, the Emperor of the State of Northern Han; Liu Jun Is Made Emperor of the State of Northern Han

After the defeat in the Battle of Gaoping, Liu Chong was so worried and indignant that he fell ill. He entrusted all the state affairs to his son Liu Jun. In November 954 Liu Chong died. Liu Jun sent an envoy to the Emperor of Liao to inform of this. The Emperor of Liao sent an envoy back to make Liu Jun Emperor of the State of Northern Han. When Liu Jun sent a letter to the Emperor of Liao, he called himself son of the Emperor of Liao; when the Emperor of Liao sent a letter to Liu Jun, he called Liu Jun "Son Emperor."

3.4. The War against the State of Southern Tang

The State of Southern Tang was a big state. It was situated to the south of the Huai River. Its eastern boundary reached Quzhou (Now Quzhou, in the west part of Zhejiang Province) and Wuzhou (now Jinhua, Zhejiang Province); its western boundary reached Dongting Hu Lake (now Dongting Hu Lake, Hunan Province) and Xiang Jiang River (now Xiang Jiang River, Hunan Province); and southward it extended to Nan Ling Mountain (situated between Hunan Province and Guangdong Province). The capital of the State of Southern Tang was Jinling (now Nanjing, Jiangsu Province).

Li Jing, the Emperor of the State of Southern Tang, was ambitious. He wanted to be the emperor of all of China. He sent envoys to collude with the Emperor of Liao to invade Central China.

On 1 November, 954, Emperor Guo Rong of the Later Zhou Dynasty appointed Li Gu as the Commander-in-chief of the Huainan branch of the army. He appointed Wang Yan Chao, Regional Military Governor of Zhongwu, as the deputy commander-in-chief of this army. They commanded twelve generals including Han Ling Kun, the commander of the cavalry of the Royal Guards, to carry out an expedition against the State of Southern Tang.

Shouzhou (now Shouxian, Anhui Province) which was situated to the southern bank of the Huai Shui River (now Huai He River, Anhui Province) would be the first city to be attacked by the Later Zhou army. When the Southern Tang army defending Shouzhou got the news that the Later Zhou armies were coming, they were afraid. The Commander of the Southern Tang army defending Zhouzhou was Liu Ren Shan. He was resolute to defend the city of Shouzhou. When Li Jing, Emperor of the State of Southern Tang, heard that the Later Zhou army was coming, he appointed General Liu Yan Zhen as the commander-in-chief of the Northern Branch to command twenty thousand men to march to Shouzhou to prevent the Later Zhou army from marching south. He appointed Huang Fu Hui, Regional Military Governor of Fenghua, as the commander-in-chief of the backup army, and Yao Feng as the supervisor of this army. They commanded an army of thirty thousand men to station in Dingyuan (now Dingyuan, Anhui Province).

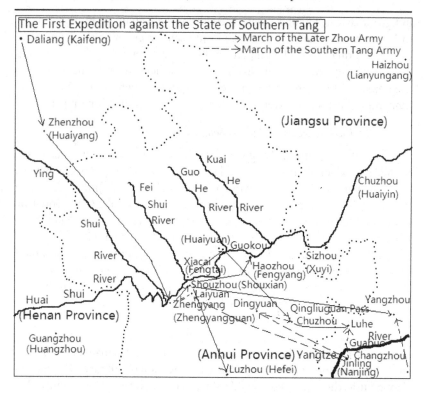

Map of the First Expedition against the Southern Tang

   Li Gu marched his army to the northern bank of the Hui Shui River opposite to Zhengyang (now Zhengyangguan which is thirty-five kilometers to the southwest of Shouxian, Anhui Province). Li Gu ordered the soldiers to build floating bridges on the Huai Shui River. The Later Zhou army crossed the Huai Shui River on the floating bridges and entered Zhengyang. Then the Later Zhou army marched northeastward towards Shouzhou. On 10 December, 954, the Later Zhou army fought a battle with the Southern Tang army under the city of Shouzhou. The Later Zhou army won the battle. On 3 January 955 they fought another battle in Shangyao (a place to the south of Shouxian, Anhui Province). Again the Later Zhou army won the battle.

   On 6 January 955 Emperor Guo Rong of the Later Zhou Dynasty issued an imperial order informing his ministers and generals that he would personally command the expedition against the State of Southern Tang. He appointed Xiang Xun, the Regional Military Governor of Zhen'an, as the commander-in-chief of the army defending Daliang, the capital of the Later Zhou Dynasty. He ordered Li Chong Jin, Regional Military Governor of Guide, to command an army to march to Zhengyang and he ordered Bai Chong jin, Regional Military Governor of Heyang, to command an army to be stationed in Yingshang (now Yingshang, Anhui Province). On 8 January

955 Emperor Guo Rong started south from Daliang.

Li Gu commanded the Later Zhou army to attack the city of Shouzhou and they fought for a long time but could not take it. General Liu Yan Zhen of the State of Southern Tang sent an army to recue Shouzhou. His army reached Laiyuan Town (which was situated to the southwest of Shouxian, Anhui Province). Li Jing, the Emperor of the State of Southern Tang, sent several hundred warships to sail along the Huai Shui River towards Zhengyang. The floating bridges were threatened by the warships. Li Gu called a council of all his subordinates to discuss the situation. He said, "We cannot fight the enemy warships on the river. If they destroy our bridges, we will be attacked by enemies from the front and the rear. Then we will not be able to go back. We'd better retreat to Zhengyang to defend our floating bridges and wait for His Majesty to come."

When Emperor Guo Rong learned of Li Gu's plan, he immediately sent an envoy to stop Li Gu from retreating. But when the envoy arrived, the Later Zhou army under Li Gu had already burned all the food supply and had retreated to Zhengyang. On 13 January, Emperor Guo Rong reached Chenzhou (now Huaiyang, Henan Province). He urged Li Chong Jin to march quickly to the Huai Shui River. The warships of the State of Southern Tang were sailing up the river and the Southern Tang army under Liu Yan Zhen was marching on Zhengyang. Li Chong Jin commanded his army to cross the Huai Shui River on the floating bridges and reached Zhengyang. At that time the Southern Tang army under Liu Yan Zhen was marching towards Zhengyang. Li Chong Jin commanded his army to intercept the Southern Tang army. A great battle broke out. The Southern Tang army was defeated and Liu Yan Zhen, their commander, was killed. More than ten thousand Southern Tang soldiers were slaughtered. The Later Zhou army got thirty thousand pieces of equipment from the Southern Tang army.

When Huang Fu Hui and Yao Feng received this news, they commanded their army to retreat from Dingyuan to Qingliuguan Pass, which was situated twelve kilometers west to Chuzhou (now Chuzhou, Anhui Province).

On 20 January 955 Emperor Guo Rong of the Later Zhou Dynasty reached Zhengyang. He appointed Li Chong Jin as Commander-in-chief of the army of the Huainan Branch to replace Li Gu. He appointed Li Gu as Governor of Shouzhou. On 22 January Emperor Guo Rong arrived at the foot of the city wall of Shouzhou. He ordered the soldiers to pitch camp on the northern bank of Feishui River (now Fei He River, Anhui Province). And he ordered his army to lay siege to the city of Shouzhou. He also had the floating bridges moved from Zhengyang to Xiacai (now Fengtai, Anhui Province).

At that time the Southern Tang troops warships sailed along the Huai Shui River and more than ten thousand Southern Tang troops camped at the foot of Tushan Mountain (in the southeast of Huaiyuan, Anhui Province). On 26 January 955 Emperor Guo Rong ordered Zhao Kuang Yin to lead an army to attack the Southern Tang army at the foot of Tushan Mountain. When Zhao Kuan Yin arrived there, he ordered a hundred cavalrymen to attack the camps. When the Southern Tang troops came out of their camps to fight, the Later Zhou cavalrymen pretended to be overwhelmed and retreated. More than ten thousand Southern Tang troops went after them. When they reached Guokou (in the northeast of Huaiyuan, Anhui Province), the Southern Tang troops fell into a trap. He Yan Xi, their commander, was killed. The Later Zhou army under Zhao Kuang Yin captured more than fifty warships.

On 2 February 955 Emperor Guo Rong ordered Zhao Kuang Yin to lead an army to make a surprise attack on Qingliuguan Pass (12.5 kilometers west of Chuzhou, Anhui Province). This pass was strategically located and difficult of access. It was located north of the Yangtze River and south of the Huai Shui River. The mountains there were steep and the valleys were deep. When the vanguards of the Later Zhou army arrived, Huang Fu Hui deployed his army at the foot of Chingliu Mountain ready to fight them. But suddenly Zhao Kuang Yin and his army appeared behind the mountain. Huang Fu Hui was shocked. He immediately commanded his army to retreat into the city of Chuzhou and break the bridge over the moat around the city.

Undeterred, Zhao Kuang Yin urged his horse to jump into the moat and swam across and reached the foot of the city wall. The soldiers with him crossed the city moat the same way. Standing atop the city wall, Huang Fu Hui shouted to Zhao Kuang Yin, "You fight for your master and I fight for my own master. Will you allow me to come out of the city and deploy my army in battle formation? Then we can have a fair fight." Zhao Kuang Yin smiled and said, "All right." He ordered his soldiers to turn back a little.

Then Huang Fu Hui commanded his soldiers to come out of the city, and he deployed them in battle formation. When Zhao Kuang Yin saw this, he dropped the reins and just holding his horse by the neck, he urged his horse to gallop forward to the enemy battle formation as fast as it could. While the horse was racing ahead, Zhao Kuang Yin called out, "I will only kill Huang Fu Hui. The rest are not my enemy!" When he reached the battle formation of the enemy, Zhao Kuang Yin waved his sword like a whip and beat Huang Fu Hui on the head. Huang Fu Hui was badly wounded and was captured. Yao Feng, another general of the Southern Tang army, was also captured. Then Zhao Kuang Yin commanded his army to go into the city of Chuzhou.

Several days later, Zhao Hong Yin, Zhao Kuang Yin's father, who was also a high ranking commander of the army of the Later Zhou Dynasty, led an army to the foot of the city wall of Chuzhou at midnight. Zhao Hong Yin shouted from the foot of the city wall, demanding his son to open the city gate and let him in. Zhao Kuang Yin shouted to his father from the top of the city wall, "Father and son are of the closest relationship. But I am guarding the city gate for the Emperor. I cannot open the city gate at midnight even though you are my father." Zhao Hong Yin had to stay outside the city all night long. He entered the city when dawn came.

Zhao Kuang Yin sent some envoys to escort Huang Fu Hui, who had been badly wounded and was lying on a stretcher, and Yao Feng to Emperor Guo Rong. When Huang Fu Hui saw Emperor Guo Rong, he said, "I have done my best to serve my master. In the past I fought against the Khitan army many times. But I have never seen any soldiers as keen as those under the command of Zhao Kuang Yin!" He highly praised the valor of Zhao Kuang Yin. Emperor Guo Rong released Huang Fu Hui and Yao Feng. Several days later Huang Fu Hui died.

After Zhao Kuang Yin took Chuzhou, Premier Fan Zhi recommended Zhao Pu, a scholar, as the chief of staff of the army stationed in Chuzhou. Zhao Kuang Yin talked with him and found that he was really very intelligent. At that time Zhao Hong Yin, Zhao Kuang Yin's father, fell ill in Chuzhou. Zhao Pu took good care of him. Zhao Hong Yin was deeply moved. Since Zhao Pu bore the family name of Zhao, Zhao Hong Yin treated Zhao Pu as a close relative descended from the same ancestor.

At that time a hundred robbers were captured and were going to be executed. Zhao Pu suspected that there would be innocent people among them. He talked to Zhao Kuang Yin. Zhao Kuang Yin asked Zhao Pu to interrogate the suspects; Zhao Pu found that seventeen of them were innocent and they were released.

Zhao Kuang Yin became more and more famous. Every time before going into battle he decorated his horse with red tassels and he wore bright colored armor. A fellow general said, "You will attract the attention of the enemies and will be identified by them." Zhao Kuang Yin said, "That is exactly what I want to do. I intentionally let them identify me on the battlefield."

It came to the attention of Emperor Guo Rong of the Later Zhou Dynasty that the Southern Tang army in Yangzhou (now Yangzhou, Jiangsu Province) was not prepared for war. So he sent General Han Ling Kun with an army to attack. On 21 February 956 Han Ling Kun, commanding his army, secretly reached Yangzhou. He ordered General Bai Yan Yu to take several hundred cavalrymen and ride into the city. The Southern Tang did not know they were soldiers of the Later Zhou Dynasty. Then Han Ling Kun arrived with the main force. Jia Chong, the commanding general of the Southern Tang army, ordered his men to set fire to the official buildings and the houses of the people. Then they abandoned the city and fled through the southern gate of the city. The Later Zhou army under Han Ling Kun took the city of Yangzhou without much of a fight.

On 17 March 956 Li Jing, Emperor of the State of Southern Tang, sent Li De Ming as his envoy to see Emperor Guo Rong of the Later Zhou Dynasty. Li De Ming conveyed the message that the Later Zhou army would withdraw back to the north on the following conditions: Li Jing would give up the title of emperor; the State of Southern Tang would cede Shouzhou (now Shouxian, Anhui Province), Haozhou (now Fengyang, Anhui Province), Sizhou (now Xuyi, Jiangsu Province), Chǔzhou (now Huaiyin, Jiangsu Province), Guangzhou (now Huangchuan, Henan Province), and Haizhou (now Lianyungang, Jiangsu Province) to the Later Zhou Dynasty; and the State of Southern Tang would contribute certain quantities of gold and silver and bundles of silk to the Later Zhou Dynasty. Emperor Guo Rong refused to accept the terms because half of the land in the area to the north of the

Yangtze River had been occupied by the Later Zhou Dynasty. Emperor Guo Rong's intention was to get the whole area to the north of the Yangtze River.

Li De Ming saw that the Later Zhou army was indeed very powerful. He told Emperor Guo Rong that he would go back to persuade Emperor Li Jing of the State of Southern Tang to cede the whole area to the north of the Yangtze River to the Later Zhou Dynasty. But when Li De Ming went back to Jinling and put forward the suggestion, Emperor Li Jing was outraged and put him to death for the crime of betraying the State of Southern Tang for personal gain.

On 2 April 956 Emperor Guo Rong of the Later Zhou Dynasty appointed Li Chong Jin as the Commander-in-chief of the armies attacking Shouzhou and Luzhou (now Hefei, Anhui Province). He appointed Wu Xing De as the Commander-in-chief of the army attacking Haozhou (now Fengyang, Anhui Province).

On 2 April 956 General Lu Meng Jin of the Southern Tang army commanded an army of over ten thousand men to march from Changzhou (now Changzhou, Jiangsu Province) to attack Yangzhou. Han Ling Kun gave up the city of Yangzhou and ran away. Emperor Guo Rong sent Zhang Yong De with an army to rescue Yangzhou and he ordered Han Ling Kun to go back there. At the same time Emperor Guo Rong ordered Zhao Kuang Yin to lead an army of two thousand men and station them in Luhe (now Luhe, Jiangsu Province). Zhao Kuang Yin issued an order to his men, "If the soldiers of the Zhou army in Yangzhou defect and go past Luhe, cut their legs off!" When Han Ling Kun heard about this, he thought he'd better fight this time and defend the city of Yangzhou. On 7 April 956 the Later Zhou army under Han Ling Kun fought the Southern Tang army under Lu Meng Jun, in a place east of the city of Yangzhou. The Southern Tang army was defeated and Lu Meng Jun was captured.

Li Jing Dan, King of Qi of the State of Southern Tang, commanded twenty thousand men in crossing the Yangtze River to Guabuo (now Guabuo, Jiangsu Province) and marched his army northward. The Southern Tang army pitched camp in a place ten kilometers east of the city of Luhe. They planted piles of logs around their camps as fences to defend themselves. The Generals under Zhao Kuang Yin wanted to attack them.

Zhao Kuang Yin said, "Our enemies have pitched camp to defend themselves. This shows that they are afraid of us. Now we have only two thousand men. If we go to attack them, they will find out that they outnumber us. It would be better for us to wait until they come to attack us. Then we will fight against them and we will surely defeat them." Several days later the Southern Tang army came out of their camps and marched to Luhe. Zhao Kuang Yin led his army out and defeated them. More than five thousand Southern Tang soldiers were killed or captured. About ten thousand Southern Tang soldiers survived. Many Southern Tang soldiers ran away to the bank of the Yangtze River and jumped into the water, trying to escape, but many of them were drowned. From then on the special troops of the Southern Tang army were wiped out.

In this battle, some Later Zhou soldiers had not really been fighting. Zhao Kuang Yin was supervising the military operation. When he saw the soldiers who were not engaged seriously, he nicked the rims of their leather hats with his sword. When the battle was over, he examined everyone's leather hats and picked out those soldiers whom he had noticed. About thirty men were executed for their cowardice. From then on all the soldiers under Zhao Kuang Yin would do their best in battles.

On 25 April Emperor Guo Rong arrived at Guokou. He wanted to go to Yangzhou, but Fan Zhi, the Premier, said that the soldiers were very tired and the food supply was short, and that it was time for the Emperor to go back to the capital. On 7 May, Emperor Guo Rong of the Later Zhou Dynasty ordered Li Chong Jin to continue the siege at Shouzhou. On the same day he started his journey back to Daliang from Guokou. On 24 May Emperor Guo Rong made it back to Daliang.

Zhang Yong De, High Ranking Commander of the Royal Guard Army and Regional Military Governor of Yicheng, stationed his army in Xiacai (now Fengtai, Anhui Province). In August 956 Lin Ren Zhao, a general of the State of Southern Tang, commanded the naval forces and land forces to reinforce Shouzhou. He ordered his soldiers to fill small boats with dry straw, then set them on fire and let the wind blow the boats down the Huai Shui River to burn the Later Zhou army's floating bridges. But suddenly the direction of the wind changed and the boats were blown back towards the Southern Tang army. The army under Lin Ren Zhao had to withdraw.

Zhang Yong De ordered that an iron chain be made, a thousand feet long. He ordered his soldiers to plant great logs of wood ten feet away from the floating bridges and then the iron chain was laid across the Hui Shui River to protect the bridges. From then on the Southern Tang soldiers could not get close.

In October 956, the Southern Tang army attacked the Later Zhou army under Zhang Yong De in Xiacai. One night Zhang Yong De ordered good swimmers in his army to swim to the bottoms of the ships and fix chains on them. The next day Zhang Yong De ordered his soldiers to attack the Southern Tang army. The Southern Tang ships were pretty helpless — they could not move forward and could not move backward, either. In order to escape, many Southern Tang soldiers jumped to the river and many were drowned. In December Emperor Guo Rong made Zhang Yong De Commander-in-chief of Royal Guard Army.

The Later Zhou army had already laid siege to Shouzhou for more than two years. Li Jing Da, King of Qi of the State of Southern Tang, was in Haozhou (now Fengyang, Anhui Province). In January 957 Li Jing Da sent Xu Wen Zhen, Regional Military Governor of Yong'an, General Bian Gao and General Zhu Yuan to command a great army of over thirty thousand men to rescue Shouzhou. They reached Zijinshan Mountain (now Bagong Shan Mountain, Anhui Province), two kilometers north of Shouzhou (now

Shouxian, Anhui Province). The Southern Tang troops pitched more than ten camps there. They built a road protected by walls on both sides to transport food supplies to Shouzhou.

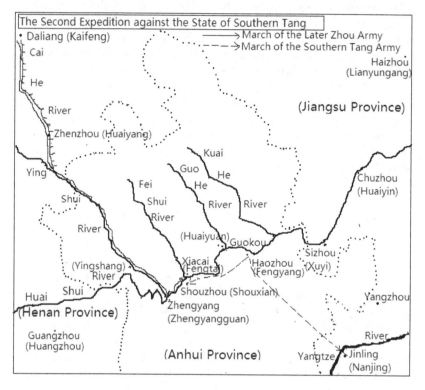

Map of the Second Expedition against the Southern Tang

On 20 January, 957, Emperor Guo Rong of the Later Zhou Dynasty informed his ministers and generals that he would be going to the area south of the Huai Shui River next month. During the previous expedition against the State of Southern Tang Emperor Guo Rong had found that the warships of the Southern Tang army moved very agily. Bbecause the Later Zhou army had no warships on the Huai Shui River, the Southern Tang army had great advantage there. So after Emperor Guo Rong came back to Daliang from Shouzhou, he ordered that several hundred warships should be built on the Bian Shui River (now Bian He River, a section of Tongji Canal) which flowedd past the west of Daliang. When the warships were built, he ordered the Southern Tang naval soldiers who had been captured to teach the naval soldiers of the Later Zhou army how to fight battles on rivers.

On 17 February 957 Emperor Guo Rong started from Daliang. The warships of the Later Zhou Dynasty sailed from Daliang along Cai He River southward into Ying Shui River. Then they sailed southward along Ying

Shui River to Zhengyang, and from there into the Huai Shui River. When the Southern Tang soldiers saw the warships of the Later Zhou Dynasty, they were very much taken by surprise.

On 27 February Emperor Guo Rong reached Xiacai (now Fengtai, Anhui Province). On 2 March he crossed the Huai Shui River and reached the city of Shouzhou, and stationed his army in Zijinshan Mountain. He ordered Zhao Kuang Yin to lead an army to attack the two camps of the Southern Tang army in Zijinshan Mountain. Three thousand Southern Tang soldiers were killed. Then the Later Zhou army under Zhao Kuang Yin destroyed the road protected by the walls through which the Southern Tang army had been provisioning Shouzhou. From then on the Southern Tang armies were cut in two and the Southern Tang army defending Shouzhou could not get food supplies and reinforcements from outside.

On 5 March, Emperor Guo Rong ordered the Later Zhou armies to attack the camps of the Southern Tang armies in Zijinshan Mountain. The Southern Tang were defeated and more than ten thousand Southern Tang soldiers were killed. Generals Xu Wen Zhen, Bian Gao and Yang Shou Zhong were captured. Emperor Guo Rong personally commanded an army to pursue the defeated Southern Tang army along the northern bank of Huai Shui River. The generals of the Later Zhou army pursued the Southern Tang army along the southern bank of the river; and the warships of the Later Zhou army sailed down the river. About forty thousand Southern Tang soldiers were killed or surrendered.

Li Jing Da, King of Qi of the State of Southern Tang, and Chen Jue escaped back to Jinling from Haozhou. When Liu Ren Zhan, Regional Military Governor of Qinghuai and Commander-in-chief of the Southern Tang army defending Shouzhou, was informed that the Southern Tang armies reinforcing Shouzhou had been defeated, he was disheartened. On 12 March Emperor Guo Rong came to Xiacai from Guokou. On 13 March he sent an envoy to Shouzhou to deliver a letter to Liu Ren Zhan demanding that he surrender. There was no immediate response. On 17 March Emperor Guo Rong arrayed a great army at the foot of the city wall of Shouzhou to display the strength of the Later Zhou army. At that time Liu Ren Zhan was deathly ill and had lost consciousness. On 19 March Zhou Ting Gou, the supervisor of the Southern Tang army defending Shouzhou, wrote a letter in the name of Liu Ren Zhan saying that he would surrender. He sent an envoy to deliver the letter to Emperor Guo Rong of the Later Zhou Dynasty. On 20 March Emperor Guo Rong sent Zhang Bao Xu as his envoy to go into Shouzhou with an imperial letter acknowledging that he would accept Liu Ren Zhan's surrender; and on 21 March Emperor Guo Rong commanded his great army to the northern gate of Shouzhou to accept the surrender of the Southern Tang army.

Liu Ren Zhan was carried on a stretcher out the city gate, accompanied by Zhou Ting Gou and his subordinate generals of the Southern Tang army. Emperor Guo Rong went forward to Liu Ren Zhan and comforted him, telling him to go back into the city to regain his health. On 24 March Emperor Guo

Rong appointed Liu Ren Zhan Regional Governor of Tianping and issued an imperial order to praise Liu Ren Zhan's devotion to his master. On that day Liu Ren Zhan died of illness. On 29 March Emperor started his journey back to Daliang from Xiacai. On 13 April Emperor Guo arrived in Daliang.

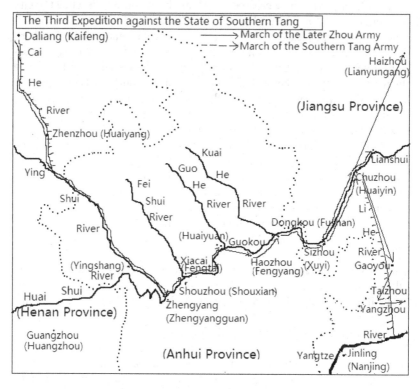

Map of Third Expedition against the Suthern Tang

On 19 October 957 Emperor Guo Rong started from Daliang to the south to carry out his third expedition against the State of Southern Tang. On 4 November Emperor Guo Rong reached Guokou. On that night the Emperor crossed the Huai Shui River. On 5 November he reached a place west of the city of Haozhou (now Fengyang, Anhui Province). There was a sandy island in the Huai Shui River nine kilometers northeast of the city of Haozhou. The troops of the Southern Tang army had pitched their camps on this sandy island. They thought that they would be protected by the river water. On 6 November Emperor Guo Rong ordered Kang Bao Yi, a commander of the Royal Guard Army, to send several hundred soldiers across the river by riding on the humps of camels. Zhao Kuang Yin urged his horse to jump into the water and they floated to the sandy island. The cavalrymen under his command all crossed over to the island by the same way. Then they started a fierce attack on the camps. They defeated the Southern Tang army and captured many warships.

On 11 November Emperor Guo Rong personally commanded the attack on Haozhou. All the strongholds around Haozhou were taken by the Later Zhou army. More than seventy warships of the Southern Tang army were burned. More than two thousand Southern Tang soldiers were killed. Guo Ting Wei, the commander-in-chief of the Southern Tang army defending Haozhou, sent a letter to Emperor Guo Rong stating that he would surrender but he hoped that Emperor Guo Rong would allow him to delay the surrender for a few days so that he could ask permission from Li Jing, the Emperor of the State of Southern Tang, because Guo Ting Wei's whole family was in Jinling. Emperor Guo Rong of the Later Zhou Dynasty gave his consent. On 19 November Emperor Guo Rong was informed that several hundred warships were sailing down the Huai Shui River to rescue Haozhou and had already reached the confluence of the Huan Shui River (now Kuai He River, Anhui Province) with the Huai Shui River.

Emperor Guo Rong ordered his warships to sail down the Huai Shui River to meet the warships of the Southern Tang army. Emperor Guo Rong personally commanded the army to march along the bank of Huai Shui River eastward to intercept the enemy. He ordered Zhao Kuang Yin to lead a group of special cavalrymen as the vanguard of the whole army. On 21 November a great battle was fought in Dongkou (now in Fushan, Anhui Province) which was situated fifty kilometers east of Haozhou. The Southern Tang army was defeated. More than five thousand Southern Tang soldiers were killed and two thousand surrendered. The Later Zhou army captured three hundred warships of the Southern Tang army.

Carrying on this momentum, Emperor Guo Rong commanded his victorious army to pursue the defeated Southern Tang army eastward along the Huai Shui River. On 23 November the Later Zhou army reached Sizhou (now Xuyi, Jiangsu Province). Zhao Kuang Yin ordered an attack on the city of Sizhou first. The Later Zhou army under Zhao Kuang Yin set fire to the southern gate of the city and took a moon-shaped stronghold outside the city. On 3 December 957 Fan Zai Yu, the commanding general of the Southern Tang army defending Sizhou, surrendered and handed over the city of Sizhou to the Later Zhou army.

On 6 December Emperor Guo Rong ordered Zhao Kuang Yin to march forward along the southern bank of the Huai Shui River. He himself commanded an army along the northern bank. Their warships sailed along the Huai Shui. On 9 December the Later Zhou army reached a place northwest of Chǔzhou (now Huaiyin, Jiangsu Province). A battle was fought and the Southern Tang army was defeated once again; they ran away along the river. Emperor Guo Rong personally commanded his army to rtack them down. Zhao Kuang Yin commanded the troops under him as the vanguard of the whole army. They marched for thirty kilometers and caught up with the enemy. After one more battle, Zhao Kuang Yin captured Chen Cheng Zhao, the commander-in-chief of the Southern Tang army rescuing Haozhou, Sizhou, Chuzhou and Haizhou. The Later Zhou army captured three hundred warships and seven thousand Southern Tang soldiers.

From then on no more warships of the Southern Tang army could be found on Huai Shui River. On 10 December Guo Ting Wei, the commander-in-chief of the Southern Tang army defending Haozhou, surrendered and handed over the city to the Later Zhou army. On 13 December Cui Wan Di, the commander-in-chief of the Southern Tang army defending Lianshui (now Lianshui, Jiangsu Province) surrendered with the city of Lianshui. Emperor Guo Rong sent General Wu Shou Qi with several hundred cavalrymen to Yangzhou (now Yangzhou, Jiangsu Province). When the Later Zhou cavalrymen reached Gaoyou (now Gaoyou, Jiangsu Province), the Southern Tang soldiers forced the people of Yangzhou to leave their homes and cross the Yangtze River to the south, then they set fire to the government offices and all the houses. When General Wu Shu Qi reached Yangzhou, there was nothing left.

On 25 December the Later Zhou army took the city of Taizhou (now Taizhou, Jiangsu Province). On 1 January 958 Emperor Guo Rong arrived at the foot of the city of Chǔzhou (now Huaiyin, Jiangsu Province). He sent General Wang Han Zhang to attack Haizhou (now Lianyungang, Jiangsu Province). On 5 January 958 the Later Zhou army under Wang Han Zhang took Haizhou. On 8 January 958 Emperor Guo Rong mobilized the able bodied men outside Chǔzhou to dig a short canal (which became the Guan He River) in the northwest of Chǔzhou to link the Huai Shui River with the Li Yunhe Canal which flowed southward into the Yangtze River. Then several hundred warships of the Later Zhou army sailed from the Huai Shui River through the Li Yunhe Canal into the Yangtze River.

On 23 January Emperor Guo Rong personally commanded the army to attack Chǔzhou (now Huaiyin, Jiangsu Province). Zhao Kuang Yin attacked the city from the north. He fought day and night without a rest against a rain of arrows and stones. On 24 January Zhao Kuang Yin commanded his soldiers to climb the city wall and at last took they the city of Chǔzhou.

On 10 March Emperor Guo Rong went to Yingluan Town (in Jiangdu, Jiangsu Province). On 12 March he went to the place where the canal reached the Yangtze River, where he saw over thirty Southern Tang army warships. He ordered Zhao Kuang Yin to command the Later Zhou army warships to attack. When the Southern Tang troops saw the Later Zhou warships coming, they sailed away. Zhao Kuang Yin commanded the warships to sail to the southern bank of the Yangtze River, and they destroyed the Southern Tang army camps there. Then he commanded his victorioys army back to the northern bank.

On 17 March Emperor Li Jing of the State of Southern Tang sent Liu Cheng Yu, one of his ministers, as his envoy to Emperor Guo Rong with a letter offering to cede Luzhou (now Hefei, Anhui Province), Shuzhou (now Qianshan, Anhui Province), Qizhou (now Qichun, Hubei Province) and Huangzhou (now Xinzhou, Hubei Province) to the Later Zhou Dynasty; and suggesting that he hoped that the Yangtze River would be the demarcation for the boundary between the Later Zhou Dynasty and the State of Southern Tang. Emperor Guo Rong accepted Li Jing's conditions for peace.

From then on the area south of the Hui Shui River and north of the Yangtze River belonged to the Later Zhou Dynasty. In this area there were fourteen prefectures, sixty counties, and two hundred and twenty-two thousand households. On 4 April Emperor Guo Rong started his journey back to Daliang from Yangzhou.

3.5. Northern Expedition

On 20 March 959 Emperor Guo Rong of the Later Zhou Dynasty announced that he would carry out a northern expedition to take back some of the prefectures which had been captured by the State of Liao. On 23 March he ordered Han Tong, a high ranking commander of the Royal Guard Army, to lead an army to march north first. On 30 March Emperor Guo Rong set out from Daliang. On 17 April he reached Cangzhou (now Cangzhou, Hebei Province). On that day Emperor Guo Rong commanded an army of over thirty thousand men to march northward to the territory of the State of Liao. On 18 April Emperor Guo Rong reached Ningzhou (now Qingxian, Hebei Province) which was situated fifty kilometers north to Cangzhou. Wang Hong, the governor of Ningzhou of the State of Liao, surrendered and handed the city of Ningzhou to the Later Zhou army.

On 18 April Emperor Guo Rong divided his army into two parts. One part of his army would go on boats up the Canal (now Nan Yunhe Canal). The commander of this part of the army was Zhao Kuang Yin. The other part of the army would go by land. This part of the army was commanded by Han Tong. On 23 April Emperor Guo Rong went on board a dragon boat and sailed northward up the Canal. On 25 April the fleet reached Duliukou (now Duliu, Hebei Province) where the Canal and Daqing He River joined. Then the fleet turned west into Daqing He River. On 27 April the fleet reached Yijinguan Pass (the old site of the pass is in Bazhou, Hebei Province). Zhong Ting Hui, the commander of the Liao army defending Yijinguan Pass, surrendered. The river narrowed from this section onward and big boats could not sail any further west. On 28 April Emperor Guo Rong and his army had to give up the boats and went by land. They had to spend the night in the wild. Emperor Guo Rong arrived ahead of his main force, and there were only five hundred soldiers defending him. The officials following the Emperor were extremely nervous. In those days, the Liao army cavalry frequently popped up unexpected. But Zhao Kuang Yin was very calm. He simply commanded the officers and men of the Royal Guard Army to defend Emperor Guo Rong.

On 29 April Zhao Kuang Yin and his troops reached Waqiaoguan Pass (the old site of the pass is in the southwest of Xiongxian, Heber Province). Yao Nei Bin, the commander of the Liao army defending Waqiaoguan Pass surrendered and handed the pass over to Zhao Kuang Yin, and on that day Emperor Guo Rong himself entered Waqiaoguan Pass.

On 30 April Liu Chu Xin, the Governor of Mozhou (now Renqiu, Hebei Province) of the State of Liao, surrendered with the city of Mozhou. On 1 May the main force of the Later Zhou army commanded by Li Chong Jin arrived. On that day Gao Yin Hui, the Governor of Yingzhou (now Hejian, Hebei Province) of the State of Liao, surrendered with the city of Yingzhou. From then on, the area to the south of Waqiaoguan Pass had been pacified. In this expedition, the army of the Later Zhou Dynasty gained three prefectures, seventeen counties, and eighteen thousand three hundred and sixty households.

In this northern expedition Emperor Guo Rong collected all the books on the way and read them. One day, a bag made of reeds was found along their route. There was a wooden ruler of about three feet long in the bag. Several characters were carved on it which read, "The Commander-in-chief of the Royal Guard Army will become Emperor." This aroused Emperor Guo Rong's suspicion. At that time the Commander-in-chief of the Royal Guard Army was Zhang Yong De. Zhang Yong De was the son-in-law of the late Emperor Guo Wei. He had indeed both the possibility and ability to become emperor. In order to make sure that his son would succeed to the throne, Emperor Guo Rong decided to deprive Zhang Yong De of his title of Commander-in-chief of the Royal Guard Army.

On 2 May 959 Emperor Guo Rong held a banquet to celebrate the victory. After the banquet a meeting was held. The Emperor said that he would go on north to take Youzhou (now the area around Beijing). But the generals did not agree with Emperor Guo Rong's opinion. They said, "Your Majesty has left the capital for forty-two days. The areas to the south of Youzhou have been taken without a battle. You have done great deeds, Your Majesty. Now the cavalrymen of the State of Liao have been gathered in the north part of Youzhou. It is not suitable for Your Majesty to go deep into enemy territory." Emperor Guo Rong did not like the remarks of the generals. Ion any event, that night Emperor Guo Rong fell ill, so he had to give up the idea of attacking Youzhou. On 5 May Emperor Guo Rong ordered that Waqiaoguan Pass be renamed as Xiongzhou. On 8 May Emperor Guo Rong started his journey back to Daliang from Xionzhou, and made it back by 30 May.

3.6. Emperor Guo Rong is Succeeded by the Seven-Year-Old Guo Zong Xun

On 6 June 959 Emperor Guo Rong made his eldest surviving son Guo Zong Xun King of Liang. On 15 June, Emperor Guo Rong appointed Premier Fan Zhi and Premier Wang Pu as members of the Privy Council. He appointed Wei Ren Pu, the head of the Privy Council, to be in charge of the Emperor's secretariat work also. He appointed Han Tong the Deputy Commander of the Royal Guard Army guarding the Emperor. He promoted Zhang Yong De to the position of a premier and minister of the Ministry Department. But his title of Commander-in-chief of the Royal Guard Army was taken away and he no longer held any military power. Emperor Guo Rong appointed Zhao Kuang Yin as Commander-in-chief of the Royal Guard Army to replace Zhang Yong De.

On 19 June 959 Emperor Guo Rong passed away at the age of thirty-nine. On 20 June, the will of the late Emperor was read before Guo Zong Xun,

King of Liang, ordering him to ascend the throne before of the coffin of the late Emperor. Guo Zong Xun ascended the throne of the Later Zhou Dynasty at the age of seven. The Temple Title of the late Emperor Guo Rong was Shizong (meaning Ancestor of the Generations).

CHAPTER THREE: THE ESTABLISHMENT OF THE SONG DYNASTY AND THE REIGN OF EMPEROR ZHAO KUANG YIN

1. Zhao Kuang Yin Is Draped with a Yellow Robe by His Subordinates at the Courier Station of Chenqiao

On 1 January 960 all the officials of the Later Zhou Dynasty were gathered at the court to express their congratulations to Emperor Guo Zong Xun and to celebrate the New Year. Suddenly, envoys from Zhenzhou (now Zhengding, Hebei Province) and from Dingzhou (now Dingzhou, Hebei Province) came hurriedly in and reported to the Emperor that great armies of the State of Liao had marched southward and had joined forcess with the armies of the State of Northern Han. After discussion with Premier Fan Zhi and Premier Wang Pu, the seven-year-old Emperor issued an order that Zhao Kuang Yin, the Grand Commandant and the Commander-in-chief of the Royal Guard Army, should command the generals and men of the Royal Guard Army to march north to cope with the threat.

On 2 January, General Murong Yan Zhao led the vanguard army on the march north. On 3 January Zhao Kuang Yin commanded the main force of the Royal Guard Army to march from Daliang to the north. At that time there was a prophecy spreading among the people of Daliang that the Commander-in-chief of the Royal Guard Army would become Emperor. On the day when the army began to march, Miao Xun, an officer of the Royal Guard Army, who could read the indications of the phenomena of the sun, the moon and the stars, saw that there was another sun under the sun. The friction of light of the two suns could be seen. He pointed at the two suns and said to Chu Zhao Fu, the head of the bodyguards of Zhao Kuang Yin, and said, "This is the will of Heaven!"

On that day Zhao Kuang Yin commanded his great army to march northward. They marched out of Daliang, the capital city of the Later Zhou Dynasty, and marched for about fifteen kilometers and reached the southern bank of the Yellow River. They crossed the Yellow River and reached the northern bank. Then they turned northeastward. They marched for about twenty more kilometers and arrived at a place named Chenqiao (now Chenqiao Village, Chenqiao Town, in the southeast of Fengqiu, Henan Province). There was a courier station in Chenqiao Village. Zhao Kuang Yin decided to let his army to stay in Chenqiao Village for the night. There was a great piece of flat land in front of the Courier Station of Chenqiao. He ordered the troops to camp there. He entered the Courier Station and tied his horse by a pagoda tree and went into a house behind this tree.

The flat land in front of the Courier Station of Chenqiao

That night Zhao Kuang Yin drank some wine and went to bed. Very soon he fell into a sound sleep. The generals and men of the army sat together and held a discussion. One of the officers said, "Now the Emperor is very young and weak. He would not appreciate us even if we fought very hard to defeat the enemies. It would be better for us to make the Commander-in-chief Emperor. Then we will go on the northern expedition." All the officers and men agreed. Li Chu Yun, an officer, went to see Zhao Kuang Yi, Zhao Kuang Yin's younger brother, and Zhao Pu, the Secretary of the army, and told them what was happening in the army. Before he could finish his words, the generals suddenly came with swords in their hands. They informed Zhao Kuang Yi and Zhao Pu that the officers and men of the army had reached an agreement to make the Commander-in-chief Emperor. Zhao Kuang Yi said to them, "Although it is the will of Heaven that changes the Emperor, it also has a lot to do with the popular sentiment. If you can discipline the officers and men under you and strictly prohibit them from looting, then the people in the capital will feel at ease and the whole country will be in peace. Then you may enjoy wealth and rank." All the generals agreed with him.

The stone tablet marks the place where Zhao Kuang Yin was draped with a yellow robe. The house behind the stone tablet was the house in which Zhao Kuang Yin had slept for the night

The tree to which Zhao Kuang Yin tied his horse

Then Zhao Kuang Yi sent Guo Yan Yun, an officer, to ride quickly to tell the news to Shi Shou Xin, a High Ranking Commander of the Royal Guard Army, and Wang Shen Qi, Supervisor of the Royal Guard Army. Shi Shou Xin and Wang Shen Qi both were devoted to Zhao Kuang Yin.

All the generals and men were lined up in formation and were waiting for the morning to come. Zhao Kuang Yin was still sound asleep in the room and did not know what had happened outside. At dawn of 4 January the generals pushed the door of the bedroom open and entered the room with their armor on and swords in their hands. They said, "Now we do not have a master. We will make you Emperor!"

Zhao Kuang Yin was so surprised that he jumped up from his bed. Before he could give an answer, a general had draped a yellow robe on him. All the generals and men knelt down and shouted, "Long live!" Then they helped Zhao Kuang Yin to mount his horse and began to march south. Zhao Kuang Yin could do nothing about it. Finally, he reined in his horse and said to the generals, "You are making me Emperor because you want wealth and rank. Now I will give an order. Will you obey my order?" All of the generals dismounted, knelt down on their knees and said, "We will obey your order!" Then Zhao Kuang Yin said, "I have served under the Emperor and the Empress Dowager. You must not frighten them. All the ministers are my fellow colleagues. You must not bully and humiliate them. You must not loot the treasure houses of the court and the houses of the officials and ordinary people. Those who obey these orders will be rewarded. Those who violate these orders will be put to death!" All the generals touched their heads to the ground and said, "Yes. We will obey these orders!" When the army reached the capital, all the officers and men entered the city through Renhe Gate (one of the east gates of the city wall of Kaifeng) in great discipline, and the soldiers did not cause the slightest trouble to the people.

The next morning Zhao Kuang Yin sent Pan Mei, the army's officer in charge of external affairs, as his envoy to the court to see the magnates in power and to inform them what had happened. At that time Premier Fan Zhi and Premier Wang Pu had just finished morning court and had not yet left. When they received this information, Premier Fan Zhi held the hand of Wang Pu very tightly and went out of the palace. Fan Zhi said, "It is our fault for sending out the general in such a great hurry!" He held Wang Pu's hand so tight that his finger nails dug into the flesh of Wang Pu's hand and nearly caused it to bleed. Wang Pu was in such great pain that he could not say anything. Han Tong, the Deputy Commander of the Royal Guard Army, rushed out of the palace intending to go home and summon the officers and men under him to resist Zhao Kuang Yin. But Wang Yan Sheng, a commander of the Royal Guard Army, who entered Daliang in the vanguard, saw Han Tong. He urged his horse to run after Han Tong. Wang Yan Sheng rode into Han Tong's home and killed Han Tong, his wife and son.

2. Zhao Kuang Yin Becomes Emperor

The generals helped Zhao Kuang Yin go up the Mingde Gate (one of the gates of the Palace City in Kaifeng). Then Zhao Kuang Yin ordered the officers and men to go back to their camps. He himself went back to the Office of the Commander-in-chief. He took off the yellow robe and sat down on his chair. A moment later the generals escorted Fan Zhi and Wang Pu into the Office of the Commander-in-chief. When Zhao Kuang Yin saw them, he cried bitterly with tears in his eyes and said, "Emperor Shizong granted me many favors and rewards. But now the officers and men under me have forced my hand. I am very sorry to have failed the expectation of Emperor Shizong. What shall I do?" Before Fan Zhi and Wang Pu could give an answer, Luo Yan Hun, a commander of the Royal Guard Army, said in a stern voice with one hand on the grip of his sword, "We don't have a master. We need an emperor today!" Fan Zhi and Wang Pu looked at each other and did not know what to do. Then Wang Pu, who apparently could also read Heavenly signs, stepped back a few steps and knelt down facing Zhao Kuang Yin and touched his head to the ground. Fan Zhi had to do the same.

This throne is the throne on which Emperor Zhao Kuang Yin once sat. The Chinese characters on the pillar on the right mean: "He was draped with a yellow robe in the Courier Station of Chenqiao; this great man brought peace to the whole realm." The characters on the pillar on the left mean: "This great emperor sat on the throne in the golden palace in the Eastern Capital; he used his great power to unify China." The characters on the horizontal board mean: "He did all he could to make the country prosperous."

Then Zhao Kuang Yin was shown to the court of Chongyuan Hall of the Palace of Daliang. A ceremony for the abdication of Emperor Guo Zong Xun and handing over the throne to Zhao Kuang Yin was to be held there. All the ministers and generals were summoned to that hall. At about three o'clock in the afternoon all the ministers and generals arrived. Tao Gu, the Secretary of the Grand Secretariat in charge of drawing up imperial orders, produced Emperor Guo Zong Xun of the Later Zhou Dynasty's Imperial Order of abdication. After the Imperial Order of Abdication was read, Zhao Kuang Yin was invited to the dais. After Zhao Kuang Yin had taken his place, all the ministers and generals knelt down and expressed their congratulations. Then the premiers helped Zhao Kuang Yin further up the steps of Chongyuan Hall. They helped Zhao Kuang Yin to put on the robe for an emperor with dragon designs on it. Then Zhao Kuang Yin ascended the throne of the Emperor. All the ministers and generals chanted their congratulations. Zhao Kuang Yin granted the title of King of Zheng to the abdicated Emperor, and granted Empress Dowager Fu the title of Empress Dowager of Zhou, and they were moved to the Western Palace. On 5 January Zhao Kuang Yin issued an imperial order that the name of the new Dynasty was Song. And thus the Song Dynasty was established.

Emperor Zhao Kuang Yin sent out envoys to all the prefectures to inform the governors that the Song Dynasty had replaced the Later Zhou Dynasty. On 6 January envoys were sent out to announce the imperial order to the commanders of the armies stationed in different places. On 8 January Emperor Zhao Kuang Yin issued an imperial order to grant Han Tong a high ranking honorary title and Han Tong was buried with a grand funeral ceremony.

Dragon Pavilion, the palace of the Song Dynasty

3. Emperor Zhao Kuang Yin Grants Rewards to Those Who Made Great Contributions in Making Him Emperor

On 11 January Emperor Zhao Kuang Yin granted rewards to those who had helped make him Emperor. He named Shi Shou Xin, originally a High Ranking Commander of the Royal Guard Army, the Regional Military Governor of the Army of Guide stationed in the area of Shangqiu (now Shangqiu, Henan Province) and Deputy Commander of the Infantry and Cavalry of the Royal Guard Army; he made Gao Huai De, originally Commander of the Cavalry of the Royal Guard Army, the Regional Military Governor of the Army of Yicheng stationed in the area of Huazhou (now Huaxian, Henan Province) and Deputy Commander-in-chief of the Royal Guard Army; he made Zhang Ling Duo, originally Commander of the

Infantry of the Royal Guard Army, the Regional Military Governor of the Army of Zhen'an stationed in Chenzhou (now Huaiyang, Henan Province) and Supervisor of the Infantry and Cavalry of the Royal Guard Army; he made Wang Shen Qi, originally Supervisor of the Infantry and Cavalry of the Royal Guard Army, the Regional Military Governor of the Army of Taining stationed in Yanzhou (now Yanzhou, Shandong Province) and High Ranking Commander of the Royal Guard Army. He made Zhang Guang Han, originally a Supervisor of the army, the Regional Military Governor of the Army of Jiangning stationed in Kuizhou (now Fengjie, Sichuan Province); he made Zhao Yin Wei, originally a Commander of the Royal Guard Army, the Regional Military Governor of the Army of Wuxin stationed in Suizhou (now Suining, Sichuan Province. And all the generals and officers who took part in this action got promotions.

On 19 January Emperor Zhao Kuang Yin promoted Han Ling Kun, who had been sent to command an army to patrol the northern border area, to Regional Military Governor of the Army of Tianping, stationed in Yunzhou (now Yuncheng, Shandong Province) and Commander of the Infantry and Cavalry of the Royal Guard Army. He made Murong Yan Zhao, who had been sent to command the vanguard army to Zhenzhou to resist the Liao army, Commander-in-chief of the Royal Guard Army and the Regional Military Governor of the Army of Zhaohua stationed in Jinzhou (now Ankang, Shaanxi Province) and Commander-in-chief of the Royal Guard Army. On 22 January Emperor Zhao Kuang Yin appointed the wise Zhao Pu as Chief Imperial Advisor. On 23 January Emperor Zhao Kuang Yin appointed Fu Yan Qing as Grand Tutor; he appointed Wang Jing as Grand Guardian; he appointed Li Yi Yin as Grand Commandant; he appointed Gao Bao Yong as grand Protector. On 24 January Emperor Zhao Kuang Yin appointed his younger brother Zhao Kuang Yi Supervisor of the Royal Guard Army and Commander-in-chief of the army in Muzhou (now Changyan, Hubei Province), and granted him the name of Zhao Guang Yi.

On 29 January Guo Chong, the commander of the army stationed in Zhenzhou (now Zhengyang, Hebei Province), reported to the Emperor that the Liao armies and the armies of the State of Northern Han had retreated.

4. Emperor Zhao Kuang Yin Makes His Mother Lady Du Empress Dowager

When Zhao Kuang Yin came back from Chenqiao, he sent Chu Zhao Fu, the head of his bodyguards, to inform his mother Lady Du that everything was alright and he'd made it home. When Lady Du heard that her son Zhao Kuang Yin had become Emperor, she said, "My son is always ambitious. Now he has really become an emperor!"

On 5 February Emperor Zhao Kuang Yin made his mother Lady Du Empress Dowager. A ceremony was held. Empress Dowager Du sat in a chair in a hall of the palace. Emperor Zhao Kuang Yin stood in front of her, bowed to her and expressed his congratulations. All the ministers and generals were also present to express their congratulations. But Empress Dowager Du looked sad, not happy. A courtier said to her, "We have heard that there is a saying which goes, 'A son of high status brings his mother greater respect.' Now your son has become Emperor. Why are you unhappy?" Empress Dowager Du said, "It is very difficult to be an emperor. The Emperor is above millions of people. If he can rule the people correctly, then the position of emperor is respected. But if he loses control of the situation, it is impossible for him to become an ordinary man again even if he wants to. This is my worry." Emperor Zhao Kuang Yin bowed again and said, "I will always remember your teachings."

5. Appointments of Officials of the Government

Emperor Zhao Kuang Yin respected the three premiers of the Later Zhou Dynasty. So Emperor Zhao Kuang Yin appointed Fan Zhi Premier, Chief Minister of Interior and Director of the Chancellery. He appointed Wang Pu Premier and Chief Minister of Public Works. He appointed Wei Ren Pu Premier and Director of the Secretariat. He appointed Wu Ting Zuo as the Head of the Privy Council which was in charge of military affairs. In the past during the Tang Dynasty and the period of Five Dynasties, it was the general practice that the emperor would invite the premiers to discuss important matters over tea. But after Fan Zhi, Wang Pu and Wei Ren Pu were appointed premiers of the Song Dynasty, they thought that, having been premiers of the Later Zhou Dynasty, it was uncomfortable to sit face to face with Emperor Zhao Kuang Yin. Zhao Kuang Yin was such a capable emperor that they were in awe of him. So they suggested to the Emperor that they would present their opinions on important matters by delivering memorandums to the Emperor instead of discussing such matters over tea. Emperor Zhao Kuang Yin accepted their suggestion. From then on the practice of discussing important matters over tea with the emperor was cancelled.

6. Suppression of Li Jun's Rebellion

Li Jun, the Regional Military Governor of the Army of Zhaoyi, had been appointed by Emperor Guo Rong of the Later Zhou Dynasty. The Army of Zhaoyi was stationed in Luzhou (now Changzhi, Shanxi Province). On 9 April 960 Emperor Zhao Kuang Yin sent an envoy to Luzhou to declare the Emperor's decision to promote Li Jun to Head of the Secretariat. Li Jun had in mind refusing the appointment. But the officers and officials under him tried very hard to persuade him to accept it. So he held a banquet to entertain the envoy. During the banquet Li Jun suddenly hung up a portrait of Emperor Guo Rong of the Later Zhou Dynasty on the wall and cried bitterly. All the officers and officials under Li Jun were very afraid. They told the envoy that Li Jun had been drunk and acted unusually. They asked the envoy not to mind.

When Liu Jun, the Emperor of the State of Northern Han, heard about this, he sent a secret letter to Li Jun suggesting that they should unite with each other and raise armies to attack the Song Dynasty. Li Shou Jie, Li Jun's eldest son, wept bitterly and tried his best to talk his father out of it. But Li Jun would not listen to his son's advice. Although Li Jun sent a reply to Emperor Zhao Kuang Yin to tell him that he would accept the appointment, he had already made up his mind to rebel.

The Emperor personally wrote a letter to comfort Li Jun and summoned Li Shou Jie to Daliang, the capital of the Song Dynasty. Li Jun sent Li Shou Jie to Daliang to observe the situation. When Li Shou Jie arrived at Daliang, Emperor Zhao Kuang Yin received him at court. The Emperor asked, "Crown Prince, why have you come?" Li Shou Jie was surprised to hear that and immediately knelt down and touched his head to the ground. He asked, "Why has Your Majesty said that? There must be somebody who has said something against my father." The Emperor said, "I have heard that you have tried several times to persuade your father to give up his plan to rebel, but he would not listen to you. He has sent you to the court and he hopes I will kill you. Now tell this to your father when you go back. 'If I were not the Emperor, you could do anything you like. Since I have become the Emperor, can you give in a little for me?'"

Li Shou Jie left Daliang and rode very quickly back to Luzhou and told what the Emperor had said to his father. Li Jun ordered one of his officials to draft a document denouncing Emperor Zhao Kuang Yin. The document listed all the crimes Zhao Kuang Yin had committed. On 15 April 960, Li Jun arrested Zhou Guang Xun, the supervisor of the army. He sent General Liu Ji Chong to deliver Zhou Guang Xun to the State of Northern Han and ask Liu Jun, the Emperor of the State of Northern Han, to send an army to help him. Then Li Jun sent an army southward to carry out a surprise attack on Zezhou (now Jincheng, Shanxi Province) and took it. Zhang Fu, the governor of Zezhou, was killed.

Qiu Zhong Qing, a subordinate of Li Jun, said to him, "You have carried out a rebellion alone. It is very dangerous. Although you depend on help from the State of Northern Han, you cannot get much help from them. The armies of the Song Dynasty are powerful. Your army is no match. It would be better for you to command your army to march westward, then go to Huaizhou and Mengjin, take Hulao and occupy Luoyang. Then you may fight eastward against the Song army and try to take control of the whole realm. This is by far the best plan for you." Li Jun said, "I am a general of the Zhou Dynasty. Emperor Guo Rong treated me as his brother. Many generals of the Royal Guard Army are my good friends. Once they hear that I have begun a rebellion, they will turn to my side. My cause will surely be successful." He turned down Qiu Zhong Qing's suggestion.

On 18 April the news that Li Jun had rebelled reached Daliang. Wu Ting Zuo, the Head of the Privy Council, said to Emperor Zhao Kuang Yin, "The City of Luzhou is a strong city and protected by the Taihang Mountains. If Li Jun defends this city with its natural barriers, we cannot take it in a month, even in a year. But Li Jun is proud. He is brave but he is not a man of resources. If we send an army to march northward, I am sure Li Jun will leave Luzhou to meet our army. Once he has left Luzhou, we can easily capture him." On 20 April Emperor Zhao Kuang Yin sent General Shi Shou Xin and General Gao Huai De to head the vanguard armies in carrying out an expedition against Li Jun. Before they started, Emperor Zhao Kuang Yin said to them, "Don't let Li Jun go to the Taihang Mountains. You must act quickly and occupy the important passes. Then he will be surely defeated." On 2 May Emperor Zhao Kuang Yin ordered General Murong Yan Zhao, the Regional Military Governor of the Army of Zhenning which was stationed in Chanzhou (now Puyang, Henan Province), Wang Quan Bin, the Regional Military Governor of the Army of Zhangde which was stationed in Xiangzhou (now Anyang, Henan Province), to command their armies to join forces with Shi Shou Xin and Gao Huai De from the east.

Liu Jun, the Emperor of the State of Northern Han, sent Li Bi, a general of the State of Northern Han, to see Li Jun with an imperial letter written; he also sent the usual emoluments of gold, silk and horses. Then Li Jun again sent Li Ji Chong to Jinyang (now Taiyuan, Shanxi Province), the capital of the State of Northern Han, to ask Liu Jun to command all the men he could raise in a march southward, and to tell Liu Jun that he himself would command his army as the vanguard. Then Liu Jun sent an envoy to ask the Emperor of Khitan to send an army too. But before the Khitan armies had gathered, Liu Ji Chong told Liu Jun that Li Jun did not want the Khitan army to come. So on 3 May Liu Jun, the Emperor of the State of the Northern Han, commanded all the armies he could raise to march southward through Tuanbogu Valley (which is situated to the southeast to Qixian, Shanxi Province).

The ministers of the State of Northern Han saw the Emperor off by the side of Fenshui River (now Fen He River, Shanxi Province). Zhao Hua, one of the premiers of the State of Northern Han, said to Liu Jun, "Li Jun has launched this rebellion rashly. He will surely fail. Now Your Majesty has raised all the armies to help him. I don't think it is a wise act." But Liu Jun would not listen to his advice. When the Northern Han armies reached Taipingyi, a place situated to the northwest of Luzhou (now Changzhi, Shanxi Province), Li Jun personally led all the generals and officials under him into Taipingyi to meet Liu Jun. There Liu Jun made Li Jun King of Pingxi and asked him to sit in a place more honorable than Wei Rong, the Prime Minister of the State of Northern Han.

When Li Jun saw that Emperor Liu Jun had a small honor guard of men who were less than robust, he felt regret about asking Emperor Liu Jun to send his armies to help him. So Li Jun told Liu Jun that he had put up the rebellion because he had been granted so many favors by Emperor Guo Rong of the Later Zhou Dynasty, and he was not hard-hearted enough to betray the Later Zhou Dynasty. These words made Emperor Liu Jun very unhappy because the Later Zhou Dynasty had been a diehard enemy of the State of Northern Han for several generations. Before Li Jun went back to Luzhou, Liu Jun appointed Lu Zhan, an official of the State of Northern Han, as supervisor of Li Jun's army. This made Li Jun very angry. When they went back to Luzhou, Lu Zhan wanted to see Li Jun to discuss matters. Li Jun refused to see him. Lu Zhan was so angry that he left. When Emperor Liu Jun heard what was going on between Li Jun and Lu Zhan, he sent Wei Rong, the Prime Minister of the State of Northern Han, to mend their relationship.

Li Jun left his son Li Shou Jie to defend the area of Shangdang (the area around Luzhou, now the area of Changzhi, Shanxi Province), and he himself commanded thirty thousand men to march southward. On 5 May Li Jun's army met the Song army under the command of Shi Shou Xin in Changping (now a place to the northwest of Gaoping, Shanxi Province). The Song army defeated Li Jun's army and over-ran the camps of Li Jun's army there.

On 6 May Emperor Zhao Kuang Yin issued an imperial order to deprive Li Jun of all his titles. On 19 May Emperor Zhao Kuang Yin announced to all the generals and ministers that he was going to personally command the expedition against Li Jun. He ordered Zhao Guang Yi and Wu Ting Zuo to stay in the capital to take care of daily affairs. He also suggested that Zhao Pu stay in the capital. But Zhao Pu said, "I would rather go with Your Majesty to suppress Li Jun's rebellion." Emperor Zhao Kuang Yin smiled and asked, "You are a scholar. Are you strong enough to wear heavy armor?" But anyway, Emperor Zhao Kuang Yin let Zhou Pu go with him.

On 21 May Emperor Zhao Kuang Yin started from Daliang. On 24 May Emperor Zhao Kuang Yin and his army reached Xingyang (now Xingyang, Henan Province). General Xiang Gong, the commander-in-chief of the garrison army in Luoyang (now Luoyang, Henan Province) went to Xingyang to see the Emperor. He said, "Li Jun has been in Luzhou for a long time. He has a great army and this army will grow stronger. I suggest that Your Majesty should cross the Yellow River immediately and go over the Taihang Mountains and attack Li Jun when his armies are not yet gathered. If we act slowly, his army will grow stronger and it would not be easy to overcome him." Zhao Pu also said to the Emperor, "Li Jun thinks that Your Majesty has just established the new dynasty and Your Majesty cannot carry out an expedition against him. If we march quickly and attack him when he is not yet prepared, we will overcome him." The Emperor accepted their suggestions.

The Song army under Shi Shou Xin and Gao Huai De fought a battle with Li Jun's army of thirty thousand men on 29 May in a place south to the city of Zezhou (now Jincheng, Shanxi Province). Li Jun's army was defeated. The Song army captured Fan Shou Tu, the Regional Military Governor of Heyang of the State of Northern Han, and killed Lu Zhan, the supervisor of Li Jun's army appointed by Liu Jun, Emperor of the State of Northern Han. Li Jun commanded his army to withdraw into the city of Zezhou.

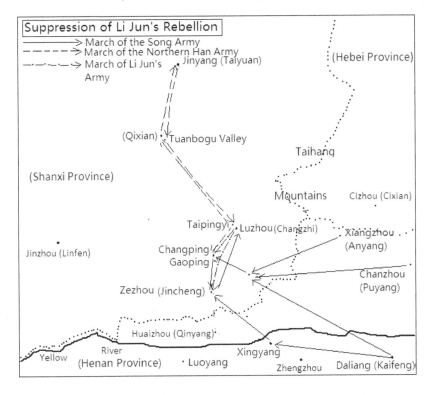

On 1 June Emperor Zhao Kuang Yin reached Zezhou. He ordered the armies to lay siege to the city and to attack it. The attack went on for more than ten days but the Song army could not take the city. On 13 June the Emperor summoned Ma Quan Yi, the commander of the guards of the Emperor, and asked him to suggest a plan to take the city. Ma Quan Yi offered to lead some elite troops to climb up the city wall. Then Ma Quan Yi commanded the ready-to-die soldiers to climb up the city wall with ladders, in the face of volley after volley of arrows and stones. Suddenly an arrow hit Ma Quan Yi and pierced his arm. Ma Quan Yi pulled out the arrow with great pain and went on fighting. The Emperor personally commanded his guards to follow the attack. On that day the Song army took the city of Zezhou. Li Jun built a fire and walked right into the fire and burned himself to death. The Emperor ordered his remains to be buried. Wei Rong, the prime minister of the State of Northern Han, was captured.

On 16 June Emperor Zhao Kuang Yin issued an order to exempt the people of the area of Zezhou from the land tax of that year. On 17 June the Song army attacked the city of Luzhou. On 19 June Li Shou Jie, Li Jun's son, surrendered. On the same day Emperor Zhao Kuang Yin entered the city of Luzhou. He released Li Shou Jie and appointed him commander-in-chief of the army stationed in Shanzhou (now Shanxian, Shandong Province). On 23 June Emperor Zhao Kuang Yin issued an order to exempt the people of the area of Luzhou from the land tax of that year. He ordered a record to be made of the names of the sons and grandsons of the generals and officers who had died in the battles to put down Li Jun's rebellion, and exempted them too from taxes for three years.

When Liu Jun, the Emperor of the State of Northern Han, got wind that Li Jun had been defeated, he immediately withdrew his army from Taipingyi and went back to Jinyang. He said to Zhao Hua (who had tried to persuade him not to help Li Jun) "Li Jun is really inept. He has totally failed, as you predicted. I am lucky enough to have made it back with all of my army. But I have lost Wei Rong and Lu Zhan."

On 29 June Emperor Zhao Kuang Yin started his journey back to Daliang from Luzhou. On 10 July Emperor Zhao Kuang Yin arrived at Daliang.

7. Suppression of Li Chong Jin's Rebellion

Li Chong Jin, the Regional Military Governor of Huainan appointed by Emperor Guo Rong of the Later Zhou Dynasty, was the nephew of Emperor Guo Wei of the Later Zhou Dynasty. Li Chong Jin was the son of the eldest daughter of Emperor Guo Wei. During the reign of Emperor Guo Rong Li Chong Jin and Zhao Kuang Yin both held great military powers and they had commanded great armies fighting for Emperor Guo Rong. Li Chong Jin was in awe of Zhao Kuang Yin because he was such a capable and mighty man.

When Emperor Guo Zong Xun succeeded to the throne of the Later Zhou Dynasty, Li Chong Jin was sent to Yangzhou (now Yangzhou, Jiangsu Province) to command the armies there. When Zhao Kuang Yin became the Emperor of the Song Dynasty, he ordered Han Ling Kun to replace Li Chong Jin and he ordered Li Chong Jin to transfer to Qingzhou (now Qingzhou, Shandong Province). This made Li Chong Jin uneasy. He requested to go to Daliang to see Emperor Zhao Kuang Yin. The Emperor sent an envoy to tell him that it was not necessary for him to go to the court.

When Li Jun held an armed rebellion in Luzhou in May 960, Li Chong Jin sent Zhai Shou Xun, one of his trustworthy officers, to go by a secret route to Luzhou to collude with Li Jun. On his way back from Luzhou, Zhai Shou Xun secretly went to Daliang and reported to the Emperor that Li Chong Jin was planning to rebel in collusion with Li Jun. The Emperor granted Zhai Shou Xun a high ranking position and many rewards. The Emperor asked Zhai Shou Xun to go back to Yangzhou and to try his best to persuade Li Chong Jin to postpone his rebellion; then the Emperor could concentrate his armies and cope with Li Jun first. Zhai Shou Xun went back to Yangzhou and pressed Li Chong Jin not to carry out the rebellion rashly and without thinking things through. Li Chong Jin accepted his opinion.

After Emperor Zhao Kuang Yin had put down Li Jun's rebellion, he sent Chen Si Hui to bring an iron plaque to Li Chong Jin that guaranteed Emperor

Zhao Kuang would exempt Yin Li Chong Jin from the death penalty. But Li Chong Jin thought that, as a close relative of the emperors of the Later Zhou Dynasty, he could not escape penalty. So he arrested Chen Si Hui. He ordered his army to fortify the city of Yangzhou and to prepare for war. He sent an envoy to the State of Southern Tang but King Li Jing did not dare to give him any help.

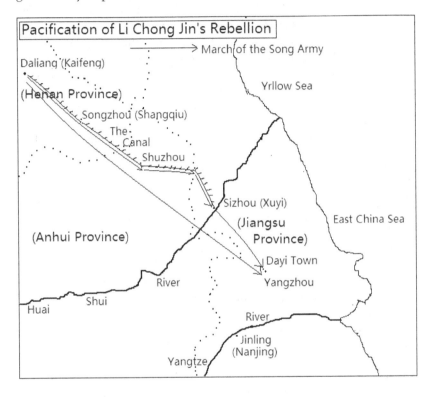

On 23 September 960 when Emperor Zhao Kuang Yin was informed that Li Chong Jin had held an armed rebellion, he appointed Shi Shou Xin as the commander-in-chief of the expedition army, and Wang Shen Qi as the deputy commander-in-chief of this army, with Li Chu Yun as the supervisor of this army. He ordered them to command the Royal Guard Army to march to Yangzhou and break up Li Chong Jin's rebellion. Emperor Zhao Kuang Yin said to the ministers and generals, "I treat the original ministers and generals of the Zhou Dynasty equally fair. I am not suspicious of them. Li Chong Jin does not understand my intention. He insists on holding a rebellion. So my soldiers have to expose themselves to the wild. I will go there to share weal and woe with them." On 27 September Emperor Zhao Kuang Yin issued an imperial order to deprive Li Chong Yin of all his titles. Emperor Zhao Kuang Yin also consulted with Zhao Pu on the matter of Li Chong Jin's rebellion. Zhao Pu said, "Li Chong Jin depends on the natural barriers of the Huai

Shui River and the Yangtze River for protection. He has fortified the city of Yangzhou. Yangzhou is now an isolated city. He cannot get help from other states. And Yangzhou does not have much food in storage. It is better for us to take Yangzhou as quickly as possible." The Emperor agreed with him.

On 21 October Emperor Zhao Kuang Yin informed all his ministers and generals that he would command the expedition personally. He appointed Zhao Guang Yi and Wu Ting Zuo to stay in the capital to take care of daily affairs. On 24 October the Emperor started from Daliang. The Emperor and his officials and soldiers got on board the ships and sailed along the canal to the east. On 7 November the Emperor and his army reached Sizhou (now Xuyi, Jiangsu Province). Then they left the ships and marched southward on land. Then they reached Dayi Town near Yangzhou. At that time the Song army under Shi Shou Xin had already laid siege to Yangzhou and attacked it. The city of Yangzhou would be taken very soon. Shi Shou Xin sent an envoy to see the Emperor in Dayi Town to inform the Emperor that the Song army would take Yangzhou very soon and to ask the Emperor to go to Yangzhou to supervise the battle. On 10 November Emperor Zhao Kuang Yin reached Yangzhou. The Song army took Yangzhou that day. When the city of Yangzhou was about to fall into the hands of the Emperor, Li Chong Jin's officers and officials tried to persuade him to kill Chen Si Hui, the envoy sent by Emperor Zhao Kuang Yin. Li Chong Jin said, "I and my whole family will kill ourselves by fire. It is no use killing him." Then Li Chong Jin made a big fire. He and his family members threw themselves into the fire and were burned to death. Chen Si Hui was killed by the officers under Li Chong Jin.

Emperor Zhao Kuang Yin entered the city of Yangzhou. He ordered the arrest of several hundred officers and officials under Li Chong Jin who had conspired in the rebellion. All of them were put to death. The Emperor ordered them to find Zhai Shou Xun. When Zhai Shou Xun came, the Emperor granted him a high position in the Royal Guard Army. On 12 November the Emperor ordered that a deca-liter of rice be given to each grown up person, and half a deca-liter to children under ten years old, to relieve the hardship of the people of Yangzhou. He ordered the release of all the people who had been forced to join the army of Li Chong Jin. On 13 November he ordered that the relatives of Li Chong Jin and Li Chong Jin's subordinates be pardoned of any crimes..

On 24 November Li Jing, King of the State of Southern Tang, sent his son Li Chong Jian and Feng Yan Lu, the minister in charge of civil affairs, to Yangzhou to see Emperor Zhao Kuang Yin. Emperor Zhao Kuang Yin said to Feng Yan Lu sternly, "Why has your king colluded with my traitorous minister?" Fen Yan Lu said, "Your Majesty only knows the fact that our King has colluded with Li Chong Jin. Your Majesty does not know for certain that our King was involved in his planned rebellion." The Emperor asked Fen Yan Lu why he had said that. Feng Yan Lu said, "The envoy sent by Li Chong Jin was lodged in my home. Our King sent an official to ask the envoy to convey the following words to Li Chong Jin, 'It is common practice for a man to rebel when he feels frustrated. This happens in history. But the timing of your rebellion is not right. At the time when the Emperor of the Song Dynasty ascended the throne, the situation was unstable. It was natural for Li Jun to rebel at that time. You did not hold a rebellion at that time. Now the situation has been stabilized. You want to resist the elite troops sent by the Emperor with your several thousand rabble-rousers. Even if the most capable general Han Xin had been still alive, he could not save you from destruction. Although I have many soldiers and a lot of food, I dare not send soldiers and provide any food to support you.' Li Chong Jin failed at last because he could not get any help from other states." Emperor Zhao Kuang Yin said, "What you have said is right. Well, then, the generals under me have suggested that I should carry on the momentum of my victory to cross the Yangtze River to attack the State of Tang. What do you think about that?" Feng Yan Lu said, "Li Chong Jin thought that he was a hero and that he was invincible. But when Your Majesty came, Li Chong Jin was defeated in a very short time. Ours is a small state. It is impossible for us to resist the powerful army of Your Majesty. But still there is something that Your Majesty should bear in mind. There are over thirty thousand brave soldiers in our state. They were all guards of the late king of our state. They have sworn to fight to death to defend the state. If Your Majesty is willing to sacrifice tens of thousands of the lives of your soldiers to fight the dare-to-die soldiers (China has a long history of loyal people willing to become martyrs) of our state, Your Majesty will be successful. Still, the Yangtze River is a natural barrier. There are unpredictable high waves and strong winds. If Your Majesty cannot take the capital of our state quickly, the transportation of food for the army will become a problem. These are the things Your Majesty should be worried about." The Emperor said, "I was only joking. Don't take it seriously."

Emperor Zhao Kuang Yin ordered his army to hold exercises in Yingluan (in Jiangdu, Jiansu Province). This made Li Jing, King of the State of Southern Tang, very nervous. He made up his mind to move the capital to another place.

On 28 November Emperor Zhao Kuang Yin appointed Li Chu Yun the Governor of Yangzhou. Li Chu Yun took proper measures to reduce the burdens of the people of Yangzhou who had just suffered the consequences of war. The situation in Yangzhou soon became stabilized. On 2 December Emperor Zhao Kuang Yin started his journey back to Daliang. On 20 December Emperor Zhao Kuang Yin arrived at Daliang.

8. Li Jing, King of the State of Southern Tang, Moves His Capital From Jinling to Nanchang

In February 961 Li Jing, King of the State of Southern Tang, decided to make Nanchang (now Nanchang, Jiangxi Province) his new capital. He made his son Li Cong Jia crown prince and ordered him to stay in Jinling to attend to state affairs. He ordered Yan Xu, one of the premiers, and Tang Yue, a member of the Privy Council, to assist Li Cong Jia. Then King Li Jing left Jinling and sailed westward along the Yangtze River. On the way the ships met with a wind storm and were nearly blown to the northern bank of the Yangtze River. In March King Li Jing of the State of Southern Tang reached Nanchang, a small city. The newly built palaces were simple and crude. Only two out of ten officials could live in the palace. The ministers longed to go back to Jinling. King Li Jing looked gloomier every day. He really wanted to kill those who had been in favor of moving the capital to Nanchang. Tang Hao, the deputy head of the Privy Council who had suggested the move, was so afraid that he fell ill and died.

9. The Death of Empress Dowager Du

On 1 May 961, Empress Dowager Du felt very ill. Emperor Zhao Kuang Yin attended his mother all day long. He personally served medicine to Empress Dowager Du. When she took a turn for the worse, she ordered that Zhao Pu be summoned to her bedroom. She asked Emperor Zhao Kuang Yin, "Do you know why you became the Emperor?" The Emperor was very sad and was crying so bitterly that he could not answer his mother's question. The Empress Dowager said, "I am talking to you about a most important matter. Why are you crying like that?" Then she asked the same question again. Emperor Zhao Kuang Yin said, "I have become Emperor because I have the blessings of my grandfather, my father and you." Empress Dowager Du said, "That is not the reason. You became Emperor because Emperor Guo Rong of the Zhou Dynasty passed his throne to a child. Nobody would submit himself to this child. You and Guang Yi are my children. When you die, you should pass the throne to Guang Yi. It is a blessing for the realm to have a grown-up man as the successor to the throne." Emperor Zhao Kuang Yin bowed to his mother and said, still weeping, "I will absolutely follow your teaching." Then she looked at Zhao Pu and said, "Now you write down what I have said. What I have said should not be violated." Then the faithful Zhao Pu wrote down the vow made by Emperor Zhao Kuang Yin in front of the Empress Dowager, and signed his name. Then the vow was put in a gold safe and the gold safe was kept in the palace. On 2 June, Empress Dowager Du died at the age of sixty.

10. The Death of Li Jing, King of the State of Southern Tang; Li Yu Ascends the Throne of the State of Southern Tang

Ever since King Li Jing of the State of Southern Tang went to Nanchang, the new capital of the State of Southern Tang, he was very unhappy. On 8 June 961 he died at the age of forty-six. In July his dead body was transported back to Jinling and was buried there. His son Li Cong Jia ascended the throne of the State of Southern Tang and changed his name to Li Yu. King Li Yu sent an envoy to Emperor Zhao Kuang Yin to report the death of King Li Jing and to ask Emperor Zhao Kuang Yin to reinstate the title of emperor to the late king. Emperor Zhao Kuang Yin gave his permission. So King Li Yu gave his father a posthumous title as Emperor of Mingdao Chongde Wenxuan Xiao. His temple title was Emperor Mingzong.

11. Emperor Zhao Kuang Yin Relieves the Great Generals of their Military Power

After the pacification of Li Jun and Wang Chong Jin, Emperor Zhao Yin had some worries. He was afraid that someone would use his military position to usurp the throne. So he transferred Murong Yan Zhao, the Commander-in-chief of the Royal Guard Army and Regional Military Governor of Zhenning to Regional Military Governor of Shannan. Morong Yan Zhao was no longer Commander-in-chief of the Royal Guard Army. And from then on Emperor Zhao Kuang Yin never appointed anyone to the position of Commander-in-chief of the Royal Guard Army.

One day he summoned Zhao Pu to the palace. They had a heart to heart talk. The Emperor asked Zhao Pu, "Since the fall of the Tang Dynasty, eight houses of emperors of different family names have been replaced in these several decades. The wars have never stopped. Many people have been killed. Can you tell me the reason why? I intend to put an end to this situation. What can I do to make the Song Dynasty last a long time?" Zhao Pu said, "It is a blessing for the realm and the people that Your Majesty has talked about this. The reason why there have been frequent changes of houses of emperors and the wars have never stopped is that the power of the military governors in different prefectures is too great. The emperors were weak but the military governors were too powerful. If Your Majesty wants peace and order in the realm, the power of the military governors should be reduced. The money and food provisions for them should be reduced. The elite troops under them should be taken away. Then there will be peace in the realm."

At that time Shi Shou Xin, Wang Shen Qi and Gao Huai De were good friends of Emperor Zhao Kuang Yin. They were in command of the Royal Guard Armies. Zhao Pu had put forward suggestions to remove them from their present positions and appoint them to other positions. The Emperor said, "They will certainly not betray me. What are you worried about?" Zhao Pu said, "I'm not worried about them, either. But as I can see, they are not good at controlling their subordinates. In case certain officers under them do something against their will, there is nothing they can do about it." Then the Emperor realized the danger.

One day in July, 961, after afternoon court, Emperor Zhao Kuang Yin asked Shi Shou Xin, Wang Shen Qi, Gao Huai De and Zhang Ling Duo to stay on. Emperor Zhao Kuang Yin invited them to have some drinks. After several cups they were warm with wine. The Emperor asked the servants to leave the room. Then he said to them, "Without your help I would not have been emperor. But it is very hard to be an emperor. The life of a military governor is much happier than the life of an emperor. I have never had a night of sound sleep." Shi Shou Xin asked, "Why?" The Emperor said, "It is not difficult to understand. Everybody wants to be an emperor." Shi Shou Xin asked, "What makes Your Majesty say that? Now the whole realm is in peace. Heaven has appointed Your Majesty as the emperor. Who would dare to take the throne from Your Majesty?" The Emperor said, "You are devoted to me and I am sure you will not do that. But if one of your subordinates, who want wealth and high rank, puts a yellow robe on you — what can you do? You will be forced to be an emperor even if you don't want to." Shi Shou Xin, Wang Shen Qi, Gao Huai De and Zhang Ling Duo all knelt down on their knees and touched their heads to the ground and said, "We are very foolish and have never thought of that. Will Your Majesty point out a way for us to avoid destruction?" Emperor Zhao Kuang Yin said, "Life is short. It is as short as the blink of an eye. Everyone wants wealth and high rank. They only want to be wealthier and spend their days happily. And they hope that their children and grandchildren will not be poor. Why don't you retire and relieve yourselves of your military power and go out to the big prefectures to be the governors there? You may select good land and good houses and buy them. Then you may leave plenty of family property and land for your children and grandchildren. You can invite singers and dancers to your home and enjoy their songs and dancing. You can drink wine every day and have a good time every day. You may spend your life happily. I will establish relationships with you through marriage. Then there will be no mistrust between you and me. Is that a good idea?" Shi Shou Xin, Wang Shen Qi, Gao Huai De and Zhang Ling Duo all touched their heads to the ground and expressed their hearty thanks to the Emperor, saying, "It is very considerate of Your Majesty to think of a way out for us. Your Majesty has saved us from destruction."

The next day Shi Shou Xin, Wang Shen Qi, Gao Huai De and Zhang Ling Duo all presented their resignations to the Emperor on the excuse that they were ill. Emperor Zhao Kuang Yin accepted their resignations and granted them sums of gold. On 9 July, Emperor Zhao Kuang Yin appointed Shi Shou Xin Regional Military Governor of Tianping in Yunzhou (now Dongping, Shandong Province), Gao Huai De Regional Military Governor of Guide (now Shangqiu, Henan Province), Wang Shen Qi Regional Military Governor of Zhongzheng in Shouzhou (now Shouxian, Anhui Province), and Zhang Ling Duo Regional Military Governor of Zhenning in Chanzhou (now Puyang, Henan Province).

Emperor Zhao Kuang Yin kept his promise to establish relationships with them through marriage. Gao Huai De had already married Emperor Zhao Kuang Yin's younger sister. So Gao Huai De was already his brother-in-law. Emperor Zhao Kuang Yin married his second daughter, Princess Yanqing, to Shi Shou Xin's second son Shi Bao Ji. So Shi Shou Xin's second son Shi Bao Ji became the son-in-law of Emperor Zhao Kuan Yin. Zhao Kuang Yin married his eldest daughter, Princess Zhaoqing, to Wang Shen Qi's son Wang Cheng Yan. So Wang Shen Qi's son Wang Cheng Yan became Emperor Zhao Kuang

Yin's son-in-law. Emperor Zhao Kuang Yin's third younger brother Zhao Guang Mei married Zhang Ling Duo's third daughter. So Emperor Zhao Kuang Yin maintained very good relations with Shi Shou Xin, Wang Shen Qi, Gao Huai De and Zhang Ling Duo.

Emperor Zhao Kuang Yin relieves the great generals of their military power by inviting them to a drinking party.

12. The Conquest of the Area of Jingnan (the State of Nanping) and the Area of Hunan (the State of Chu)

In January 960 Emperor Zhao Kuang Yin, who had just ascended the throne of the Song Dynasty, appointed Gao Bao Rong to be Grand Protector. He was already Regional Military Governor of Jingnan (in the area of now the southern part of Hubei Province) and King of Nanping. But that August Gao Bao Rong fell seriously ill. His son Gao Ji Chong was still young and could not attend to civil and military affairs. So he ordered his younger brother Gao Bao Xu to take over civil and military affairs in Jingnan. On 27 August Gao Bao Rong died. Gao Bao Xu became Regional Military Governor of Jingnan.

On 29 September 962 Zhou Xing Feng, the Grand Commander-in-chief of Langzhou and the Regional Military Governor of Wuping in the area of Hunan (now the area of Hunan Province), fell seriously ill. He summoned all the generals and officers under him to his room and entrusted them to assist his son Zhou Bao Quan. Zhou Xing Feng said to them, "Zhang Wen Biao, the

Governor of Hengzhou, rose through the ranks together with me when we were both ordinary men. He has always been resentful because he was not appointed as the chief of staff of the army. After I die, he will certainly rebel. If he rebels, General Yang Shi Fan should command an army to suppress his rebellion." After Zhou Xing Feng died, Zhou Bao Quan succeeded him at the age of eleven. At that time Zhang Wen Biao was the Governor of Hengzhou (now Hengyang, Hunan Province). In October, when Zhang Wen Biao learned that an eleven-year-old had become Grand Commander-in-chief of Langzhou and the Regional Military Governor of Wuping, he was very angry. He said, "Zhou Xing Feng and I both rose through the ranks and made great contributions to the success of our emperor. How can I be a subordinate to this child and serve him as my master?"

At that time Zhou Bao Quan sent soldiers to replace those who had been garrisoned in Yongzhou (now Yongzhou, in the southwest part of Hunan Province). They passed Hengzhou. Zhang Wen Biao took these soldiers as his own and forced them to rebel. He put on white clothes to pretend that he was going to Langzhou (now Changde, Hunan Province) to attend the funeral of Zhou Xing Feng. Zhang Wen Biao commanded his army to march northward towards Tanzhou (now Changsha, Hunan Province). Sima Liao Jian, the commander of the army in Tanzhou, had always looked down upon Zhang Wen Biao. When he learned that Zhang Wen Biao was marching his army towards Tanzhou, he did not make any preparation to resist. When Zhang Wen Biao reached Tanzhou, Sima Liao Jian was holding a banquet in his home, entertaining his subordinates. When an officer reported to him that Zhang Wen Biao had arrived, he still did not seem to care. He said to the generals and officers attending the banquet, "When Zhang Wen Biao comes, he will be arrested. Don't worry about it." He drank wine and laughed as before. In a short time Zhang Wen Biao sent his soldiers into the banquet hall. Sima Liao Jian was so drunk that he could not hold up his bow. He could do nothing but spit out curses at Zhang Wen Biao. Zhang Wen Biao killed Sima Liao Jian and all those at the banquet. Zhang Wen Biao took the seal and proclaimed himself commander of the army in Tanzhou.

When the report that Zhang Wen Biao had taken Tanzhou reached Langzhou, Zhou Bao Quan immediately ordered Yang Shi Fan to take an army to suppress Zhang Wen Biao's rebellion. He told Yang Shi Fan that his father had expected Zhang Wen Biao would rebel and had named Yang Shi Fan to suppress the rebellion. At the same time Zhou Bao Quan sent envoys to Jingnan asking Gao Bao Xu to send an army to help him. He also sent envoys to Emperor Zhao Kuang Yin to ask him for help.

In November Gao Bao Xu, the Regional Military Governor of Jingnan, felt that his days were coming to an end. He summoned Liang Yan Si, the commander-in-chief of the army in Jiangling (now Jiangling County in Jingzhou, Hubei Province), and said to him, "I am going to die. Who do you think should succeed me?" Liang Yan Si said, "The late King of Nanping did not let his son Gao Ji Chong succeed him. He entrusted all the civil and military affairs to you. Now Gao Ji Chong has grown up. You can entrust all the civil and military affairs to him." And Gao Bao Xu did entrust all the civil and military affairs to Gao Ji Chong. On 20 November 962 Gao Bao Xu died.

When Gao Bao Xu died, Emperor Zhao Kuang Yin sent Lu Huai Zhong as his envoy on a mission to Jingnan. Before Lu Huai Zhong set out, Emperor Zhao Kuang Yin said to him, "I want to know the sentiment of the people, the situation and the geography of Jiangling. Report this information to me when you come back from this mission." When Lu Huai Zhong came back, he reported to Emperor Zhao Kuang Yin, "Gao Ji Chong has an army of no more than thirty thousand men. Although there is a good harvest this year, the people are still very poor because the government of Jingnan levies exorbitant taxes on them. Jingnan is unstable. It is very easy to conquer this state." On 7 January 963 Emperor Zhao Kuang Yin appointed Murong Yan Zhao, the Regional Military Governor of Shannandongdao in Xiangzhou (now Xiangfan, Hubei Province), as the commander-in-chief of the Hunan Branch of the army. He appointed Li Chu Yun, the deputy head of the Privy Council, as the supervisor of this army. He ordered Li Chu Yun to head an army and set out from the capital to meet Murong Yan Zhao in Xiangzhou.

Before Li Chu Yun left the capital, Emperor Zhao Kuang Yin told him of his plan to take the area of Jingnan. On 13 January the Emperor appointed Zhang Xun commander-in-chief of the cavalry of the Hunan branch of the army, and Lu Huai Zhong as the Supervisor of the cavalry of this branch. On 23 January Emperor Zhao Kuang Yin issued an imperial order to Jiangling for Gao Ji Chong to send three thousand naval soldiers to Tanzhou to attack Zhang Wen Biao. General Yang Shi Fan commanded an army to Tanzhou to attack Zhang Wen Biao. At first the attack was not successful. The two armies were in a stalemate. But in one battle Yang Shi Fan defeated Zhang Wen Biao and took both the town of Tanzhou and the miscreant Zhang Wen Biao. After the soldiers under Yang Shi Fan entered Tanzhou, they set fire to the city and went looting. Then Zhang Wen Biao was executed in the market place of Tanzhou.

Gao Ji Chong, the Military Governor of Jingnan, thought that he was still too young to handle civil and military affairs well. So he entrusted the civil affairs to Sun Guang Xian, the manager of the office of the Regional Military Governor, and he entrusted the military affairs to Liang Yan Si, the commander-in-chief of the guards.

When Li Chu Yun arrived at Xiangzhou, he sent an envoy to sound out Gao Ji Chong. Arriving in Jiangling, the envoy asked Gao Ji Chong to let the army of the Song Dynasty pass Jiangling so as to go to the area of Hunan to attack Zhang Wen Biao, and asked Gao Ji Chong to provide food to the Song army. Gao Ji Chong discussed this matter with his subordinates. Then Gao Ji Chong asked the envoy to convey his reply to Li Chu Yun that in order not to intimidate the people of Jiangling, he would provide food to the Song army fifty kilometers outside the city. Li Chu Yun again sent the envoy to ask Gao Ji Chong to let the Song army pass Jiangling. Sun Guang Xian and Liang Yan

Si tried to persuade Gao Ji Chong to allow the Song army to pass Jiangling. But Li Jing Wei, the deputy commander of the army of Jingnan, said to Gao Ji Chong, "Although the Song army will primarily pass Jiangling to take the area of Hunan, I am afraid that they will launch a surprise attack on us. I hope you will give me three thousand men. I will set an ambush in the strategic vantage point in Jingmen. When the Song troops march towards Jiangling at night through that place, I will launch a surprise attack on them and capture their commanding general. Then the Song army will retreat. Then we shall send an army to Hunan to attack Zhang Wen Biao and capture him. We will present Zhang Wen Biao to the court of the Song Dynasty. In this way you will demonstrate your great merit. Otherwise you will suffer the consequence of asking mercy from the Emperor of the Song Dynasty." But Gao Ji Chong did not think he needed to take such precautions. He said, "The House of Gao has been an outstanding supporter to the Emperor of the Song Dynasty every year. I don't think the Emperor will treat me like that." Sun Guang Xian said, "Li Jing Wei is not a man of resources. The Dynasties in Central China have tried to unify China since Emperor Guo Wei of the Zhou Dynasty. Since the establishment of the Song Dynasty, Emperor Zhao Kuang Yin has shown himself to be an emperor with foresight and he has taken great measures to unify China. Now Emperor Zhao Kuang Yin has sent an army to carry out an expedition against Zhang Wen Biao. It will be very easy for the Song army to conquer Hunan. If the Song army conquers Hunan, will they pass by without taking Jingnan too? It would be better for you to present the territory of Jingnan to the court of the Song Dynasty. In this way we can avoid disaster. And you may still enjoy wealth and high rank." Then Gao Ji Chong said he agreed with this idea; but Li Jing Wei understood that Gao Ji Chong had turned down his suggestion. He said with a sigh, "Jingnan will perish. What is the use of living in this world?" He went home and committed suicide.

Gao Ji Chong sent Liang Yan Si and Gao Bao Yin, his own uncle, to go out of Jiangling to welcome the Song army with meat and wine. And their task was to see what the Song army would do. On 9 February 963 the Song army reached Jingmen (now Jingmen, Hubei Province), fifty kilometers from Jiangling. Li Chu Yun greeted Liang Yan Si and Gao Bao Yin politely. Liang Yan Si was very relieved and sent an envoy back to Jiangling to report to Gao Ji Chong that there was nothing to be worried about. That night Murong Yan Zhao held a banquet to entertain Liang Yan Si and Gao Bao Yin in his tent. Li Chu Yun secretly commanded several thousand light cavalrymen to ride at double speed towards Jiangling. Gao Ji Chong was waiting for Liang Yan Si and Gao Bao Yin to return. Suddenly it was reported to him that the Song army was marching towards Jiangling. Gao Ji Chong was panic-stricken and went out of the city of Jingling to welcome the Song army in a great hurry. He met Li Chu Yun fifteen kilometers north of Jiangling.

Li Chu Yun got down from his horse and bowed to Gao Ji Chong and asked Gao Ji Chong to stay there to wait for Murong Yan Zhao. Then Li Chu Yun jumped on his horse and rode very quickly with his cavalrymen to the city of Jingling. Li Chu Yun and his men entered the city of Jingling and went up to the top of the city wall at the north gate. By the time Gao Ji Chong went back with Murong Yan Zhao, the Song troops had occupied all the strategic points and were guarding all the streets in the city. Gao Ji Chong was terrified. So he submitted to the Song army and wrote a memorandum to Emperor Zhao Kuang Yin to present all the territory of Jingnan to the Song Dynasty. In total, there were three prefectures, seventeen counties and one hundred and forty-two thousand three hundred households in the territory of Jingnan.

On 10 February Li Chu Yun and Murong Yan Zhao commanded the Song army and the army in Jiangling to march towards Langzhou. Now Zhou Bao Quan was very afraid. He summoned Li Guan Xiang, one of his subordinates, to discuss the situation. Li Guan Xiang said, "Zhang Wen Biao has been killed. But the Song army has not gone back. Their intention is to take the whole territory of Hunan. Now Gao Ji Chong of Jingnan has submitted to the Song Dynasty. The area of Jingnan was originally a protection for Hunan but now Jingnan has been taken by the Song army. Hunan will not be able to survive. It would be better to submit ourselves to the rule of the Emperor of the Song Dynasty. Then you will still enjoy wealth and high rank." Gao Bao Quan was about to take his advice, but Zhang Chong Fu, the commander-in-chief of the army of Hunan, and others strongly opposed Li Guan Xiang's opinion. Then Zhou Bao Quan discussed with them how to make a plan to resist the Song army.

On 17 February the memorandum written by Gao Ji Chong was received by Emperor Zhao Kuang Yin. Then Emperor Zhao Kuang Yin again appointed Gao Ji Chong as the Regional Military Governor of Jingnan. He sent Wang Ren Shan, a member of the Privy Council, to Jingnan as an inspector. When the Emperor heard about Li Jing Wei's suggestion of resisting the Song army, he said, "Li Jing Wei is really a devoted man." He ordered Wang Ren Shan to comfort the family members of Li Jing Wei and awarded them a lot of money. At the same time Emperor Zhao Kuang Yin sent an envoy to Langzhou with a letter to Zhou Bao Quan and his generals and officers. The letter read, "I have sent a great army to help you. Why have you resisted my army? By doing so you will destroy yourselves." But Zhou Bao Quan did not give any reply to Emperor Zhao Kuang Yin. Then Emperor Zhao Kuang Yin ordered his army to attack Hunan. The Song army under Murong Yan Zhao defeated Zhou Bao Quan's army in Sanjiangkou (in Yueyang, Hunan Province) and then took Yuezhou (now Yueyang, Hunan Province). In March Zhou Bao Quan sent Zhang Chong Fu to command an army to march to Lizhou (now Lixian, Hunan Province). When the army of Hunan reached a place south to Lizhou, they met with the Song army under Li Chu Yun. The army of Hunan under Zhang Cong Fu broke down in utter confusion without a fight. The Song army under Li Chu Yun gave a hot pursuit to the army of Hunan. They captured many Hunan soldiers. Li Chu Yun selected several tens of fat soldiers of Hunan and ordered his soldiers to cook them and eat them. He ordered his soldiers to make tattoos on the faces of the rest of the captives and then sent them back to Langzhou. When the People of Langzhou got the news that the Song soldiers ate human beings, they were in great panic. They set fire to the city of Langzhou and ran away to the mountains to hide themselves so that they would not be captured and eaten by the Song Soldiers. General Wang Duan of Langzhou escorted Zhou Bao Quan and his family members to leave Langzhou and to hide them in a cave in a mountain. On 9 March Murong Yan Zhao commanded his army to enter the city of Langzhou. The Song soldiers captured Zhang Chong Fu in a mountain west to the city of Langzhou and killed him. Tian Shou Qi, a general under Li Chu Yun, commanded some troops to go in the mountains to search for Zhou Bao Quan. When General Wang Duan saw the coming Song soldiers, he abandoned Zhou Bao Quan and ran away. General Tian Shou Qi captured Zhou Bao Quan and brought him back. Then the whole territory of Hunan was occupied by the Song army. There were fourteen prefectures, sixty-six counties and ninety-seven thousand two hundred and eighty-eight households in the territory of Huanan. On 24 July Zhou Bao Quan was escorted to Daliang and he waited for the verdict of punishment by Emperor Zhao Kuang Yin. Emperor Zhao Kuang Yin issued an imperial order to set Zhou Bao Quan free and appointed him as a general of the royal guards.

13. Zhao Pu Becomes the Manager of Governmental Affairs

On 6 January 964 Premier Fan Zhi, Premier Wang Pu and Premier Wei Ren Pu presented their resignations to Emperor Zhao Kuang Yin. Emperor Zhao Kuang Yin accepted their resignations. On 10 January Emperor Zhao Kuang Yin appointed Fan Zhi as the Grand Tutor of the Crown Prince, Wang Pu as the Grand Guardian of the Crown Prince, and Wei Ren Pu as the adviser of the Emperor. So there were no premiers.

At that time Zhao Pu was the Head of the Privy Council. On 12 January Emperor Zhao Kuang Yin appointed Zhao Pu as the Director of the Chancellery and Manager of Governmental Affairs. Zhao Pu held the power of a premier. Emperor Zhao Kuang Yin appointed Li Chong Ju, a general, as the Head of the Privy Council to take the place of Zhao Pu who had been appointed as the Director of the Chancellery and Manager of Governmental Affairs. According to government rules, orders issued by the government to local officials should be signed by a premier. Since there was no premier, nobody could sign the orders issued by Zhao Pu. Zhao Pu went to the palace to see Emperor Zhao Kuang Yin and asked him what should be done. Emperor Zhao Kuang Yin said, "You just write the orders and present them to me. I will sign the orders for you." Zhao Pu said, "Signing orders of the government is the job of the government officials. It is not the job for an emperor." Then the Emperor sent for the scholars of Hanlin Academy. Dou Yi, a scholar from Hanlin Academy, said, "Zhao Guang Yi is the Governor of Kaifeng and also a Joint Manager of Governmental Affairs. He is equal to a premier. The orders issued by Zhao Pu can be signed by Zhao Guang Yi." Emperor Zhao Kuang Yin agreed with him. From then on the orders issued by Zhao Pu were signed by Zhao Guang Yi, Emperor Zhao Kuang Yin's younger brother.

14. The Expedition against the State of Shu

Having conquered the area of Jingnan and the area of Hunan, Emperor Zhao Kuang Yin planned to carry out an expedition against the State of Later Shu. Mu Zhao Si, a medical officer at Hanlin Academy, once served the House of Gao as a doctor in the State of Later Shu. Emperor Zhao Kuang Yin summoned him to the palace several times and asked him about the geography of the area of Shu. Mu Zhao Si said to the Emperor, "Jiangling, the capital of Jingnan, is a big city which is situated beside the Yangtze River. Now that the whole area of Jingnan has been taken by Your Majesty, the army of the Song Dynasty can enter the territory of the State of Shu by water and by land." Emperor Zhao Kuang Yin was very glad to hear his suggestion.

Meng Chang, the King of the State of Later Shu, was a proud and ambitious man. During the reign of Emperor Guo Rong of the later Zhou Dynasty, Meng Chang referred to himself as the "Emperor of the Great Shu" in a letter to Emperor Guo Rong. Emperor Guo Rong was very angry with him and did not reply. Meng Chang thought that perhaps he had gone a little too far. He made thorough preparations to resist an attack by the army of the Later Zhou Dynasty. He sent armies to Jianmen (now Jianmenguan Pass, in the area of Guangyuan, Sichuan Province), Kuizhou (now to the east of Fengjie, Sichuan Province) and Xiazhou (now Yichang, Hubei Province) and ordered them to store a lot of food in these places and be prepared for an attack by the Later Zhou Dynasty army. He named his son Meng Xuan Zhe crown prince. He entrusted the military and civil affairs to Wang Zhao Yuan, Yi Shen Zheng, Han Bao Zheng and Zhao Chong Tao. Wang Zhao Yuan was the Head of the Privy Council; he had only been given this position because he and Meng Chang had been companions when they were young.

Lady Li, Meng Chang's mother, once said to him, "I have seen how your father fought against the army of Khitan and how he commanded the army to enter the area of Shu and put down the uprisings of the Eastern Shu and the Western Shu. Your father only appointed those who had established military credentials to commanding positions. He never appointed those who had not proven themselves in battle. This is the reason why all the officers and men respected and obeyed the generals appointed by your father. But now Wang Zhao Yuan got his position only because he was your friend in school. Han Bao Zheng and Zhao Chong Tao are the sons of high-ranking generals. They have never commanded any troops and never fought in real battles. If there is an emergency in the border areas, do they have the ability and astuteness and resourcefulness to push back the enemies? Gao Yan Chou is a friend of your father. He is a devoted man. He has experienced many battles. You may entrust important military affairs to him." But Meng Chang would not listen to his mother's advice.

After Emperor Zhao Kuang Yin had taken the area of Jingnan and the area of Hunan, Meng Chang wanted to send envoys to pay tribute to Emperor Zhao Kuang Yin. Wang Zhao Yuan and others strongly opposed the idea of paying tribute to the Emperor of the Song Dynasty. Meng Chang had to give up the idea. Zhang Ting Wei, a subordinate of Wang Zhao Yuan, said to him, "You have no experience in military strategy or in battle. Now you are in the position of the Head of Privy Council which is in charge of military affairs. How can you convince others that you have the ability to occupy this position? I have a suggestion. You should persuade the King to send an envoy to the King of the State of Han and establish friendly relations with him. The envoy should ask the King of the State of Han to send armies to march south across the Yellow River to attack the Song Dynasty from the north. Then we may send an army to head north through Ziwugu Valley to coordinate with the army of Han. Then the Song Dynasty will be attacked from the north and from the south. We may take this chance to occupy the area to the west of the Hanguguan Pass." Wang Zhao Yuan took his advice. He went to the palace and said to Meng Chang, "Let's unite with the King of Han to attack the territory of the Song Dynasty. We should persuade the King of Han to send an army to attack from the north. We can attack the territory of the Song Dynasty from the south. Then the Song army will be easily defeated and we may take the part of the territory of the Song Dynasty." Meng Chang said, "That is a very good idea. Who can be sent to the State of Han to convey my idea of working together with the King of Han to attack the Song Dynasty?" Wang Zhao Yuan said, "Sun Yu, Zhao Yan Tao and Yang Juan can take up this mission." So Meng Chang wrote a letter to Liu Jun, the King of the State of Han, which read, "Last year I sent a letter to you seeking to establish friendly relations with you. We have united with each other like two brothers. Let us be united in attacking the Song Dynasty. I have stationed armies in Baoxiegu Valley and Hanzhong. Once your armies cross the Yellow River to attack the Song Dynasty, my army will march through Baoxiegu Valley to attack the Song Dynasty from the south."

Sun Yu, Zhao Yan Tao and Yang Juan set off on their mission along secret pathways. When they reached a place close to Daliang, Zhao Yan Tao took the secret letter to Daliang to present it to Emperor Zhao Kuang Yin. When Emperor Zhao Kuang Yin received the letter presented by Zhao Yan Tao, he said with a smile, "This letter has given me a justification to send out armies against the State of Shu!" The Emperor rewarded Zhao Yan Tao handsomely and set Sun Yu and Yang Juan free. He asked Zhao Yan Tao, Sun Yu and Yang Juan to draw up maps of the mountains and rivers, the strategic places of the State of Shu and the places where the Shu armies were stationed.

On 2 November, 964, Emperor Zhao Kuang Yin appointed Wang Quan

Bin, the Regional Military Governor of Zhongwu, the Commander-in-chief of the Fengzhou branch of the army. He appointed Cui Yan Jin, Regional Military Governor of Wuxin, the Deputy Commander-in-chief of this branch of the army. He made Wang Ren Shan, Deputy Head of the Privy Council, the supervisor. There were thirty thousand infantry and cavalrymen in this branch of the army. This branch would march into the area of Shu from Fengzhou (now Fengxian, in the southwest part of Shaanxi Province). Emperor Zhao Kuang Yin appointed Liu Guang Yi, the Regional Military Governor of Ningjiang, to be Commander-in-chief of the Guizhou branch of the army. He appointed Cao Bin, a member of the Privy Council, to be its supervisor. They had thirty thousand infantry and cavalrymen. They would march into the area from Guizhou (now Zigui, Hubei Province).

Emperor Zhao Kuang Yin issued an imperial order to prohibit the troops marching into the Shu area from burning the people's houses, looting officials and people, robbing graves or destroying crops in that area. Anyone who dared to go against this imperial order would be punished according to military law. He also ordered the officials in charge of civil engineering to build a grand mansion by the southern bank of Bianshui River to house Meng Chang and his family members when they were captured and escorted to Daliang, the capital of the Song Dynasty.

On 3 November Emperor Zhao Kuang Yin held a banquet in Chongde Hall of the palace to entertain Wang Quan Bin, Wang Ren Shan, Liu Guang Yi, Cao Bin and the generals who were going to march into the area of Shu. The Emperor gave the maps and pictures of Shu, drawn by painters according to the information provided by Sun Yu, Zhao Yan Tao and Yang Juan, to Wang Quan Bin and Liu Guang Yi and other generals. The Emperor asked Wang Quan Bin, "Do you think that you can take the area of Shu?" Wang Quan Bin said, "With the great might of Your Majesty and the detailed plan by Your Majesty, we are sure to win and take the whole territory of the State of Shu in a short time." General Shi Yan De came forward and said to the Emperor, "If the State of Shu was in the sky, we could not go up to the sky. Then we can do nothing about it. But the State of Shu is on the earth. With our present military force, the area of Shu will be ours as soon as our armies reach there." Emperor Zhao Kuang Yin highly praised their resolute determination. Emperor Zhao Kuang Yin said to Wang Quan Bin, Liu Guang Yi and other Generals, "When you have taken a city, you will confiscate all the military supplies and food. The money and cloth will be distributed to the soldiers. What I want is the territory of the State of Shu."

When Meng Chang, King of the State of Shu, was told that Emperor Zhao Kuang Yin was sending armies to attack him, he appointed Wang Zhao Yuan as the commander-in-chief of the Shu army, Zhao Chong Tao as the supervisor of the army, Han Bao Zheng as the commander of an expedition army, Li Jin as the deputy commander of this expedition army. Meng Chang said to Wang Zhao Yuan, "The Song armies are actually coming against us because of you. Now you should do your best to hold off the Song army and show your heroism." Wang Zhao Yuan was a conceited man. He read a lot of military history and he thought that he was mighty smart. He compared himself to Zhuge Liang, the greatest strategist in the period of "Three Kingdoms" (316–384). When Wang Zhao Yuan commanded his army to leave Chengdu (now Chengdu, Sichuan Province), the capital of the State of Shu, Meng Chang ordered Li Hao, the Premier of the State of Shu, to hold a banquet outside the city of Chengdu to see off Wang Zhao Yuan and his men. When Wang Zhao Yuan was warm with the wine, he said excitedly to Li Hao, "This time I will not only defeat the coming Song enemy. It will be very easy for me to command these thirty thousand men to occupy the area of central China." When the army began to march, holding his scepter made of iron and pointing it here and there, Wang Zhao Yuan issued orders to his army as if he was really Zhuge Liang.

Wang Quan Bin commanded his army to march from Fengzhou southward into the area of the State of Shu. On 19 December the Song army under Wang Quan Bin attacked the strongholds of Qianqüdu and Wanrenyanzi which were situated to the north of Xingzhou (now Lüeyang, in the southwest part of Shaanxi Province) and took these two strongholds. Then the Song army marched southward to attack Xingzhou and defeated seven thousand Shu soldiers and took Xingzhou. The Song army got 548,000 bushels of grains for the army stored in Xingzhou. Lan Si Wan, the Governor of Xingzhou of the State of Shu, retreated to Xixian (now Mianxian, in the southwest part of Shaanxi Province).

Wang Quan Bin confidently commanded his army to attack the strongholds south of Xingzhou and took about twenty of them, including the strongholds of Shituyuguan and Baishuige. Han Bao Zheng (the general sent by Meng Chang, the King of the State of Shu, to challenge the Song army), heard that Xingzhou had been taken by the Song army. He gave up Shannan (now Nanzheng, Shaanxi province) and marched his army to Xixian to join forces with Lan Si Wan to defend Xixian. Then Wang Quan Bin sent Shi Yan De, the Commander of the cavalrymen of Fengzhou branch of the army, to command the cavalry to attack Xixian.

Han Bao Zheng, son of a military man, was in fact a coward. When the Song cavalry under Shi Yan De arrived, he did not dare to fight. He ordered over thirty thousand soldiers to build camps against the mountainside to resist the onslaught. Shi Yan De ordered his men to attack the camps of the Shu army, and Han Bao Zheng ran away. The Song army went in hot pursuit and captured Han Bao Zheng and Li Jin, the deputy commander of the Shu army. They got 411,000 bushels of grains for the army. Cui Yan Jin, the Deputy Commander-in-chief of the Fengzhou branch of the Song army, and General Kang Yan Ze, the Supervisor of the cavalry of the Song army, pursued the defeated Shu army. They passed Sanquan (now Yangpingguan Pass in the northwest of Ningqiang, Shaanxi Province). Then the Song army reached Jialing (now a place to the west of Guangyuan, Sichuan Province). After they passed it, the Shu troops destroyed the plank road which was built along the precipice of the mountain so that the Song army could not pursue them. The Shu army retreated to Jiameng (now a place to the southwest of Guangyuan, Sichuan Province).

In December, Liu Guang Yi, the Commander-in-chief of the Guizhou branch of the Song army, commanded the Song army under him to march westward into the area of Shu from Guizhou (now Zigui, Hubei Province). The Song army entered the territory of the State of Shu by water. The warships of the Song army sailed along the Yangtze River. The Song army attacked the strongholds of Songmu, Sanhui and Wushan and took them all. They killed Nan Hai Guang, the commander of the Shu army in that area, and killed and captured over five thousand Shu soldiers. They fought a battle with the navy of the State of Shu. They captured Yuan De Hong, the commander of the navy of the State of Shu, and captured more than two hundred warships of the Shu military. They killed and captured six thousand men from the Shu navy. The Shu army had built a floating bridge across the Yangtze River to block the river in the section of the river of Kuizhou (now a place to the east of Fengjie, Sichuan Province). Three layers of sharp iron bars were planted on the floating bridge to prevent enemy warships from getting though. Big stone launchers were lined up on both banks of that section of the river, ready to destroy the enemy ships.

Before Liu Guang Yi left Daliang to Guizhou, Emperor Zhao Kuang Yin pointed at the section of the Yangtze River near Kuizhou on the map and said to him, "When your warships sail to this part of the river, you must not fight the enemy on boats. You should send infantry and cavalry to attack the enemy by land. When the enemies have retreated, the warships can sail into that part of the river and destroy the enemy defense." So when the warships of the Song army reached the section of the river in the area of Kuizhou, fifteen kilometers away from the floating bridge, Liu Guang Yi ordered the foot soldiers and cavalrymen to attack the Shu army by land. The Song army launched a surprise attack. The Shu troops were only watching the river, waiting for the Song warships to come. They did not expect that the Song troops would attack them by land. So very soon the Shu troops were defeated and ran away. The Song troops took the floating bridge. Then the warships of the Song army sailed down the river close to Kuizhou. The Song army did not attack the city of Kuizhou. They just stopped at Baidicheng (now Baidicheng, a place to the east of Fengjie, Sichuan Province). Gao Yan Chou, the commander-in-chief of the Shu army defending Kuizhou, said to Zhao Chong Zhi, the deputy commander-in-chief, and Wu Shou Qian, the supervisor of the Shu army, "The Song troops have travelled a long way here. It would be advantageous for them to fight a quick battle. We'd better not fight them. Perhaps we can just stay inside the city and defend the city and wait for our chance." Wu Shou Qian said, "The Song troops have come to the foot of the city but they have not started an attack. This is a good chance for us to defeat them."

On 26 December Wu Shou Qian commanded one thousand Shu soldiers to exit the city to fight the Song army. Liu Guang Yi sent Zhang Ting Han, the commander of the cavalry of the Guizhou branch of the Song army, to command the cavalrymen under him to meet the Shu troops under Wu Shou Qian. Wu Shou Qian was defeated and ran back. Zhang Ting Han commanded his men to go forward triumphantly and climbed the city wall. Gao Yan Chou fought very hard to defend the city but very soon the Song army overcame them. Gao Yan Chou was seriously wounded. All his followers had deserted. With great pain he ran back to his home and dressed neatly. Then he made several bows to the northwest. Then he set fire to his house and burned himself to death.

Several days later Liu Guang Yi found the bones of Gao Yan Chou in the ashes of his house. He ordered his soldiers to bury Gao Yan Chou's bones with great honor. Then Liu Guang Yi sent troops to take Wanzhou (now Wanxian, Sichuan Province), Shizhou (now Enshi, Hubei Province), Kaizhou (now Kaixian, Sichuan Province) and Zhongzhou (now Zhongxian, Sichuan Province). In January 965 the Song army under Liu Guang Yi reached Suizhou (now Suining, Sichuan Province). Chen Yu, the commander of the Shu army defending Suizhou, opened the city gate and surrendered to the Song army under Liu Guang Yi. After having taken each city, Liu Guang Yi took the money and cloth from the government treasuries of the State of Shu to distribute to the generals, officers and men according to the order issued by Emperor Zhao Kuang Yin. Some generals and men wanted to kill and loot the people, but Cao Bin, the supervisor of the Guizhou branch of the army, strictly prohibited it. So this branch of the Song army marched forward with great discipline and did not do any harm to the people of the State of Shu. When Emperor Zhao Kuang Yin understood what discipline Cao Bin had instilled in his troops, he was very glad. He said, "I have appointed the right person to the right position." He issued an imperial order praising Cao Bin.

Since the Shu troops had destroyed the plank road, the Song army under Wang Quan Bin could not go forward. It was suggested that the whole army should take Luochuan Road to march south. Kang Yan Ze said to Cui Yan Jin, "Luochuan Road is a perilous road. Soldiers can only go along in single file. It would be better to divide the whole army into two parts. One part will take Luochuan Road. The other part will repair the plank road. When the plank road is repaired, that part of the army use the new road and the two parts of the army will join forces at Shendu." Cui Yan Jin conveyed Kang Yan Ze's suggestion to Wang Quan Bin. Wang Quan Bin agreed.

Wang Qaun Bin commanded the main force to take Luochuan Road. Cui Yan Jin stayed behind to lead the soldiers in repairing the plank road. Cui Yan Jin sent soldiers into the forest to fell trees. The soldiers made logs with the branches of the trees and made planks from the trunks of the trees. They sharpened one end of the logs and insert them into the holes already dug into the precipice of the mountain. Then they put planks of wood on the logs. Section by section, the plank road was repaired. Several days later the whole plank road was ready. Cui Yan Jin led his troops along the plank road and then they attacked and took Jinshan Stronghold and Xiaomantian Stronghold (situated in Mantian Mountain in the northeast of Guangyuan, Sichuan Province). The Song army under Cui Yan Jin reached Shendu (a ferry crossing of Jialing Jiang River which was situated to the south of Xiaomantian Stronghold). Very soon the main force commanded by Wang Quan Bin also reached Shendu and joined forces with the Song army under Cui Yan Jin.

The Shu troops were arranged in battle formation along the river. Cui Yan Jin sent Zhang Wan You, the commander of the infantry of the Fengzhou branch of the Song army, to command the foot soldiers to attack the battle formation of the Shu army. The Song troops defeated the Shu army and took the bridge over the river. When evening came, the Shu Troops retreated to Damantian Stronghold. The next day Cui Yan Jin divided his troops into three parts. Cui Yan Jin, Kang Yan Ze and Zhang Wan You each commanded one part of the army and they attacked Damantian Stronghold from three directions. The Shu troops in other places came to reinforce Damantian Stronghold. The Song troops defeated the Shu troops anyway, and took Damantian Stronghold. The Song troops captured Wang Shen Chao, the commander of the Shu army holding Damantian Stronghold, Zhao Chong Wo, the supervisor of the Shu army holding Damantian Stronghold, and Liu Yan Zuo, the supervisor of the Shu army in Sanquan (now Yangpingguan, Shaanxi Province) who had come to back up the Shu army in Damantian Stronghold. Wang Zhao Yuan and Zhao Chong Tao commanded the Shu army to fight against the Song army. Three battles were fought and the Shu army was defeated three times. The Song troops pursued the Shu army to the north of Lizhou (now Guangyuan, Sichuan Province). Wang Zhao Yuan and Zhao Chong Tao escaped and crossed Jialing Jiang River by the floating bridge at Jubojin Crossing. After they had crossed the river, they burned the bridge. Wang Zhao Yuan commanded the defeated Shu army to retreat to Jianmen (now Jianmenguan, Sichuan Province). On 30 December Wang Quan Bin led the Song army to occupy Lizhou. The Song army captured 1,096,000 bushels of grain for the army stored in Lizhou.

It was a very cold December that year. It snowed heavily in Daliang, the capital of the Song Dynasty. Emperor Zhao Kuang Yin set up a big tent made of wool in Jiangwu Hall in the palace. He himself put on a marten coat and wore a fur hat, but still he felt cold. One day while he was attending to matters of state, he suddenly said to the officials with him, "I have put on very warm clothes but I still feel cold. Now the marshal and generals on the western expedition are exposed to the frigid cold weather. How can they withstand such cold weather?" Then he took off his marten coat and fur hat and sent several of his body-guards as his envoys to ride very quickly to the battlefront to grant the marten coat and fur hat to Wang Quan Bin. When the Emperor's envoy delivered the coat and hat to Wang Quan Bin, Wang Quan Bin knelt down on his knees to receive them with tears in his eyes.

In January 965 Meng Chang, King of the State of Shu, learned that Wang

Zhao Yuan and Zhao Chong Tao were defeated, he was shocked. He gave the order to recruit more soldiers to be sent to defend Jianmen. He appointed Meng Zhe, the crown prince, as the marshal of the Shu army, Li Ting Gui as the chief of the general staff and Zhang Hui An as deputy chief of general staff. They would command more than ten thousand soldiers to march northward to reinforce Jianmen. All the banners were made of silk embroidered with the great characters of Shu on them. The banners were put on flag poles. When the army was ready to march, it suddenly rained. Meng Jie ordered the soldiers to take the silk banners off from the flag poles so that the banners would not get wet. But very soon it stopped raining. Meng Jie ordered the soldiers to put the banners on the flag poles again. When the banners were put on the flag poles, people found that all the banners were upside down. Meng Jie ordered many small carts to be prepared to carry all his concubines with him. And he ordered over thirty actors and actresses to go with the army. When the Shu army marched out of Chengdu (now Chengdu, Sichuan Province), the capital of the State of Shu, the on-lookers all laughed secretly.

Wang Quan Bin marched the Song army from Lizhou to Jianmen. On the way, the Song army stopped in Yiguang (now Zhaohua, Sichuan Province). There, Wang Quan Bin held a military conference with all his officers. Wang Quan Bin said, "Jianmen Pass is a natural barrier. There is a saying describing this place: 'If one man guards the pass, ten thousand are unable to get through.' Now each of you may present your plan to take Jianmen." Xiang Tao, an officer of the guards, said, "Mu Jin, a Shu soldier who has surrendered, told me, 'From Yiguang along the east bank of Jialing Jiang River there are several mountains. If you cross these mountains, you will come to a narrow path named Laisu. The Shu army has established a stronghold on the west bank of the river. You can cross this section of the river. From there you may reach Qingjiang, a place ten kilometers south of Jianmen Pass. You will see a road leading to Jianmen Pass. Then you may take Jianmen Pass easily.' " Wang Quan Bin thought that sounded perfectly acceptable.

But Kang Yan Ze said, "Laisu path is a narrow path. It is not necessary for the commander-in-chief to use this path. We have defeated the Shu army many times. Now all the troops of the Shu army have retreated to Jianmen. It would be better for us to attack Jianmen directly with our main force. You may send a general to command a detachment to march to Laisu. When our troops under this general reached Qingjiang, they may attack Jianmen from the south. If our main force attacks from the north and this detachment attacks from the south, we will surely take Jianmen."

Wang Quan Bin agreed with Kang Yan Ze's suggestion. He ordered Shi Yan De to take command of a detachment and go through Laisu Path. When Shi Yan De with his detachment reached Laisu (a place in the area to the east of Jiange, Sichuan Province), he ordered his soldiers to build a floating bridge over Jialing Jiang River. When the Shu troops holding the stronghold on the west bank saw that a bridge had been built, they gave up the stronghold and ran away. Then the Song troops under Shi Yan De marched to Qingjiang.

When Wang Zhao Yuan heard that the Song troops under Shi Yan De had reached Qingjiang, he and Zhao Chong Tao commanded the main force of the Shu army to Hanyuanpo (in the area to the east of Jiange, Sichuan Province), leaving a general in command of the Shu troops defending Jianmen. Wang Quan Bin commanded the main force of Song army to attack Jianmen fiercely and took Jianmen Pass. Then the main force of the Song army marched southward to Huanyuanpo. Seeing that the Song troops were coming, Zhao Chong Tao arranged the Shu troops in battle formation to resist the Song troops. He galloped forward to meet the Song troops. But very soon he was captured. When Wang Zhao Yuan saw the oncoming Song troops, he may not have considered himself such a great strategist after all. He was so afraid that he just stayed in his bed and could not get up. Then he threw away his armor and weapons and ran away. On 2 January 965 Wang Quan Bin took Jianzhou (now Jiange, Sichuan Province). In this battle more than ten thousand Shu soldiers and officers were killed. Wang Zhao Yuan fled to the east part of Sichuan and hid himself in a store house. He could do nothing but weep all day long. He wept so much that his eyes were swollen. He kept reciting a bit of poetry, "Luck has deserted the hero. The hero will lose his freedom." Very soon the pursuing Song troops reached the place where Wang Zhao Yuan was in hiding and captured him. Then Wang Quan Bin sent a group of soldiers to escort Wang Zhao Yuan and Zhao Chong Tao to Daliang to present them to Emperor Zhao Kuang Yin.

When they were escorted to Daliang, Emperor Zhao Kuang Yin set them free.

Meng Jie, the crown prince of the State of Shu, and Li Ting Gui, commanded the Shu troops to go north to reinforce the Shu army in Jianmen. On the way they had all kinds of frolics. They did not care that the State of Shu was in peril. When they reached Mianzhou (now Mianyang, Sichuan Province), they heard that the Song army had taken Jianmen. On 4 January 965 Meng Jie and the Shu army ran back to Chengdu, burning all the houses and grain storage barns on their way back.

Meng Chang, the King of the State of Shu, was told that Jianmen had been taken by the Song army, and by that time, Meng Jie had run back. Meng Chang was so afraid that he was at a total loss as to what he should do. He summoned all the generals and officials to the palace to discuss what measures they should take. Shi Bin, an old general, said, "The Song troops have come from afar. They cannot stay for long. We may gather all our troops to defend Chengdu. If we stand fast for long enough, the Song troops will be tired out. Then we may defeat them." Meng Chang said with a long sigh, "My father and I have maintained an army for over forty years. We have provided the soldiers with good food and good clothes. But now when they meet the enemy in the battlefront, they will not fight for me. If I gather all the troops to defend the capital, who will be willing to fight to the death for me?" Li Hao, the minister of works, suggested that Meng Chang should surrender. Meng Chang took his suggestion. Then he ordered Li Hao to draft the petition of surrender. On 7 January Meng Chang deputized Yi Shen Zheng to go to the Song army to present the petition of surrender to Wang Quan Bin, the commander-in-chief of the Song army.

On 13 January Wang Quan Bin reached Weicheng (now Weicheng in the area of Mianyang, Sichuan Province) and stationed his army there. Yi Shen Zheng arrived at Weicheng with the petition of surrender on the same day. He presented the petition to Wang Quan Bin. Wang Quan Bin accepted it and sent Tian Jin Zuo, an officer under Wang Quan Bin, with a party of soldiers to ride quickly to Daliang to present Meng Chang's petition to Emperor Zhao Kuang Yin. Then he sent Kang Yan Ze, the commander-in-chief of the Fengzhou branch of the cavalry, with a hundred cavalrymen, to go to Chengdu to see Meng Chang, King of the State of Shu. When Kang Yan Ze reached Chengdu and saw Meng Chang, he told him that Emperor Zhao Kuang Yin had given orders to treat Meng Chang kindly. He sealed all the treasure houses of the State of Shu. Three days later Kang Yan Ze and the one hundred cavalrymen rode back to join the Song army under Wang Quan Bin. On 19 January Wang Quan Bin reached Shengxianqiao (five kilometers north to Chengdu, Sichuan Province). Meng Chang went to Shengxianqiao to see Wang Quan Bin at the gate of the camp of the Song army. A ceremony was held to accept Meng Chang's surrender.

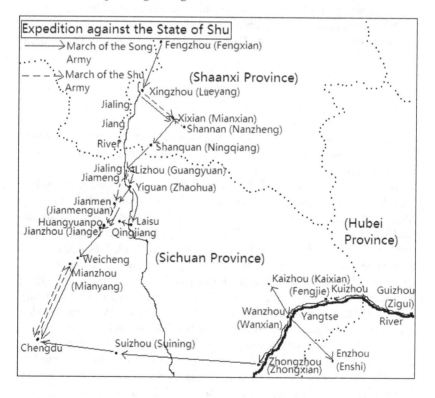

Expedition against the State of Shu

→ March of the Song Army
March of the Shu Army

Fengzhou (Fengxian)

(Shaanxi Province)

Xingzhou (Lüeyang)

Jialing

Jiang

Xixian (Mianxian)
Shannan (Nanzheng)

River

Shanquan (Ningqiang)

Jialing
Jiameng

Lizhou (Guangyuan)

Yiguan (Zhaohua)

Jianmen
(Jianmenguan)

Huangyuanpo
Jianzhou (Jiange)

Laisu
Qingjiang

(Hubei Province)

Weicheng
Mianzhou
(Mianyang)

(Sichuan Province)

Kaizhou (Kaixian)
(Fengjie) Kuizhou Guizhou
(Zigui)

Wanzhou
(Wanxian)

Yangtse

River

Chengdu

Suizhou (Suining)

Zhongzhou
(Zhongxian)

Enzhou
(Enshi)

Then Wang Quan Bin set Meng Chang free, in accordance with Emperor Zhao Kuang Yin's order, before setting out from Daliang. Several days later, Liu Guang Yi and Cao Bin also commanded the Guizhou Branch of the Song army to come to Chengdu. From the time Wang Quang Bin left Daliang to carry out the expedition against the State of Shu to the time when Wang Quan Bin entered Chengdu, only sixty-six days had passed. In this expedition, the Song Dynasty gained forty-six prefectures, two hundred and forty counties and five hundred and thirty-four thousand and twenty-nine households.

Meng Chang sent his younger brother Meng Zhi to Daliang to present a petition to Emperor Zhao Kuang Yin. The petition read, "My father was ordered by the Emperor of the Tang Dynasty to put down the unrest in the area of Shu and he established the State of Shu. When my father died, I was still young and inexperienced. After I succeeded my father, I was surrounded by ill-intentioned officials. I did not respect the rule that a small state should serve the big state and the small state should be a vassal state of the big state. So I made a mess of things. Your Majesty had to take the trouble of sending an army to punish me. The army sent by Your Majesty is invincible. I have sent several envoys with my petitions of surrender to Your Majesty. I am afraid that it is not easy to get to Daliang and my envoys may not have reached your capital. So on 19 this month I went with my brothers to the gate of the camp of the army Your Majesty sent, to surrender. My mother is nearly seventy years old and my children are still very young. I hope Your Majesty will spare them and let them live on. The marshal of Your Majesty's army has conveyed Your Majesty's kindness in sparing me. But I have committed a serious crime. So I cannot rest easy. This is the reason why I have sent my younger brother with this petition to present to Your Majesty and I await the verdict issued by Your Majesty."

Having read Meng Chang's petition, Emperor Zhao Kuang Yin issued an imperial edict. It read, "I have been assigned by Heaven to be the emperor of central China. My aim is to protect the people and practice good governance. I don't want to send armies to threaten other states. But although you are in a remote place, you had a secret plan to take over the area of central China. You colluded with the State of Han to invade the territory of the Song Dynasty. It is you who provoked the war. I had to send an army to punish you. My army is a righteous army carrying out a punitive war against you. The Song troops are invincible and they overcome their enemies wherever they go. Sometimes at midnight, lying in bed, I would think, 'What crimes have the ordinary people committed that they have to go to the battlefields and expose themselves to death?' I have done my best to save you from destruction and I have treated you with due respect. Now you have really led all your officials to surrender and ask for mercy; you have presented a petition to tell me your worries and your concerns. You want to preserve the temples of your clan; you have sealed all the treasure houses of the State of Shu for the coming Song army. That means you have given up all your wrong ways from the past and have reformed yourself. By doing so, you will gain more blessings for yourself. I have promised to pardon you. I will not go back on my own words. All your worries can be removed."

In March 965, Meng Chang and all the officials of the State of Shu with their families started their journey to Daliang, the capital of the Song Dynasty. They took boats along the Yangtze River to Xiazhou (now Yichang, Hubei Province), then made it to Jiangling (now Jiangling County in Jingzhou, Hubei Province). Emperor Zhao Kuang Yin sent Dou Si Yan, an official, to meet them. On 5 May Meng Chang and his mother arrived at Daliang. Emperor Zhao Kuang Yin sent his younger brother Zhao Guang Yi to welcome Meng Chang in the outskirts of Daliang. Then they were shown to the house built for them by the bank of Bianshui River.

On 16 May Meng Chang, his brother Meng Ren Zhi, his sons Meng Jie and Meng Yuan Jue, Premier Li Hao, thirty-three persons in all, went to the palace, standing outside the Mingde Gate of the palace. They were all dressed in white awaiting the punishment declared by the Emperor. Emperor Zhao Kuang Yin issued an imperial order to pardon them. Then they took off the white clothes. Emperor Zhao Kuang Yin received them in Chongyuan Hall of the palace. Emperor Zhao Kuang Yin granted Meng Chang a robe, a jade belt, a saddle decorated with gold, a thousand ounces of gold, ten thousand ounces of silver, one thousand bolts of brocade and ten thousand bolts of silk. Emperor Zhao Kuang Yin granted Meng Chang's mother three hundred ounces of gold, three thousand ounces of silverware, one thousand bolts of brocade, and two thousand bolts of silk. On 22 May the Emperor held a banquet in Daming Hall of the palace to entertain Meng Chang and all his brothers and sons.

Emperor Zhao Kuang Yin also invited Meng Chang's mother to the palace. Emperor Zhao Kuang Yin said, "You should take good care of yourself. You needn't miss your homeland so much. Later I will send officials to escort you back." Meng Chang's mother asked, "Where shall I go?" Emperor Zhao Kuang Yin said, "Back to the area of Shu." Meng Chang's mother said, "My original home is in Taiyuan. I wish I could go back and spend my remaining years there." Emperor Zhao Kuang Yin was glad to hear that. He said, "When I have defeated Liu Jun, I will send officials to escort you back to Taiyuan."

On 4 June Emperor Zhao Kuang Yin made Meng Chang Duke of Qin and appointed him Head of the Secretariat. He also appointed Meng Chang's brothers and sons to various positions. On 10 June Meng Chang died at the age of forty-seven. Emperor Zhao Kuang Yin did not hold court for five days, in mourning for Meng Chang. He granted Meng Chang the title of King of Chu. When Meng Chang died, his mother did not cry. She poured some wine on the floor and said, "You would not die for your country. You preferred life over honor. I still managed to live on because you were still alive. Now that you have died, there is no point for me to live on." She refused to eat anything for several days and starved herself to death.

After the Song army under Wang Quan Bin took Chengdu, Wang Qian

Bin, Cui Yan Jin and Wang Ren Shan often held parties and drank a lot of wine. They did not discipline their soldiers. The soldiers under them robbed and looted the people of Chengdu and raped the women there. Wang Quan Bin took part in it. This caused great sufferings to the people of Chengdu. Cao Bin tried many times to persuade Wang Quan Bin to withdraw the army back to Daliang. But Wang Quan Bin refused to do so. Not long later Wang Quan Bin received an imperial order from Emperor Zhao Kuang Yin ordering Wang Quan Bin to send the Shu soldiers to Daliang, the capital of the Song Dynasty. The Emperor gave ten thousand coins of money to each soldier being sent to Daliang. And the Emperor provided ten thousand coins of money and food enough for two months to those Shu soldiers who remained in Chengdu. Wang Quan Bin did not carry out the order immediately. He reduced the money which should be provided to the Shu soldiers and he allowed the soldiers under him to rob the money from the Shu Soldiers. The Shu soldiers were very angry.

When the Shu soldiers being sent to Daliang reached the area of Mianzhou (now Mianyang, Sichuan Province), they rebelled. They occupied the counties around Mianzhou. Many people joined in the rebellion. Very soon the rebellious Shu army increased to more than a hundred thousand men. Quan Shi Xiong, a former general of the State of Shu, was on his way to Daliang with his whole family. When the Shu soldiers brought their rebellion to the area of Mianzhou, he was afraid that he would be implicated in it, so he took his whole family to hide in the house of a farmer by the river. But several days later he was found by the Shu soldiers and was forced to serve as the marshal of this army.

They named this army "the Army of Rejuvenating the State of Shu." Wang Quan Bin sent Mi Guang Xu, a supervisor of the army, to go to Mianzhou to offer amnesty to the rebelling Shu soldiers. When Mi Guan Xu reached Mianzhou, he searched and found Quan Shi Xiong's family hiding in the farm house. He took Quan Shi Xiong's daughter as his own wife and killed the rest of the family. When Quan Shi Xiong heard that, he dismissed the idea of surrendering himself to the Song army. Instead he became very resolute in fighting against the Song army. He commanded the Shu soldiers to attack Mianzhou but they were defeated. Then Quan Shi Xiong commanded his army to attack Pengzhou (now Pengzhou, Sichuan Province) which was situated to the southwest of Mianzhou. The Shu army drove Wang Ji Tao, the Governor of Pengzhou, away and killed Li De Rong, the supervisor of the army defending Pengzhou. The Shu army under Quan Shi Xiong took Pengzhou. The Shu people of the ten counties around Chengdu rose up in arms and joined the rebel forces led by Quan Shi Xiong.

Quan Shi Xiong declared himself the "Great King of Rejuvenating the State of Shu." He established his own court and appointed court officials and appointed generals to his army. He ordered his generals to command troops to occupy Guankou County (Now Guankou Town, to the west of Dujiangyan, Sichuan Province), Daojiang County (now Dujianyan, Sichuan

Province), Pixian (now Pixian, Sichuan Province), Xinfan (now Xinfan, Chengdu, Sichuan Province) and Qingcheng (now a place to the west of Dujiangyan, Sichuan Province).

Cui Yan Jin, Zhang Wan You, and Tian Qin Zuo commanded the Song troops to launch a punitive expedition against Quan Shi Xiong. But they were defeated by the troops under Quan Shi Xiong. Gao Yan Hui was killed in battle. Tian Qin Zuo had a narrow escape. The rebelling Shu army became even stronger. Wang Quan Bin sent Zhang Ting Han and Zhang Xu to head out from Chengdu to attack the enemy, but the attack was not successful. They had to retreat back into Chengdu. Quan Shi Xiong deployed his army between Mianzhou (now Bianyang, Sichuan Province) and Hanzhou (now Guanghan, Sichuan Province). He ordered the Shu soldiers to build strongholds along Shiting Jiang River. He declared that he would command the Shu army to attack Chengdu. From then on the people of many prefectures such as Qiongzhou (now Qionglai, Sichuan Province), Shuzhou (now Chongzhou, Sichuan Province), Meizhou (now Meishan, Sichuan Province), Yazhou (now Ya'an, Sichuan Province), Guozhou (now Nanchong, Sichuan Province), Suizhou (now Suining, Sichuan Province), Yuzhou (now Chongqing, Sichuan Province), Hezhou (now Hechuan, Sichuan Province), Zizhou (now Zizhong, Sichuan Province), Jianzhou (now Jianyang, Sichuan province), Changzhou (now Yongchuan in the Chongqing area, Sichuan Province), Puzhou (now Anyue, Sichuan Province), Jiazhou (now Leshan, Sichuan Province), Rongzhou (now Yibin, Sichuan Province), Lingzhou (now Renshou, Sichuan Province), rose to join the rebellion led by Quan Shi Xiong.

Communication between the court of the Song Dynasty in Daliang and the commander of the Song army in Chengdu was cut off for more than a month. This made Wang Quan Bin very afraid. At that time he had more than twenty thousand Shu soldiers in Chengdu. Wang Quan Bin felt that these Shu soldiers might rebel and join Quan Shi Xiong. The generals under Wang Quan Bin suggested that all of the soldiers should be killed. Kang Yan Ze suggested that they should pick out the old soldiers, under-aged soldiers and the sick soldiers and release them; there would be seven thousand of them; the rest should be taken back to Daliang by boats along the river; if the rebel Shu army came to save them, then it would not be too late to kill them all. Wang Quan Bin turned down his suggestion. Still, one day all the Shu soldiers in Chengdu, twenty seven thousand in all, were driven into a narrow place and killed.

In June Liu Guang Yi and Cao Bin commanded the Song army under them to fight a battle against the rebel Shu army under Quan Shi Xiong in Xinfan (now Xinfan, a place to the north of Chengdu, Sichuan Province). The Song army won a great victory. They captured more than ten thousand Shu soldiers. Quan Shi Xiong retreated to Pixian (now Pixian, Suchuan Province). Wang Quan Bin and Liu Ren Shan sent the Song army to defeat Quan Shi Xion in Pixian. Quan Shi Xiong led the soldiers under him to retreat to a stronghold in Guankou (now west of Dujiangyan, Sichuan Province).

Lü Han, a commander of the Song army stationed in Jiazhou (now Leshan, Sichuan Province), rebelled because he felt that he was unfairly treated by his superior. He killed Wu Huai Jie, the governor of Jiazhou, and Liu Han Qing, the supervisor of the naval forces. He joined forces with Liu Ze, a general appointed by Quan Shi Xiong. Their army developed into an army of fifty thousand men. Song De Wei, a commander of the Song army stationed in Guozhou (now Nanchong, Sichuan Province), killed Wang Yong Chang, the governor of Guozhou, Liu Huan and Zheng Guang Bi, the supervisors of Guozhou, and rebelled. Wang Ke Liao, a high ranking officer of the Song army stationed in Suizhou (now Suining, Sichuan Province), led the people of Suizhou to rebel. Liu Ren Shan commanded an army to carry out an expedition against Lü Han in Jiazhou. Lü Han was defeated and escaped into Yazhou (now Ya'an, Sichuan Province). Liu Ren Shan commanded his army to pursue Lü Han to Yazhou and defeated him again. Lü Han ran away to Lizhou (now Hanyuan, Sichuan Province). Not much later, Lü Han was killed by his subordinates. His dead body was thrown into water.

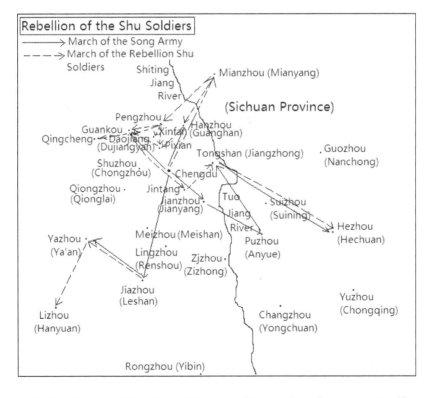

In July Emperor Zhao Kuang Yin learned about a brutal act committed by a high ranking officer of the Song army in Chengdu. This high ranking officer had cut off the breasts of a woman and then killed her. Emperor Zhao Kuang

Yin was very angry. He issued a severe order to escort the high ranking officer to Daliang. When the officer was brought in, many officials tried to save him. Emperor Zhao Kuang Yin said, with tears in his eyes, "I raised an army to punish the King of the State of Shu who has committed crimes in plotting to attack our territory. What crime has this woman committed that she should be killed in such a vicious way? This high ranking officer should be executed right away, according to law, so as to pay for his brutal act to the woman." The high ranking officer was executed in the market place in Daliang.

In August Emperor Zhao Kuang Yin issued an order appointing Kang Yan Ze Governor of Puzhou (now Anyue, Sichuan Province). Kang Yan Ze went to see Wang Quan Bin and asked him to send soldiers to escort him to Puzhou to take up his new position. Wang Quan Bin only sent a hundred soldiers to escort Kang Yan Ze. When Kan Yan Ze reached Jianzhou (now Jianyang, Sichuan Province), he recruited run-away soldiers. He got more than one thousand of them. He trained the new recruits how to fight in battles. When he reached the area occupied by the rebels, he showed the people of that area that the rebellion would surely be pacified and the Song army would surely win. Then three thousand people joined the Song army.

Kang Yan Ze led his soldiers into battle against the rebels under Liu Ze. The thirty thousand men under Liu Ze were defeated by the Song troops under Kang Yan Ze. On 1 November, 965, Kang Yan Ze led his army into Puzhou. Not long later, Liu Ze with all the rebels under him came to Puzhou to surrender to Kan Yan Ze. Emperor Zhao Kuang Yin issued an imperial order appointing Kang Yan Ze commander of the Song army to pacify the seven prefectures in Chuandong (now the east part of Sichuan Province).

In June 966 Wang Quan Bin commanded the Song army to attack Quan Shi Xiong, the chief of the rebellion Shu army, in Guankou (now a place to the west of Dujiangyan, Sichuan Province). Quan Shi Xiong was defeated. More than two thousand rebels were captured. Quan Shi Xiong led his defeated army to run away to Jintang (now Jintang, Sichuan Province). In December Quan Shi Xiong died of illness in Jintang. The rebels elected Xie Xing Ben as the chief and Luo Qi Jun as the assistant. They retreated to Tongshan (now Jiangzhou, Sichuan Province). Kang Yan Ze commanded the Song army under him to march from Puzhou to Tongshan to fight a battle with the rebels under the command of Wang Ke Liao. The rebels under Wang Ke Liao were defeated and ran away to Hezhou (now Hechuan, Sichuan Province). Kang Yan Ze commanded the Song arm to pursue the rebels and took Hezhou. Then Kang Yan Ze commanded the Song army to Tongshan and took it. The rebellion in the Shu area was at last stamped out.

In January 967, some people of Shu went to Daliang to lodge complaints against Wang Quan Bin, Wang Ren Shan and Cui Yan Jin with Emperor Zhao Kuang Yin. The complaints revealed their unlawful acts when they occupied the area of Shu. In a careful investigation, Emperor Zhao Kuang Yin thoroughly examined all the crimes committed by the generals. Then he called all the generals in the area of Shu back to Daliang. Wang Ren Shan was the first one to be interrogated by the Emperor. Wang Ren Shan listed all the wrong doings of the other generals but failed to acknowledge his own crimes. The Emperor was very angry. He said, "Taking the Shu General Li Ting Gui's prostitute as your concubine, breaking into the Treasure House of Fengde and taking the gold from that treasure house, are these acts done by Wang Quan Bin?" Wang Ren Shan was so afraid that he could not say a word.

Emperor Zhao Kuang Yin did not want to sent Wang Quan Bin, Wang Ren Shan and Cui Yan Jin to prison because they had done great deeds in conquering the State of Shu. He entrusted the members of the Secretariat to interrogate Wang Quan Bin, Wang Ren Shan and Cui Yan Jin. Wang Quan Bin, Wang Ren Shan and Cui Yan Jin acknowledged all the crimes they had committed. Emperor Zhao Kuang Yin issued an imperial order which read, "Wang Quan Bin, Wang Ren Shan and Cui Yan Jin carried out an expedition against the State of Shu. Wearing armor and taking weapons in their hands, they fought very bravely and made great contributions to the realm. Under fierce attack by the Song army, the King of the State of Shu was brought to submission and asked for mercy. I sent an imperial order to accept his surrender and showed pity on him. I have ordered Wang Quan Bin, Wang Ren Shan and Cui Yan Jin to pacify the people of Shu and to preserve the royal house, officials, generals and men, and people of the State of Shu and let them live on peacefully. But Wang Quan Bin, Wang Ren Shan and Cui Yan Jin did not carry out my order and did not discipline the officers and men under them. They went against my order and killed the Shu soldiers who had surrendered of their own will; they opened the treasure houses and took the treasures as their own; they forced the women to be their concubines; they robbed the people of their property. These have caused great complaints from the people. And these caused rebellions everywhere in the Shu area. We had to use the army to put down the rebellions. And the rebellions were pacified only after great efforts. I had to call them back. Originally I did not want to investigate this matter. But thousands of complaints were sent to the court. Wang Quan Bin, Wang Ren Shan and Cui Yan Jin were accused of taking the gold, silver and jade from the treasure houses as their own; they have taken one hundred and sixty thousand coins of money; they opened the Treasure House of Defeng and two hundred and eighty thousand coins of money were lost. I have ordered the members of the Secretariat to investigate into these matters. Wang Quan Bin, Wang Ren Shan and Cui Yan Jin have admitted all their crimes. Now, I order the Minister of Law and all the generals and officials to discuss in court what punishment should be given to them."

On 23 January Emperor Zhao Kuang Yin summoned the Minister of Law and all the generals and officials to the court to discuss what punishment should be given to Wang Quan Bin, Wang Ren Shan and Cui Yan Jin. After discussion, the Minister of Law and all the generals and officials agreed that Wang Quan Bin, Wang Ren Shan and Cui Yan Jin deserved the death penalty. According to law, they would be executed by being cut into pieces. They asked Emperor Zhao Kuang Yin to approve their decision. Then Emperor Zhao Kuang Yin issued an imperial order which read, "I intended to conquer the State Shu without a war, although I raised a righteous army. But the unwise King of the State of Shu first plotted to attack the Song Dynasty by uniting with the State of Han. So I sent an army to punish him. Very soon the King of the State of Shu was brought to submission and surrendered. I ordered our troops to discipline themselves and not to commit the slightest offence against the people's interest and let the people of Shu live peacefully. Wang Quan Bin, the Regional Military Governor of the Army of Zhongwu, Cui Yan Jin, the Regional Military Governor of the Army of Wuxin, commanded the elite troops to march into the State of Shu and successfully conquered the State of Shu in accordance with my plan. They should understand my intention was to conquer the State of Shu and let the people of Shu to live peacefully. They should have returned triumphantly as soon as they conquered the State of Shu. In that case, they would have been granted rewards for their great contributions and their names and deeds would be written in history. But they lingered in the Shu area and would not return. They were insatiably greedy and killed innocent people. They would not stop taking military actions. Instead they used their military power to commit all kinds of unlawful acts. They have perpetrated major crimes and should be punished severely. Considering that they have also made great contributions to the realm, I have decided to be lenient towards them. I will only take away their military power. They will be assigned positions in the army. I have shown great mercy on them. They should reflect on their wicked actions and examine their mistakes. Wang Quan Bin will be demoted to commander in the Army of Chongyi. Cui Yan Jin will be demoted to commander in the Army of Zhaohua. Wang Ren Shan will be demoted to Great General of the Right Guards."

In the expedition against the State of Shu, Cao Bin and Liu Guang Yi had maintained discipline among their officers and men, so the Guizhou branch of the Army did not commit the slightest offence against the people of Shu. In order to reward their great work, on 28 January Emperor Zhao Kuang Yin appointed Cao Bin as the Director of the Southern Court Affairs and Regional Military Governor of Yicheng, Liu Guang Yi as the Regional Military Governor of Zhen'an, Zhang Ting Han as Supervisor of the Cavalry of the Royal Guard Army and Regional Military Governor of Zhangguo.

When Wang Ren Shan was interrogated by Emperor Zhao Kuang Yin, he listed all the crimes committed by other generals, but he had only praised Cao Bin. He said, "Cao Bin was honest and clean. He was cautious. He really lived up to Your Majesty's expectations." So Emperor Zhao Kuang Yin granted him very great rewards. Cao Bin went to the court to express his gratitude to Emperor Zhao Kuang Yin and wanted to decline the rewards. He said, "The other generals have all been punished. But I am granted rewards by Your Majesty. I really feel uneasy." Emperor Zhao Kuang Yin said, "Your contributions were remarkable and you have not committed the slightest offence. You have not claimed credit for yourself and become arrogant. If you had made the slightest offence, Wang Ren Shan would not have concealed it for you. Giving punishment to those who have committed crimes and giving rewards to those who have established contributions is the general practice in a state. You don't need to decline the rewards granted to you."

15. Emperor Zhao Kuang Yin Visits Zhao Pu in a Snowing Night

Emperor Zhao Kuang Yin visits Zhao Pu in a snowing night. Emperor Zhao Kuang Yin (front on the left); Zhao Guang Yi (back on the left); Zhao Pu (back on the right); Zhao Pu's wife (front on the right)

After Zhao Kuang Yin ascended the throne of the Song Dynasty, he often went out of the palace in plain clothes to visit the homes of the officials. So after court when Zhao Pu went home, he would not take off the clothes he wore for court in case Emperor Zhao Kuang Yin would come for a visit. One night it was snowing heavily. Suddenly Zhao Pu heard someone knocking at the door of his house. He opened the door in a great hurry. He saw that Emperor Zhao Kuang Yin was standing there, in the strong wind and heavy snow. Zhao Pu knelt down and touched his head to the ground. Emperor Zhao Kuang Yin said, "I have also asked my younger brother to come." Zhao Pu invited Emperor Zhao Kuang Yin into the living room. Not long later, Zhao Guang Yi also arrived. Zhao Pu spread out thick blankets on the floor and they sat on the blankets. A stove with burning charcoal was put in the middle of the living room and they roasted meat on the stove. Zhao Pu's wife served wine for them. Emperor Zhao Kuang Yin called Zhao Pu's wife "sister-in-law."

Zhao Pu asked the Emperor, "Why has Your Majesty come out of the palace in such a cold, snowy night?" Emperor Zhao Kuang Yin said, "I lay in bed but could not fall asleep. So I got up and have come to visit you." Zhao Pu asked, "Now it is time to conquer the states in the south and in the north. Which state is Your Majesty planning to conquer next?" Emperor Zhao Kuang Yin said, "I plan to take Taiyuan." Zhao Pu was silent for some time.

Then he said, "I don't think it is a good idea." Emperor Zhao Kuang Yin asked, "Why?" Zhao Pu said, "The State of Han faces alien nationalities in the north and in the west. If we take the State of Han, then we have to be prepared to continually resist threats from the north and from the west. It would be better for us to leave the State of Han alone for the time being. When we have conquered all the other states, it will be very easy for us to conquer this small state." Emperor Zhao Kuang Yin said, "That is exactly what I am planning to do. I just wanted to hear your opinion on this matter." Then Emperor Zhao Kuang Yin said to Zhao Pu, "Wang Quan Bin killed too many people when he was in command of the army sent to pacify the State of Shu. I am still angry with him when I think of this. He cannot be entrusted with any more military tasks whatsoever." Zhao Pu recommended Cao Bin and Pan Mei. Emperor Zhao Kuang Yin accepted his suggestion.

16. The Situation in the State of Northern Han

In July 968 a spy from the State of Northern Han was brought before Emperor Zhao Kuang Yin. Emperor Zhao Kuang Yin said to the spy, "Go back and tell this to your king, 'You have been a diehard enemy of the Emperors of the Zhou Dynasty for generations. So you would not submit to the Emperors of the Zhou Dynasty. But there are no grudges between you and me. Why have you so stubbornly stood fast to this small corner in the north? If you are determined to take over the area of Central China, command your army to march south across Taihang Mountains and fight a decisive battle with me." The spy went back to Taiyuan and conveyed what Emperor Zhao Kuang Yin had said to Liu Jun, the King of the State of Northern Han. Liu Jun sent the same man back to Daliang to convey his words to Emperor Zhao Kuang Yin: "The land of the State of Han is less than one tenth of that of Central China. I have a small army, one tenth of the army of the Song Dynasty. I do my best to keep this small state only because I am afraid that the House of the State of Han will not last for long and that no one will offer sacrifices to the ancestors in the House of Kings of the State of Han." When Emperor Zhao Kuang Yin heard these words, he had pity on Liu Jun. So Emperor Zhao Kuang Yin did not carry out an expedition against the State of Northern Han during the lifetime of Liu Jun.

Liu Jun had no sons, so there was no successor to the throne of the State of Northern Han. His father Liu Chong, the former Emperor of the State of Northern Han, had a daughter. When Liu Chong was a commander of the royal guards of Emperor Shi Jing Tang of the Jin Dynasty, he married his daughter to Xue Qian, a low ranking officer of the royal guards. She gave birth to a boy. This boy was named Xue Ji En. When Liu Chong became illustrious and influential, he took his daughter and grandson back from Xue Qian. Xue Qian was very angry. One day having drunk a lot of wine Xue Qian went into Liu Chong's house and saw his wife. He drew out his sword and thrust at his wife, intending to kill her. But his wife dodged and escaped. Then Xue Qian killed himself with his own sword. At that time, Xue Ji En was still very young. So Liu Chong ordered Liu Jun to adopt Xue Ji En as his son. Xue Ji En's name was changed to Liu Ji En. Then Liu Chong married his daughter to a man by the name of He. Again she gave birth to a boy. They named this boy He Ji Yuan. Not long later, He Ji Yuan's father and mother both died. Liu Chong ordered Liu Jun to adopt He Ji Yuan as his son, too. He Ji Yuan's name was changed to Liu Ji Yuan.

Liu Ji En was a dutiful son. He went to see Liu Jun and wished him good health in the morning and in the evening every day. He punctiliously observed all the filial duties. But when Liu Ji En became the Governor of Taiyuan, he was not capable of maintaining law and order in the area of Taiyuan. Liu Jun was worried. He said to Guo Wu Wei, the Premier of the State of Northern Han, "Liu Ji En is pure and dutiful. But he does not have the ability to rule over the state. I am afraid that he will not be capable of succeeding to the throne of the State of Han." Guo Wu Wei did not give any opinion on this matter.

In July 968 Liu Jun fell seriously ill. Liu Ji En began to take up the affairs of state. On 26 July 968 Liu Jun died. Liu Ji En sent an envoy to the State of Liao to report Liu Jun's death to the Emperor of the State of Liao and told the Emperor that he was prepared to ascend the throne of the State of Northern Han. The Emperor of the State of Liao gave permission. Then Liu Ji En ascended the throne of the State of Northern Han.

On 14 August 968 Emperor Zhao Kuang Yin ordered Lu Huai Zhong and other twenty-two generals to command troops of the Royal Guard Army to station in Luzhou (now Changzhi, Shanxi Province) to prepare to attack the State of Northern Han. On 18 August Emperor Zhao Kuang Yin appointed Li Ji Xun, the Regional Military Governor of Zhaoyi (in Luzhou, now Changzhi, Shanxi Province), as the Commander-in-chief of the Expedition Army against Hedong, and appointed Dang Jin, a commander of the Royal Guard Army, as the deputy Commander-in-chief of this army, Cao Bin, the Director of the Southern Court Affairs, as the Supervisor of this army. Emperor Zhao Kuang Yin appointed He Ji Jun, Commander of the army stationed in Dizhou (now Huimin, Shandong Province), as the Commander-in-chief of the Vanguard Army, Kang Yan Zhao, Commander of the army stationed in Huaizhou (now Qinyang, Henan Province), as the Supervisor of this army. Emperor Zhao Kuang Yin appointed Zhao Zan, the Regional Military Governor of Jianxiong, as the commander-in-chief of the Fenzhou branch; he made Si Chao (the commander of the army in Jiangzhou) the deputy commander-in-chief of this branch of the army; he appointed Li Qian Pu, the Governor of Xizhou, as its supervisor.

Liu Ji En, the new King of the State of Northern Han, disliked Guo Wu Wei, the Premier of the State, because he wielded great power. He wanted to drive Guo Wu Wei out but could not. In September 968 Liu Ji En made Guo Wu Wei concurrently Minister of Works. Outwardly Liu Ji En showed great respect to Guo Wu Wei. But actually Liu Ji En became estranged from him. Liu Ji En attended to the state affairs in Qinzheng Hall of the palace and he slept in that hall at night. All his former attendants and trusted followers stayed in the office of the Governor of Taiyuan. Someone suggested that he should summon them to the palace to guard him. But Liu Ji En would not listen to this advice.

On 29 September 968 Liu Ji En held a banquet to entertain all the ministers and generals. After the banquet, he stayed in Qinzheng Hall in the palace. He slept on the bed in the hall. Hou Ba Rong, the official in charge of provision for the palace, came into the hall and killed Liu Ji En with one thrust of his sword into his chest. Liu Ji En was on the throne of the State of Northern Han for only sixty days.

When Guo Wu Wei heard that Liu Ji En had been killed by Hou Ba Rong, he ordered soldiers to go into Qinzheng Hall by climbing ladders and kill Hou Ba Rong. Then Guo Wu Wei sent some soldiers to escort Liu Ji Yuan, the other adopted son, who was at that time Governor of Taiyuan, to the palace to ascend the throne of the State of Northern Han.

By the time Liu Ji Yuan ascended the throne, the Song army had already marched into the territory of the State of Northern Han. Liu Ji Yuan sent an envoy to the Emperor of the State of Liao asking him to send army to help him. Then Liu Ji Yuan sent General Liu Ji Ye, the supervisor of the royal guard army, and General Ma Jin Ke, to head an army to defend Tuanbaigu Valley (which is situated to the southeast of Qixian, Shanxi Province). Liu Ji Yuan appointed General Ma Feng as the supervisor of the army under Liu Ji Ye. When Ma Feng commanded his army to Dongguohe River (now in the east of Qingxu, Shanxi Province), the Song army under Li Ji Xun had already got there. He Ji Jun, the commander of the vanguard army under Li Ji Xun, defeated the Northern Han army commanded by Ma Feng. More than two thousand Northern Han soldiers were killed. Then the Song army took the bridge over Fen He River. The Song troops crossed Fen He River and marched to the foot of the city wall of Taiyuan. The Song army set fire to Yanxia Gate (in the south city wall of Taiyuan). Liu Ji Yuan, King of the State of Northern Han, sent General Guo Shou Bin to command the royal guards to go out of the city to fight against the Song army. Of course, they were defeated. Guo Shou Bin himself was struck by a stray arrow, so he had to lead his troops to retreat into the city of Taiyuan.

In October Emperor Zhao Kuang Yin sent an envoy to Taiyuan with about forty letters written by Emperor Zhao Kuang Yin. One letter was for Liu Ji Yuan. In this letter Emperor Zhao Kuang Yin urged Liu Ji Yuan to surrender and promised to appoint him the Regional Military Governor of Pinglu (now in Yidu, Shandong province). One letter was for Guo Wu Wei. Emperor Zhao Kuang Yin promised to appoint Guo Wu Wei the Regional Military Governor of Anguo (in Xingtai, Hebei Province). The envoy handed all the letters to Guo Wu Wei. When Guo Wu Wei had read the letter for him, he vacillated. He really wanted to accept the offer. He took to Emperor Zhao Kuang Yin's letter to Liu Ji Yuan and tried to persuade him to surrender and accept Emperor Zhao Kuang Yin's offer. But Liu Ji Yuan refused.

In September Yelu Jing, the Emperor of the State of Liao, appointed Ta'er, a king of the State of Liao, as the commander-in-chief to command a great army to rescue the State of Northern Han. Li Ji Xun had to command the Song army to retreat back to Daliang. The Northern Han army took this chance to march southward and took Jinzhou (now Linfen, Shanxi Province) and Jiangzhou (now Xinjiang, Shanxi Province).

17. The Situation in the State of Liao

Yelu Jing, the Emperor of the State of Liao, was a cruel man. He once believed in a sorceress by the name of Xiao Gun. She told the Emperor of the State of Liao that the gall bladders of human beings could be made into medicine for longevity. So Yelu Jing killed many people to take their gall bladders to make this medicine. But later he realized that he had been deceived by this sorceress. He ordered the soldiers to take her to the woods and then he ordered the soldiers to shoot whistling arrows at her, and killed her like an animal on the hunting ground. From then on he stuck to drinking wine, and but he still took pleasure in killing human beings. He used a lot of instruments to torture officials who had made very minor mistakes.

In 21 February, 969, Yelu Jing left Shangjing (now Barin Zuoqi, Inner Mongolia Autonomous Region), the capital of the State of Liao, to go hunting in Huaizhou (now Barin Youqi, Inner Mongolia Autonomous Region). Yelu Jing saw a bear and shot an arrow at it. He killed the bear. Xiao Si Wen, the head of the attendants of Emperor Yelu Jing, Yilesiba and Yalisi brought wine to celebrate this great success. Yelu Jing drank his fill and got drunk. Yelu Jing and his followers went back to his temporary dwelling place in Huaizhou. That night Yelu Jing was murdered by Xiao Ge, one of his bodyguards, with help from Hua Ge, one of his attendants, and Xi Gun, a cook. He died at the age of thirty-nine.

On 22 February Xiao Si Wen, and Gao Xun, the head of the Southern Privy Council, escorted Yelu Xian, the second son of Emperor Yelu Yuan, to ride with two thousand cavalrymen to Huaizhou where the late Emperor was lying in state. Yelu Xian cried bitterly before the dead body of Yelu Jing. All the ministers and generals asked Yelu Xian to ascend the throne. So Yelu Xian ascended the throne of the State of Liao in the presence of the coffin of the late emperor. On 9 March Emperor Yelu Xian and the ministers and generals went back to Shangjing, the capital of the State of Liao.

18. Expedition against the State of Northern Han

On 28 January 969, Emperor Zhao Kuang Yin sent out envoys to different army commands to sent troops to station in Luzhou (now Changzhi, Shanxi Province), Jinzhou (now Linfen, Shanxi Province), and Cizhou (now Cixian, Hebei Province). On 7 February 969 Emperor Zhao Kuang Yin ordered Cao Bin and Dang Jin to command the Song army to march to Taiyuan. On 10 February Emperor Zhao Kuang Yin informed the officials and Generals that he would personally command the northern expedition.

On 11 February Emperor Zhao Kuang Yin issued an imperial order to appoint his younger brother Zhao Guang Yi, the Governor of Kaifeng Area, as the commander-in-chief of the army defending Daliang, the capital; he appointed Shen Yi Lun, the deputy head of Privy Council, as the commander-in-chief of the army defending the palace. Emperor Zhao Kuang Yin appointed Li Ji Xun, the Regional Military Governor of the Army of Zhaoyi (in Luzhou, now Changzhi, Shanxi Province), as the commander-in-chief of the vanguard army of the command of Hedong; he appointed Zhao Zan, the Regional Military Governor of Jianxiong, as the supervisor of the infantry and cavalry. Li Ji Xun and Zhao Zan commanded the armies under them to march to Taiyuan. On 16 February Emperor Zhao Kuang Yin started from Daliang.

On 19 February Emperor Zhao Kuang Yin reached Wangqiaodun (a place near Anyang, Henan Province). When the Emperor was there, Han Chong Yun, the Regional Military Governor of Zhangde in Xiangzhou (now Anyang, Henan Province), went to Wangqiaodun to see him. Emperor Zhao Kuang Yin invited him to dinner. After drinking some wine, Emperor Zhao Kuang Yin said to him, "The Emperor of Khitan knows that I am carrying out an expedition against the State of Northern Han. He will send an army to rescue the State of Northern Han. He will think that the Song armies in Zhenzhou and Dingzhou are not prepared. The Khitan armies will certainly come through this way. You should command the troops under you to march at double speed and get to Dingzhou to launch a surprise attack on the Khitan army. The Khitan army will be surely defeated." Then Emperor Zhao Kuang Yin appointed Han Chung Yun as the commander-in-chief of the Song army in the northern front. He appointed Guo Ting Yi, the Regional Military Governor of Yiwu, as the deputy commander-in-chief of this army.

On 27 February Emperor Zhao Kuang Yin reached Luzhou (now Changzhi, Shanxi Province). At that time it was raining heavily. Many carts from different prefectures, loaded with food for the army, were gathered and traffic ground to a halt. When Emperor Zhao Kuang Yin learned about this, he was angry. He was going to punish the official in charge of transportation of military supplies. Zhao Pu said to the Emperor, "The armies of different prefectures have just arrived. But the official in charge of transportation of military supplies has been punished. When our enemies learn about this, they will know that we have not transported sufficient military supplies for the army. This is not the way to show our power to the enemy. It would be better to send a man who is good at handling such situations to come here and solve the problem."

The next day Emperor Zhao Kuang Yin appointed Wang You, an official of the ministry of finance, as the temporary Governor of Luzhou. Wang You organized and dispatched all the transportation tools skillfully and very soon the roads became clear.

Liu Ji Ye and Ma Jin Ke, the generals of the army of the State of Northern Han, commanded their army to station in Tuanbaigu Valley. Liu Ji Ye sent Chen Ting Shan, a commander, to lead several hundred cavalrymen to go south to reconnoiter the movement of the Song army. It happened that the vanguards of the Song army under the command of Li Ji Xun came. Chen Ting Shan and the soldiers under him surrendered to the Song army. Liu Ji Ye and Ma Jin Ke knew that their army was greatly outnumbered by the Song army. So they commanded the army under them to go back to Taiyuan. Liu Ji Yuan, the King of the State of Northern Han, was so enraged that he stripped Liu Ji Ye of his military power. Li Ji Xun commanded the Song army under him to march to Taiyuan and laid siege to the city.

At that time Emperor Yelu Xian of the State of Liao sent Han Zhi Fan, an attendant of the Emperor of the State of Liao, as his envoy to Taiyuan to make Liu Ji Yuan Emperor of the State of Northern Han. Liu Ji Yuan ordered to open the city gate to let Han Zhi Fan into the city. On the next day Liu Ji Yuan held a banquet to welcome Han Zhi Fan. All the officials and generals of the State of Northern Han attended the banquet. During the banquet Guo Wu Wei, the premier of the State of Northern Han, cried loudly. He drew out his sword and wanted to kill himself. Liu Ji Yuan hurriedly went down the steps and stopped Guo Wu Wei from killing himself. Then he held Guo Wu Wei's hand and led him up the steps to the table of the host. Guo Wu Wei said, "Why should we stand against the million Song soldiers with this isolated city?" Guo Wu Wei's purpose was to shake the determination of generals and officials to defend Taiyuan.

Emperor Zhao Kuang Yin stayed in Luzhou for eighteen days. During that time a spy from the State of Northern Han was captured and brought before Emperor Zhao Kuang Yin. The spy was interrogated. He said, "The people in the city of Taiyuan have suffered for a long time. They are longing for Your Majesty to come. They are afraid that Your Majesty will come too late." Emperor Zhao Kuang Yin smiled. He gave the spy some decent clothes and set him free. On 15 March, Emperor Zhao Kuang Yin left Luzhou. On 21 March he reached Taiyuan. On 23 March he inspected his army outside the south gate of the city wall of Taiyuan. He ordered the soldiers to build a long wall. The next day, he went to the bank of Fen He River. He ordered the soldiers to build a new bridge over Fen He River. Emperor Zhao Kuang Yin wanted to send more troops to attack the city of Taiyuan. At that time Chen Cheng Zhao, a general, was standing beside the Emperor. He said to the Emperor, "Your Majesty already has a million soldiers by your side.

Why does Your Majesty not use them?" Emperor Zhao Kuang Yin did not get his point and looked at Chen Cheng Zhao in great surprise. Then Chen Cheng Zhao pointed at the water in Fen He River with his horsewhip. Then Emperor Zhao Kuang Yin laughed heartily.

On 28 March Emperor Zhao Kuang Yin went southeast from Taiyuan and ordered over thirty thousand people to be mobilized in the counties around Taiyuan to build a dike across Fen He River. He put Chen Cheng Zhao in charge of this project. On 30 March Emperor Zhao Kuang Yin ordered Li Ji Xun to station the army under him to the south of the city of Taiyuan; he ordered Zhao Zan to station the army under him to the west side of the city; he ordered Cao Bin to station the army under him in the north of the city and Dang Jin to station the army under him to the east side of the city. The Song army built strong camps around the city of Taiyuan.

That night the troops of the State of Northern Han stealthily went out of the west gate to launch a surprise attack on the Song army under Dang Jin in the west camp. Zhao Zan commanded the troops under him to fight against the Northern Han troops. Zhao Zan was wounded on the leg by an arrow. But he did not retreat but went on fighting bravely. That day Dang Jin had sent Li Qian Pu, the supervisor of his army, to lead some soldiers to go to the Western Hill to cut trees for military use. Li Qian Pu heard the sound of drum beating. He commanded the soldiers under him to hurry back to the battlefield. When the Northern Han troops saw the troops coming to he rescue, they immediately withdrew into the city. Emperor Zhao Kuang Yin also hurried to the battlefield. He was surprised to see that the rescuing troops were not elite troops. He asked who they were, and he knew that it was Li Qian Pu who had come to the rescue on time. Emperor Zhao Kuang Yin was very glad.

Liu Ji Ye, the general of the State of Northern Han, commanded several hundred cavalrymen to launch a surprise attack on the eastern camp of the Song army. Dang Jin, although he had been wounded by the leg, urged his horse to ride at the Northern Han cavalrymen under Liu Jing Ye. Liu Jing Ye was defeated and he got down from his horse and hid himself in a ditch by the side of the city wall. The Northern Han troops went out of the city to rescue him. The soldiers on the top of the city wall threw down one end of a rope and Liu Ji Ye climbed up the city wall with it and escaped.

On 1 April Emperor Zhao Kuang Yin went to the east of the city of Taiyuan and inspected the progress of the dike project across Fen He River. On 4 April Emperor Zhao Kuang Yin sent Sun Wan Jin, the Governor of Haizhou, to command several thousand men to lay siege to Fenzhou (now Fenyang, Shanxi Province). He Ji Jun, the commander-in-chief of the army stationed in Dizhou (now Huimin, Shandong Province), was originally the commander of the army stationed in Shilinguan Pass in the north of Yangqu (now Yangqu, Shanxi Province).

Shilingguan Pass was situated in precipitous mountains. It was a pass of critical importance. Emperor Zhao Kuang Yin got information that one of the Liao armies would be going through that pass to rescue the State of Northern Han. He immediately dispatched an envoy to speed off to Dizhou to send He Ji Jun to the Taiyuan area where the Emperor was staying. When He Ji Jun came, Emperor Zhao Kuang Yin gave him instructions as to how to defeat the Liao army in Shilingguan Pass. Emperor Zhao Kuang Yin gave him several thousand top troops to hold off the Liao army. Before He Ji Jun and the troops left for Shilingguan Pass, Emperor Zhao Kuang Yin said to He Ji Jun, "I will be waiting for your report of victory tomorrow noon."

At that time it was already summer and the weather was hot. Emperor Zhao Kuang Yin ordered the cook to prepare bean starch noodles for He Ji Jun. After eating the bean starch noodles, He Ji Jun immediately commanded the troops under him to march to Shilingguan Pass. The next day they fought and the Song troops under He Ji Jun won a resounding victory over the Liao army. The Song troops captured Wang Yan Fu, the Governor of Wuzhou of the State of Liao. More than one thousand Liao soldiers were killed.

On 12 April, He Ji Jun sent his son He Cheng Rui with a party of soldiers to ride quickly back to Taiyuan to report the great victory to Emperor Zhao Kuang Yin, bringing the heads and the armor of the Liao soldiers. Before He Cheng Rui arrived, Emperor Zhao Kuang Yin had already been standing on a raised platform waiting for the good news. When he saw a man riding very quickly from the north, he sent someone to welcome him. He was very glad to learn from He Cheng Rui that the Song army had won a great victory. The Northern Han troops had expected the Liao army to come to rescue them, so they were quite resolute. But when they saw the heads of the Liao soldiers displayed before them, they lost heart.

On 6 May a Liao army sent by the Emperor of the State of Liao to rescue the State of Northern Han reached Dingzhou (now Dingzhou, Hebei Province). General Han Chong Yun had already deployed his army in battle formation in Jiashan in Dingzhou area. When the general commanding the Liao troops saw the battle formation of this great Song army, he was shocked and commanded his troops to retreat. General Han Chong Yun gave the order to attack. The Song troops pounced on the retreating Liao troops. The Song troops won a great victory. Many Liao soldiers were killed. The Liao troops were defeated and ran away. Han Chong Yun sent an envoy to Taiyuan to report the great victory to Emperor Zhao Kuang Yin. Emperor Zhao Kuang Yin was very glad and wrote an imperial order to praise the bravery of the Song army in this battle.

On 7 May Emperor Zhao Kuang Yin went to the north of Taiyuan and issued the order lo lead the water blocked by the dike across Fen He River to flood the southern part of the city wall of Taiyuan. On 11 May Emperor Zhao Kuang Yin came to the southeast of the city of Taiyuan and ordered the troops to embark on boats loaded with bows and arrows. The soldiers rowed the boats to get close the city and attacked the Northern Han troops standing at the top of the city wall. Wang Ting Yi, the commander of the infantry and cavalry beat the drum to inspire the soldiers to attack the city. When the boats got to the city wall, General Wang Ting Yi ordered the soldiers to put ladders against the city wall. He took off his helmet and armor so as to be lighter, and he was the first to climb up a ladder. But unfortunately he was struck by an arrow on the face when he was halfway up the wall. He fell on the boat. The soldiers took him back. The Song troops had to retreat. On 13 May Wang Ting Yi died. On 14 May General Shi Han Qing, a commander of the Royal Guard Army, commanded some troops to attack the city of Taiyuan by boats. But in the battle he was shot by an arrow and fell to the water and was drowned. On 16 May Emperor Zhao Kuang Yin conferred Wang Ting Yi posthumously with the title Regional Military Governor of Jianwu, and conferred upon Shi Han Qing the posthumous title of Commander-in-chief of the army in Yuanzhou.

On 20 May Emperor Zhao Kuang Yin went to the west of Taiyuan. He ordered the Song troops to attack the west gate of the city. On the same day he sent an army to lay siege to Lanzhou (now Lanxian, Shanxi Province). Zhao Hong, the commander of the Northern Han army defending Lanzhou, surrendered. Emperor Zhao Kuang Yin appointed Zhou Cheng Yin, a general of the Emperor's bodyguards, as the commander-in-chief of the Song army stationed in Lanzhou.

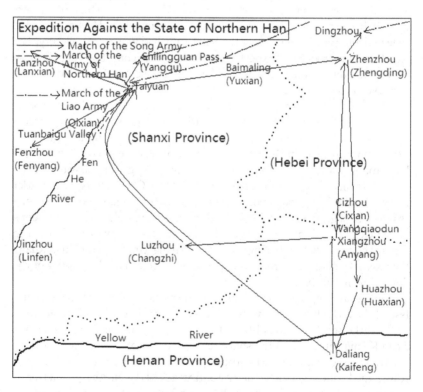

Taiyuan was surrounded by the Song army. Guo Wu Wei planned to go away from Taiyuan. He went to Liu Ji Yuan, King of the State of Northern Han, and said to him that he would personally command some troops to go out of the city of Taiyuan to attack the Song army. Liu Ji Yuan believed him and selected several thousand elite troops to be commanded by Guo Wu Wei. Liu Ji Yuan appointed Liu Ji Ye and Guo Shou Bin as deputy commanders of this army. Liu Ji Yuan went up the top of Yanxia Gate (the northern gate of the city of Taiyuan) to see this army off and he waited this army to return. At night it was dark and it was raining. When Guo Wu Wei reached Beiqiao (the Northern Bridge), he stopped his horse and summoned the generals there. Liu Ji Ye's horse had a slip and was hurt in the leg. So Liu Ji Ye had to lead the men under him to go back to the city of Taiyuan. Guo Shou Bin lost his way and misled his troops. Guo Wu Wei could not find Guo Shou Bin and his troops, so he had to go back to the city of Taiyuan.

On 3 of the second May (969 was an intercalary year which had two months of May), the foot of the southern city wall of Taiyuan had been immersed in water for over twenty days and was damaged. A hole was made by the water of Fen He River and water was flowing into the city through this hole. The people of Taiyuan were shocked. Emperor Zhao Kuang Yin went to the long dike to watch the water flowing into the city of Taiyuan. The hole was washed bigger and bigger by the water. Northern Han soldiers tried to set up barriers to block the hole. Song soldiers shot arrows at the Northern Han soldiers setting up the barriers, so they couldn't make much progress. But not long later a great ball of grass floated to the hole and stopped it up. Water could not flow into the city anymore. The arrows shot by the Song army could not go through this big ball of grass. Then the Northern Han soldiers carried out the work of repairing the city wall.

Guo Wu Wei tried again to persuade Liu Ji Yuan, the King of the State of Northern Han, to surrender but Liu Ji Yuan refused. Wei De Gui, a eunuch, said to Liu Ji Yuan, "It is very clear that Guo Wu Wei intends to betray Your Majesty. He should be killed. He cannot be spared. " So Liu Ji Yuan ordered to arrest Guo Wu Wei and put him to death.

At night of 3 of the second May the Northern Han troops went out of the city of Taiyuan through the west gate and tried to burn the offensive devices such as ladders and battering rams. The Song troops fought against the Northern Han troops. In this battle more than ten thousand Northern Han soldiers were killed. The Northern Han troops had to retreat into the city. At midnight, the soldiers inside the camps of the Song army heard a voice shouting, "The King of Han has come to surrender!" Emperor Zhao Kuang Yin ordered the guards to open the gate of the camp to accept the surrender of the King of the State of Northern Han. Zhao Sui, a commander of Emperor Zhao Kuang Yin's bodyguards, said, "Accepting surrender should be as careful as meeting the enemy in the battlefield. How can we open the gate of our camp at midnight?" Emperor Zhao Kuang Yin sent somebody out of the camp to find out what was happening. And he found out that it was a trick played by spies.

The Song army attacked Taiyuan for over two months but could not take it. Li Huai Zhong, the commander of the Royal Guard Army, said to Emperor Zhao Kuang Yin, "The city of Taiyuan is now isolated. Our enemies are now trying to protect themselves with this isolated city. They cannot have much of a military stockpile in the city and there are armies coming to the rescue from outside the city. The situation is not favorable for our enemies. If we attack the city fiercely, we may take it. I am willing to lead some elite troops to attack the city of Taiyuan."

Emperor Zhao Kuang Yin agreed to let him have a try. It was already midsummer and the weather was very hot. The attack was not successful. Li Huai Zhong was seriously wounded by an arrow but he went on fighting. But at last he had to lead his men to turn back. Zhao Ting Han, Supervisor of the Royal Guard Army, led all the soldiers under him to see Emperor Zhao Kuang Yin. They all knelt down in front of Emperor Zhao Kuang Yin. Zhao Ting Han said, "We are willing to climb up the city wall of Taiyuan and do our best to take this city. We shall keep fighting until we are killed in the battlefield." Emperor Zhao Kuang Yin said, "You were all trained by me. You are my bodyguards. I know that each of you can take on a hundred enemy soldiers. We share weal and woe. You will be sent into battle only in critical situation. I would rather give up the attack of Taiyuan than force you to go where you are sure to die." All the guards were moved to tears by his words.

At that time of the year, the Song army camped in the grasslands. It was very hot and it rained for days. Many soldiers contracted diarrhea.

Now Wuzhen, a king of the Northern Court of the State of Liao, commanded a strong army to march very quickly from Baimaling (in Yuxian, Shanxi Province) through a side road at night to a place west of Taiyuan. The Liao soldiers beat drums loudly and lit fires to tell the king of the State of Northern Han that they had come to rescue Taiyuan. When the Northern Han soldiers heard the sound of drums and saw the light of the fires, they jumped for joy and this inspired their determination to defend Taiyuan.

Li Guang Zan, the official in charge of ceremonies to offer sacrifices to Heaven, presented a memorandum to Emperor Zhao Kuang Yin which read, "Your Majesty is invincible. All the plans of Your Majesty have been realized. Those rulers of the neighboring states depended on the protection of the natural barriers and made themselves emperors and kings. In the past they were neighbors. Now they have submitted to Your Majesty. Taiyuan is a very small place. It is not necessary for Your Majesty to command the expedition personally. Now, the people have been mobilized to transport military supplies. This caused complaints from the people. If Taiyuan is conquered, it does not add much to our empire. If we lose it, it is not a disgrace for us. The best thing for the state is to stay in peace and tranquility. Heaven abhors undue trouble. I am worrying about the rulers of those neighboring states who depend on natural barriers for their protection. When they learn that a lot of treasure has been spent in this expedition against Taiyuan, and many people have been mobilized in this expedition, they will be making their secret plans. There is a teaching in history: 'The advantage of your neighbor is your disadvantage.' I suggest that Your Majesty go back to the capital. Some troops should be stationed in the area of Shangdang. These troops should get the wheat grown by the people of the State of Han in summer and get their millet and corn in autumn. In this way it is not necessary for us to send armies to fight battles and the strength of our enemy will be reduced greatly. This is an important policy to conquer the State of Han. I hope Your Majesty may consider my suggestion." Having read the memorandum, Emperor Zhao Kuang was very glad. He asked Zhao Pu's opinion. Zhao Pu also thought that it was a very good idea. Then Emperor Zhao Kuang Yin sent Zhao Pu to summon Li Guang Zan and personally praised Li Guang Zan for his good suggestion.

On 8 of the second May Emperor Zhao Kuang Yin held a meeting on the south slope of a hill which was situated east of the city of Taiyuan to discuss a retreat. In the meeting, Xue Hua Guang said, "When we fell a tree, we first cut off its leaves and branches and then cut it down from the root. Now the State of Han can get help from the State of Liao from outside and collect land taxes from the households of the State of Han from inside. I am afraid that it will be difficult for us to conquer the State of Han in a short time. It would be better for us to station armies in Shilingshan Mountain just to the north, and build strongholds in the Jingyang Village, Leping Town, Huangzeguan Pass in the east area of Xishan Mountain in the area to the north of the Yellow River to prevent the Liao army from coming to rescue the State of Han. We should move households of the State of Han to the areas of Luoyang, Xiangzhou, Dengzhou, Tangzhou, and Ruzhou and give them available lands and ask them to grow crops there. In this way the food supplies would not have to be transported to the government of the State of Han. In several years time the area of the State of Han will be pacified." Emperor Zhao Kuang Yin adopted his good suggestion. On 14 of the second May, ten thousand households in the area around Taiyuan were moved to the areas east of Xiaoshan Mountain (Xiaoshan Mountain is situated in the west part of Shaanxi Province and east part of Henan Province, which was regarded as the demarcation between the western part of China and eastern part of China in ancient times) and south to the Yellow River.

On 17 of the second May Emperor Zhao Kuang Yin started his journey back to Daliang, the capital of the Song Dynasty. At that time more than a hundred Song soldiers were captured by the Later Han troops. Emperor Zhao Kuang Yin ordered General Kong Shou Zheng to command the cavalrymen to save them. General Kong Shou Zhen and the soldiers under him fought very bravely and saved the Song soldiers who had been captured. When the Song army retreated, they left a lot of grain and supplies behind. The King of Han got about three hundred thousand catties of grain and more than thirty catties of tea and many bolts of silk.

On 23 of the second May, Emperor Zhao Kuang Yin reached Zhenzhou (now Zhengding, Hebei Province). Emperor Zhao Kuang Yin summoned Su

Cheng, a Taoist priest, to have a talk. The Emperor said, "I have ordered the building of a Taoist temple named Jinlong Temple in Daliang. I am looking for a Taoist priest of supernatural skill to be the master of this temple. Are you interested to be the master of this temple?" Su Cheng answered, "The capital is a prosperous and busy place. It is not a good place for a quiet life."

On 27 of the second May Emperor Zhao Kuang Yin went to the place where Su Cheng lived and paid him a visit. Emperor Zhao Kuang Yin asked, "You are already over eighty years old, but you look very young. Will you teach me some ways to keep good health?" Su Cheng answered, "My way of keeping health is very simple. I only do meditation and practice breathing exercise. The way for an emperor to keep good health is different from my ways. Laozi, the great thinker in ancient times, said, 'I let things take their own course and do nothing against nature. Then the people will progress from barbarity to civilization. I get rid of all my desires; then the people will act correctly'. Letting things take their own course, doing nothing against nature and getting rid of all desires will lead to great harmony. In ancient times Yellow Emperor and Emperor Yao ruled the realm in this way. They stayed on the throne for a very long time." At these words Emperor Zhao Kuang Yin was very glad and granted handsome rewards to Su Cheng.

On 1 June Emperor Zhao Kuang Yin left Zhenzhou on his way back to Daliang. On 14 June Emperor Zhao Kuang Yin reached Huazhou (now Huaxian, Henan Province). On 18 June Emperor Zhao Kuang Yin came back to Daliang, the capital of the Song Dynasty.

In June the people of the State of Northern Han drained the water in Taiyuan into a lake. After the water was drained, many parts of the city were damaged and fell down. At that time Han Zhi Fan, the envoy of the State of Liao, was still in Taiyuan. He exclaimed, "The Song troops only knew to use water to flood the city of Taiyuan. They only knew one way of using the water. If they had used water to flood the city and then drained the water, then the city of Taiyuan would have been damaged and taken by the Song army and we all would have been captured."

At that time Yelu Sezhen, the King of the South Court of the State of Liao, commanded an army to be stationed in the city of Taiyuan. Liu Ji Ye said to Liu Ji Yuan, the King of the State of Northern Han, "The Khitans are greedy and faithless. They will destroy our state someday in the future. Now the Khitan soldiers are proud and unprepared for any attack. I am willing to lead troops to launch a surprise attack on the Khitan soldiers. We may capture tens of thousands of horses. Then we may submit to the Song Dynasty with the territory of the State of Han so that the people of the State of Han can be saved from destruction. And Your Majesty may enjoy rank and wealth forever. Isn't that a good idea?" The King of the State of Northern Han refused to take his advice.

Several days later Yelu Sezhen returned to the State of Liao. The King of the State of Northern Han presented him with many gifts. Later the King of the State of Northern Han sent a rich bounty to Wuzhen who had rescued the city of Taiyuan. Wuzhen reported to the Emperor of the State of Liao that he had this money from the King of the State of Northern Han. The Emperor of the State of Liao gave an order allowing Wuzhen to accept the money presented by the King of the State of Northern Han.

19. The Situation in the State of Southern Han

Liu Chang, the King of the State of Southern Han, was a fatuous and suspicious man. He did not trust his ministers. He thought that all the ministers had their own families and their own children to take care of. They were only devoted to their own families and would not be devoted to him. He only believed the eunuchs, because the eunuchs did not have families and children to take care of and they were very close to him. He placed great power in eunuchs Gong Cheng Shu and Chen Yan Shou. If he wanted to put anyone in an important position, that man had to be castrated first.

Since he had placed great power in the hands of Gong Cheng Shu and Chen Yan Shou, King Liu Chang did not attend to state affairs. He stayed in the imperial harem all day long, having fun with the women. Chen Yan Shou brought Fan Hu Zi, a sorceress, into the palace. She said that Jade Emperor (Emperor of Heaven) had attached himself to her body. Liu Chang ordered a big tent to be set up in the inner hall of the palace and displayed all kinds of treasures in the tent. Fan Hu Zi, wearing a hat for travelling and clothes of purple color, sat in the tent and predicted all kinds of disasters and blessings. She called Liu Chang "Crown Prince Emperor." From then on all the decisions on state affairs were made by Fan Hu Zi, the sorceress. Lu Qiong Xian, a maid whom Liu Chang loved very much, and Gong Cheng Shu fawned on Fan Hu Zi. Then Fan Hu Zi said to Liu Chang that Lu Qiong Xian and Gong Cheng Shu were sent by Heaven to assist Liu Chang, and if they had committed any crime, Liu Chang should not punish them.

Zhong Yun Zhang, the premier, was appalled by all this. He said to Liu Chang several times that he should kill all the eunuchs. The eunuchs hated him. In 959 Liu Chang held a ceremony in the southern outskirts of Guangzhou (now Guangzhou, Guangdong Province) to offer sacrifices to Heaven. Three days before the ceremony, Zhong Yun Zhang and the official in charge of ceremony went up the sacrificial altar. They looked around and pointed here and there on the altar. Xu Yan Zhen, a eunuch, saw them and said to another eunuch, "They are planning a rebellion!" Xu Yan Zhen drew out his sword and went up the altar. Premier Zhong Yun Zhang went forward and scolded him. Xu Yan Zhen ran back and told Liu Chang that Zhong Yun Zhang had rebelled. Liu Chang ordered Zhong Yun Zhang be thrown into jail. Liu Chang sent Xue Yong Pi, the minister of law, to interrogate Zhong Yun Zhang. Zhong Yun Zhang and Xue Yong Pi were friends. Premier Zhong Yun Zhang said to Xue Yong Pi, with tears in his eyes, "Now, I am innocent. I have been accused falsely of committing a crime. I will not regret it even if I should die. My two sons are still very young. When they grow up, you may tell them the facts." When the eunuch Xu Yan Zhen heard Zhong Yun Zhang's words, he said, "The rebel wants his sons to avenge him!" He went to report to Liu Chang. Liu Chang ordered Zhong Yun Zhang's two sons to be arrested, and not long after Zhong Yun Zhang and his sons were all killed.

In 960 Chen Yan Shou, the other eunuch, said to Liu Chang, "The reason why you are in a position to succeed your father as King is that your father had all his brothers killed." He tried to persuade Liu Chang to kill his brother. Liu Chang took his advice and killed his younger brother Liu Xuan Xing, King of Gui.

Shao Ting Juan, a general, said to Liu Chang, "The State of Han was established during the chaotic period by the end of the Tang Dynasty and has been in this place for fifty years. Luckily enough there have been no wars in this place, although there are endless wars in Central China. And we are proud that there have been no wars in the State of Han. Now the soldiers do not have the slightest idea of what a war is like. They do not know what orders are signified by the flags and the beating of drums. The ruler does not know the importance of survival. Now China has been in chaos for a long time. It is a natural rule that if the realm is in chaos for a long time, stability and peace will reign again. Now the true Emperor has come into being. He is now doing his best to unify the whole realm. He will not stop until the unification of all of China has been realized. Your Majesty has two choices: you should train your army well to prepare for war; or you may send envoys to Central China with generous treasures to present to the Emperor of the Song Dynasty so as to establish good relations with the Emperor of the Song Dynasty." Liu Chang was such a stupid man that he ignored this sound advice suggested by Shao Ting Juan. And he deeply resented Shao Ting Juan for his words.

In 961 an auspicious symbol grew in the palace of the State of Southern Han. (It was the glossy ganoderma, a reddish brown or dark purple kidney-shaped fungus, with shiny ring-like patterns, used to make medicine.) Animals hit their heads on the gate of the palace; the goats in the imperial garden spat out pearls from their mouths; a stone lying beside a well stood up by itself and moved a hundred feet over and then fell down again. Fan Hu Zi, the sorceress, thought that all these were auspicious signs. She asked all the ministers to go into the palace to see Liu Chang and chant their congratulations to him.

Li Tuo, a eunuch, had an adopted daughter. In 962 Liu Chang took Li Tuo's adopted daughter as his concubine. He appointed Li Tuo as grand tutor and conferred great power on him. Li Tuo became a despot in the State of Southern Han.

Since Xu Yan Zhen had killed Zhong Yun Zhang, he hated Gong Cheng Shu because Gong Cheng Shu held a higher rank than him. He planned to murder Gong Cheng Shu. Gong Cheng Shu found out his plan and acted first. He sent a subordinate to tell Liu Chang that Xu Yan Zhen was planning a rebellion. Liu Chang ordered them to arrest Xu Yan Zhen and execute him.

Liu Chang was a cruel man. He set up many kinds of instruments of punishment to torture those who had committed crimes. Some criminals were cooked, burned or cut into pieces. Some were thrown into a room full of standing swords and daggers. He would order criminals to fight with tigers and elephants.

He levied heavy taxes on the people. The tax on a deca-liter of rice was five copper coins. People who wanted to go into the cities had to pay one copper coin. In short, the people of the State of Southern Han lived in poverty.

Liu Chang led a luxurious life. He ordered people to dive into the South China Sea to get pearls and catch sea tortoises to strip the tortoiseshells to decorate his palaces. He had over thirty temporary homes built around the city of Guangzhou (now Guangzhou, Guangdong Province). He often lived in these temporary homes for a long time and did not attend to the state affairs.

There was a great pipal tree in the garden of Faxing Temple in Guangzhou. It was one hundred and forty feet tall. It had a very big trunk. It was said that it had been planted by a monk from the Western Region (the area includes Xinjiang Uygur Autonomous Region of China, Middle Asia, Western Asia and Indian Peninsula) four hundred years ago. In 967, there was a great wind storm. The big pipal tree was pulled up from the ground by the great wind and fell. In that year, the bed chamber of King Liu Chang, was struck by thunder and lightning. Those who specialized in such signs prophesied that the State of Southern Han would fall.

As early as in 951 Liu Cheng, Liu Chang's father had taken advantage of the chaos in the State of Chu to send armies to occupy Guizhou (now Guilin, Guangxi Zhuang Autonomous Region), Chenzhou (now Chenzhou, Hunan Province), Hezhou (now Hexian, Guangxi Zhuang Autonomous Region) which were situated in the southern part of the State of Chu. In 968 Liu Chang sent an army to attack Daozhou (now Daoxian, in the south part of Hunan Province).

20. The Expedition against the State of Southern Han

Back in the times of Emperor Guo Rong of the Later Zhao Dynasty, General Pan Mei was a good friend of General Zhao Kuang Yin. When Zhao Kuang Ying ascended the throne of the Song Dynasty in 960, General Pan Mei became his most trusted general. When he had just ascended the throne, he sent Pan Mei to see the former ministers of the Later Zhou Dynasty, who still held great power, to analyze the situation with them and to persuade them to serve the new emperor. He successfully completed his task.

Yuan Yan, the commander-in-chief of the army stationed in Shanzhou (now Shanxian in the west part of Henan Province) was a fierce and tough man. Unfortunately, he trusted persons of vile character. He committed many unlawful acts. He trained and armed his troops well and prepared for war.

Emperor Zhao Kuang Yin suspected that Yuan Yan would carry out a rebellion. So he sent General Pan Mei to Shanzhou to be the supervisor of Yuan Yan's army. Before Pan Mei left for Shanzhou, Emperor Zhao Kuang Yin told him that he could kill Yuan Yan if necessary. Pan Mei rode to Shanzhou solo. When he arrived at Shanzhou, he said to Commander Yuan Yan, "Heaven has made Zhao Kuan Yin Emperor. As one of his subordinates you should serve him, heart and soul." Yuan Yan agreed and went to Daliang to have an audience with Emperor Zhao Kuang Yin. The Emperor was very pleased and said to himself, "Pan Mei did not kill Yuan Yan. Now Yuan Yan has come to have an audience with me. Pan Mei has completed his mission very well."

Li Chong Jin raised a rebellion in September 960, and Emperor Zhao Kuang Yin carried out an expedition against him in October. He appointed Shi Shou Xin as the commander-in-chief of the expedition army and Pan Mei as the supervisor of this army. When the expedition army captured Yangzhou (now Yangzhou, Jiangsu Province), Pan Mei was appointed as the inspector of Yangzhou to pacify the people of Yangzhou. When the Song army conquered Hunan (the State of Chu) in 962, there was turmoil in this area. Then Emperor Zhao Kuang Yin appointed Pan Mei as the commander-in-chief of the Song army stationed in Tanzhou (now Changsha, Hunan Province). Liu Chang's father Liu Cheng, the King of the State of Southern Han, had sent armies to occupied the areas of Guizhou (now Guilin, Guangxi Zhuang Autonomous Region), Chenzhou, (now Chenzhou, Hunan Province) and Hezhou (now Hexian, Guangxi Zhuang Autonomous Region) in 951. In 962 Liu Chang sent armies to attack Guiyang (now Guiyang, in the southeast part of Hunan Province) several times. Pan Mei commanded the army under him and beat back the army of the State of Southern Han.

In 964 General Pan Mei and General Ding De Yu commanded an army to take Chenzhou (now Chenzhou, Hunan Province), the territory of the former State of Chu. More than ten officials of the State of Southern Han were captured. Among them a man named Yu Yan Ye, who claimed he was the commander of the archers of the bodyguards of Liu Chang, the King of the State of Southern Han. When he was given a bow, he did not have the strength to draw the bow. General Pan Mei sent soldiers to escort these captives to Daliang to present them to Emperor Zhao Kuang Yin.

Emperor Zhao Kuang Yin asked Yu Yan Ye with a smile about the state affairs of the State of Southern Han. Yu Yan Ye told Emperor Zhao Kuang Yin the luxurious life Liu Chang had led and all the cruelties Liu Chang had done to the people of the State of Southern Han. When Emperor Zhao Kuang Yin heard all this from Yu Yan Ye, he was greatly surprised and said, "I shall save the people in this place!" Then Wang Ji Xun, the Governor of Daozhou (now Daoxian, Hunan Province), said to Emperor Zhao Kuang Yin, "Liu Chang is fatuous and brutal. The people of the State of southern Han are suffering under his rule. He has sent armies to invade the territory of the Song Dynasty several times. I hope Your Majesty shall send a great army to crush the State of Southern Han."

But at that time Emperor Zhao Kuang Yin did not want to send an army to attack the State of Southern Han. Instead he sent an envoy to Li Yu, King of the State of Southern Tang, and asked him to send an envoy of his own to persuade Liu Chang to declare himself a vassal to Emperor Zhao Kuang Yin and return the lands of the former State of Chu he had occupied. Li Yu duly sent an envoy, taking a letter written by him to Guangzhou, the capital of the State of Southern Han, to convey the orders of Emperor Zhao Kuang Yin. But Liu Chang refused to declare himself a vassal to Emperor Zhao Kuang Yin and return the lands he had occupied.

When Li Yu's envoy came back to the State of Southern Tang and reported that Liu Chang had refused to obey the orders of Emperor Zhao Kuang Yin, Li Yu sent Gong Shen Yi, one of his attendants, to take a letter to Liu Chang. The letter read, "The State of Southern Tang and the State of Southern Han have been friendly states for several generations. Your forefather and my forefather formed an alliance. So you and I are like two brothers. We share weal and woe. When differences occur between you and me, I would like to meet with you and talk face to face with you. We may explain clearly the merits and demerits of a matter, so that our worries can be removed. But the State of Southern Tang and the State of Southern Han are too far away from each other. It is impossible for us to meet with each other. I wrote a letter to you to express my suggestions, but you took my letter lightly. So my sincere advice, in the letter, were like stones sinking to the bottom of a river and I never had an answer from you. Now I am sending an envoy to you again to explain to you all my suggestions, but I am afraid that the envoy may not express my ideas fully and clearly. Therefore so I am writing this letter to state clearly all my suggestions so as to save the trouble of travelling all the way and talking with you in person. I hope you will read this letter carefully and consider carefully all my suggestions. I put forward these suggestions because I think I am a good friend to you, and you and I are like close relatives. It is up to you to decide whether you will take the advice or not. The Emperor of the Song Dynasty sent an army to carry out a southern expedition intending to take back the territory of the former State of Chu, and the Song army and your army fought with each other. So there is discord between you and the Emperor of the Song Dynasty. I have been observing the development of the situation carefully and am quite concerned for you. I hope that the Emperor of the Song Dynasty will not send armies to attack the State of Southern Han and I hope that the problem can be solved in an amicable way. Several days ago I sent an envoy to present tribute to the Emperor of the Song Dynasty. The Emperor of the Song Dynasty said to my envoy, 'If Liu Chang treats me with due respect, as a king of a small state should treat the emperor of a big state, then it is not necessary for me to carry out an expedition against him. If he dares to mobilize an army to fight against my army, I will certainly occupy the State of Southern Han.' The Emperor of the Song Dynasty has fixed a time limit for you to reform yourself. The time limit is this autumn. If you have not changed your attitude by that time, he will raise a great army to punish you. The Emperor of the Song Dynasty has asked me to send a letter to reiterate the advice which has been stated in the previous letter. As I can see, the Emperor of the Song Dynasty is not a greedy person. He is angry with your attitude towards him. What you have done has been done out of an anger from a certain time. Since ancient times there have been four reasons for those persons who have relied on military force to fight their powerful enemies, despite the fact that their forces were far inferior to those of their enemies: to avenge their fathers and mothers and ancestors who were killed by their enemies—this is the first reason they have to fight a powerful enemy; or the state is collapsing and the people are rebelling, so that fighting is the only way to survive—this is the second reason for fighting with a powerful enemy; the enemy is sure to attack and defeat them, and they will not spare them; the enemy will not allow them to sue for peace and there is no way to retreat and defend oneself—one will perish no matter whether they put up a fight or not—this is the third reason one might fight a powerful enemy; or, there are signs that Heaven will destroy one's enemies, one has the opportunity to defeat the powerful enemy—this is the fourth reason that one might fight against powerful enemies. Now the Emperor of the Song Dynasty has not killed your father or mother or any of your ancestors. There is no hatred between you and the Emperor of the Song Dynasty for that. It is not a critical moment for your survival. You are not in a situation in which you will perish whether you put up a fight or not. You don't have the opportunity to destroy the Song Dynasty. So you don't have any of the four reasons cited above that would indicate you should put up a fight. You are actually waiting for an attack by the army of the Song Dynasty. The Emperor of the Song Dynasty has allowed you to establish friendly relations with the Song Dynasty, but you have refused to accept his offer. A man who works for the interest of the state and for the interest of the people should not do this. In history there have been many persons who strived to be kings or emperors and to be outstanding figures. Also there have been many people who ceded the territory of their states to the big states and sent tribute to the big states so as to please the ruler of the big states. This happens in history. A man has to be flexible. He may take anything from others or give anything to others. It is not necessary for him to stick to one point. It is not necessary for him to pretend to be strong and treat the coming disaster lightly. You are a brilliant ruler to take care of the people of your state. The northern border of your state reaches the Five Ridges; the southern border of your state reaches the great sea. Your forefather founded the state and the throne of the state has been passed to several generations. The kings of the state brought benevolence to the people. You have an army of over three hundred thousand men. There are beautiful mountains and rivers in the territory of your state. You are proud of all these. But it is inauspicious to go against the will of Heaven. It is dangerous to be bellicose. Heaven granted many blessings to the State of Chu. But the King of the State of Chu could not resist an army sent by the Emperor of the Song Dynasty. This is because the great power of the army of the Song Dynasty is granted by Heaven. The soldiers of the Song Dynasty are brave ones. They crossed the Taihang Mountains and took the area of Shangdang. They passed the dangerous precipices of Jianmenguan Pass and occupied the State of Shu. They completed their task in very short order. From these facts we know that it is difficult to measure the great power of the Song Dynasty. And we know from this that although a state is very far from the Song Dynasty, it is impossible for this state to avoid being destroyed by the great Song army. You may fight ten battles and win nine of them. But this one battle lost may be disastrous. You may carry out six strategic plans and see that five of them are successful. But the consequences brought about by this one unsuccessful plan may be irreparable. If you think that your state is protected by natural barriers and your army is strong, you are only thinking of the strong points, but you have not considered the weak points. You only think of the victories you will win, but you have not considered the consequences of defeat. Why do I say so? The most dangerous natural barrier is Jianmenguan Pass. But it could not protect the State of Shu, and the State of Shu was destroyed by the Song Dynasty. The army of Shangdang was very strong, but this army was defeated and the area of Shangdang was taken by the army of the Song Dynasty. A man may sit at home and think that he can cross the great sea. But when he really takes a ship and travels at sea, he may meet a great wind storm and the waves may rise very high and he may lose control of the ship. This is greatly different from what he is envisioning while sitting at home. So the wise man will consider the consequences beforehand; a nimble-minded man places emphasis on predictions. He will do the difficult things when they are easy to do. While a state still exists, the king of this state should consider the consequence when his state eventually falls. People seldom plan for misfortune and often think of good fortune, because people like good fortune. Since people like good fortune, they expect much of good fortune. Since people dislike misfortune, they seldom think of misfortune. So when good fortune comes, it is within their expectation; when misfortune comes, it is often unexpected. Some ministers and generals, who want to make great military contributions, may say, 'Don't make peace with the big state. Five Ridges are dangerous natural barriers. The mountains are high and the rivers are deep there. The carts of our enemy loaded with military supplies cannot move side by side. The enemy soldiers have to march in single file. We may strengthen our defenses and clear the fields. We may cut our enemy's food transportation line. We may hide ourselves in the mountains and behind the banks of the rivers and shoot arrows at the enemy soldiers so as to stop their advance. In this way our enemies cannot go a step forward and they cannot retreat either.' Some others may say, 'Our enemies are good at fighting in the plains areas. Now they have to fight in the mountain areas. They are not good at fighting in the mountain areas. Even if they have an army of a million men, they cannot defeat us.' Still some others may say, 'If we win, we will become the strongest and the most powerful leader in this realm. If we lose, we may sail out to the sea on big boats. We shall not submit ourselves to anyone else.' This kind of talk is irresponsible. It is much easier said than done. Why? The people of the areas of the former State of Jing and the former State of Chu and the Former State of Shu are used to travelling in mountains and on rivers. More than a hundred thousand men can be mobilized in these areas. It is not necessary to send armies from Central China. The northern part of your state borders on the territory of the Song Dynasty. The lands and rivers link with the lands and the rivers of the territory of the Song Dynasty. The crowing of the roosters and the sound of barking of dogs on one side can be heard on the other side. Horses and cows can certainly travel from one side to the other. Once the border areas are taken, the Song troops will come from all directions. How can you cut the transportation lines of the Song armies and protect your cities? If your natural barriers are strongly defended, that is all right. But once they are breached, the Song armies will come through easily. And there is another possibility. The Emperor of the Song Dynasty will use the troops of the State of Wuyue. The troops of Wuyue will come from Quanzhou to your capital by sea. They will reach the city of your capital in a few days. When the people are confused as to what to do and the morale of the soldiers drops and there are enemies on land and on the water, how many of your ministers and generals will remain devoted to you? They will think of running away and they will try their best to take care of their wives and children. The development of the situation is not easily predicted. Things change very quickly. Your greater goal will be impeded by short-sighted plans. But making plans is ordinary practice in wars. Any plan may lead to success or to failure. But once you make up your plan, you should carry it out to the end. It would be a pity if you change your fixed plan because of a very minor reason. The king of a small state should serve the emperor of a big state. This is a natural rule. I will not cite examples from ancient times. I will cite an example from not long ago. The royal family of Yang established the State of Wu. The King of the State of Wu presented tributesto Zhuangzong of the Tang Dynasty. Take my own state as an example. When my forefather established the State of Southern Tang, Central China was in a state of warfare. So the rule that the king of a small state should serve the emperor of the big state was not observed. This led to war between the big state and our state. Our state was nearly destroyed. Our state was protected by the Yangtze River and there were many soldiers in our state's armies. But very soon my father realized that he could not withstand the fierce attack by the big state. So he sent an envoy to the big state to ask for peace. As soon as the envoy reached the big state, all the armies of the big state stopped attacking our state and withdrew. Peace resumed. The people of our state benefit from this. Today we still insist on this policy. Since your forefather established your state, he also established good relations with the big state in central China. You should forget your anger and give up unnecessary disputes. You should work for the survival of your state and know the consequences of its destruction. You may flexibly adopt the policy of a strong state and also adopt the policy of a weak state. You may yield to the emperor of the big state so as to give benefits to the millions of people. For the sake of stabilizing your state, you may do anything. This is a virtuous act and will benefit the people. This will not do harm to your ancestral temple or your state. As soon as you send out the envoy to present tribute to the big state, there will be peace and no more wars. It is an easy thing to do and your state will surely survive. It is not necessary to carry out wars with the big state to show your bravery. There is a saying which goes, 'A virtuous act is not a difficult thing to do. But very few people will adopt it. I will resolutely do it.' And there is another saying which goes, 'If the king of a state knows what he should do and what he should not do, his state will last forever.' This is the great cause of a sacred and virtuous man. Why do you think it shameful and not do it? The Emperor of the Song Dynasty is an outstanding and wise emperor. He has inherited the former fiver dynasties and has ascended the throne. All the kings of the states around the Song Dynasty have submitted themselves to him. Now he has halted his army's advance and he is waiting for your answer. He has shown great kindness and patience with you. You should give up your anger. You should do things which are good for your ancestral temples, good for your people, good for your state and good for yourself. If you ignore the benefits to your ancestral temples, to your people, to your state and to yourself, you will be an enemy of the Song Dynasty. Disasters will fall on the State of Southern Han. Why will you do this? If you luckily win, you will not be able to stop your state from destruction in the future. If you are defeated, your state will no longer exist. Recently I received an imperial edict from the Emperor of the Song Dynasty. In this imperial edict the Emperor of the Song Dynasty informed me that you had refused to establish friendly relations with him and so he will raise a great army to attack your state this autumn. He ordered me to drop all relations with you. But I still want to save you from destruction. Although I still want to keep friendly relations with you forever, I have to obey the order from the Emperor of the Song Dynasty. I do not want to go against the order because I have to insist on the principle that a king of a small state must serve the emperor of the big dynasty. But I still have pity on you and I have written this letter to you. This is my last letter. I am sorry that I have to sever all relations with you."

When Liu Chang read the letter from Li Yu, he was furious. He threw Gong Shen Yi, Li Yu's envoy, into jail. He wrote a letter back to Li Yu. The letter was full of harsh and impolite words. Li Yu sent an envoy to take this letter to Emperor Zhao Kuang Yin. Then Emperor Zhao Kuang Yin made up his mind to attack the State of Southern Han.

On 1 September 970 Emperor Zhao Kuang Yin appointed Pan Mei, the commander-in-chief of the Song army in Tanzhou (now Changsha, Hunan Province), as the Commander-in-chief of the Hezhou branch of the Song army; he appointed Yin Chong Ke, the commander-in-chief of the Song army in Langzhou (now Changde, Hunan Province), as the deputy commander-in-chief of this branch of the Song army; he appointed Wang Ji Xun, the Governor of Daozhou (now Daoxian, Hunan Province), as its supervisor.

Then Emperor Zhao Kuang Yin sent envoys to order the armies in ten prefectures to gather outside the city of Hezhou (now Hexian, Guangxi Zhuang Autonomous Region) to prepare to attack Hezhou. On 29 September General Pan Mei commanded an army to attack Fuzhou (now Zhaoping, Guangxi Zhuang Autonomous Region), a city which was situated to the southwest of Hezhou, and took it. Then he commanded his army to march towards Hezhou. Chen Shou Zhong, the Governor of Hezhou of the State of Southern Han, sent an envoy to Liu Chang asking him to send troops to rescue Hezhou. At that time many of the generals of the State of Southern Han had been killed by Liu Chang because the eunuchs said slanderous words against them and falsely accused them of rebellion. The military power was in the hands of several eunuchs. The city walls were in disrepair and the warships and the weapons and city defense devices were also broken down and could not be used because all the money had been spent in decorating the palaces.

When the envoy sent by the Governor of Hezhou arrived at Guangzhou, Liu Chang, all the officials and people were shocked. Liu Chang, King of the State of Southern Han, sent Gong Cheng Shu, the eunuch who held such great power, to cheer the fighting spirits of the army in Hezhou. At that time the soldiers of the State of Southern Han had been stationed in the border area for a long time. They lived in poverty. They hoped that Gong Cheng Shu would bring them money to improve their life. But to their great disappointment, Gong Cheng Shu had just brought a letter of comfort written by the King of the State of Southern Han. Then the soldiers defending the city of Hezhou began to desert.

When the Song armies were approaching the city of Hezhou, Gong Cheng Shu ran away and came back to Guangzhou by a small boat. In early October the Song armies lay siege to the city of Hezhou. The King of the State of Southern Han summoned all the ministers to court to discuss what to do. All the ministers asked Liu Chang to send Pan Chong Che to command an army to rescue Hezhou. Pan Chong Che had been very unhappy because his military power had been taken away by the eunuchs. So he refused to go, on the excuse that he had an eye disease. Liu Chang was very angry. He said, "Why must we send Pan Chong Che? I will send Wu Yan Rou. He is also good at strategic planning!" Then he sent Wu Yan Rou to command an army to rescue the city of Hezhou. The Southern Han army under Wu Yan Rou took boats to sail from Guangzhou westward up the Pearl River. When they reached Fengzhou (now Fengkai, Guangxi Zhuang Autonoumous Region) they sailed northward along He Jiang River. On 19 September General Pan Mei got word Wu Yan Rou was commanding an army to sail up He Jiang River to rescue Hezhou. He ordered his troops to retreat for ten kilometers and secretly laid an ambush behind the east bank of the river in Nanxiang (a place to the south of Hezhou just beside He Jiang River).

The Southern Han army under Wu Yan Rou reached Nanxiang at night. The boats lay at anchor for the night. In early morning, the Southern Han soldiers began to go ashore. Sitting on his bed, Wu Yan Rou directed his soldiers to disembark. At this time the Song troops started their sudden attack from behind the bank where they had laid an ambush. The Southern Han troops were in a great confusion. Seven or eight out of ten of the Southern Han soldiers were killed. The Song troops captured Wu Yan Rou and killed him. They showed the head of Wu Yan Rou to the defenders of Hezhou. But the defenders would not surrender but continued to resist the attack by the Song troops. Wang Ming, the officer in charge of transportation of military supplies for the Song armies, said to Pan Mei, "Support is coming. We should start a fierce attack on the city as soon as possible." But the other generals still hesitated. The next morning, Wang Ming commanded more than a hundred soldiers under him who were responsible for escorting the transportation team, and the several thousand men who were engaged in transportation, to fill the deep ditch around the city with hoes, spades and shovels. After the deep ditch had been filled, the Song troops marched to the gate of the city wall. The defenders of the city of Hezhou were terrified. On 12 October they opened the city gate to let the Song army into the city. The city of Hezhou was taken.

Then General Pan Mei declared that he would command his troops to sail to Guangzhou along He Jiang River and the Pearl River. Liu Chang was very worried and did not know what to do. Then he promoted Pan Chong Che to the position of grand tutor and commander-in-chief of the cavalry and foot soldiers of the State of Southern Han. He ordered Pan Chong Che to station thirty thousand men along He Jiang River to prevent the Song troops from sailing down the He Jiang River.

But the Song troops did not sail southward along the river. General Pan Mei commanded his troops to march northwest to Zhaozhou (now Pingle, Guangxi Zhuang Autonomous Region). Pan Chong Che and the troops under him waited by the He Jiang River for the Song troops, but Song troops never came.

In November Pan Mei and the other generals of the Song Dynasty commanded the Song troops under them to attack Kaijian Stronghold (which was situated to the south of Zhaozhou) of the army of Southern Han. On 23 October the Song troops killed several thousand Southern Han soldiers and captured Jin Hui, the commander of the Southern Han army in Kaijian Stronghold. Tian Xing Chou, the governor of Zhaozhou of the State of Southern Han, abandoned the city of Zhaozhou and ran away. Li Cheng Gui, the governor of Guizhou (now Guilin, Guangxi Zhuang Autonomous Region) of the State of Southern Han, also abandoned the city of Guizhou and ran away. So on 3 November the Song army occupied Zhaozhou and Guizhou.

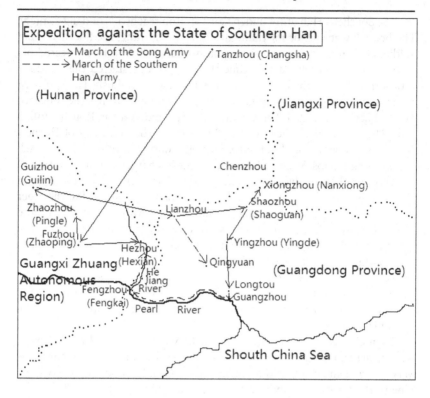

Expedition against the State of Southern Han

————→ March of the Song Army
– – – → March of the Southern
　　　　Han Army

Tanzhou (Changsha)

(Hunan Province)

(Jiangxi Province)

Guizhou
(Guilin)

Chenzhou

Xiongzhou (Nanxiong)

Zhaozhou
(Pingle)

Lianzhou

Shaozhou
(Shaoguan)

Fuzhou
(Zhaoping)

Hezhou
(Hexian)

Yingzhou (Yingde)

Guangxi Zhuang
Autonomous
Region)

He
Jiang
River

Fengzhou
(Fengkai)

Qingyuan

(Guangdong Province)

Longtou
Guangzhou

Pearl　River

Shouth China Sea

There were rich deposits of silver in the mountains in the area of Guizhou. Emperor Zhao Kuang Yin read statistics about the yearly silver production in Guizhou. Then he said to Zhao Pu, the premier, "We may benefit greatly from the silver mining in the mountains. But the miners have to work very hard to produce this amount of silver." On 6 November Emperor Zhao Kuang Ying issued an order to reduce the former production of silver by one third so as to relieve the hardship of the miners.

On 3 December the Song army under Pan Mei took Lianzhou (now Lianzhou, in the northwest part of Guangdong Province). Lu Shou, the commander of the Southern Han army in this area, commanded his army to retreat to Qingyuan (now Qingyuan, Guangdong Province). When Liu Chang, King of the State of Southern Han, got the news that the Song army had occupied Lianzhou, he said to the officials around him, "Zhaozhou, Guizhou, Lianzhou and Hezhou were originally territory of the State of Chu. Now that the Song troops have taken all these places, they are satisfied and will not come further south."

Pan Mei commanded the Song army to march to Shaozhou (now Shaoguan, in the north part of Guangdong Province). Li Cheng Wo, the commander-in-chief of the army of the State of Southern Han in Shaozhou area, had an army of more than a hundred thousand men. This army stationed at the foot of Penghuafeng Mountain. He trained elephants to line up in battle formation.

Each elephant carried more than ten soldiers on its back. All of the soldiers carried weapons. When there was a battle, Li Cheng Wo would put the elephants at the front of the battle formation so as to terrify the enemies. On 22 December when the Song army came, Li Cheng Wo arranged his battle formation with the elephants at the front. Pan Mei ordered all the archers to stand at the front of his battle formation. The archers shot arrows at the elephants. When the elephants were struck by the arrows, they were hurt so they began to run in all directions. The soldiers on the backs of the elephants were tossed to the ground. The elephants stamped their big feet on the Southern Han soldiers and killed many of them. The Southern Han army lost its battle formation and they were in great confusion. Pan Mei ordered the Song soldiers to attack the Southern Han army. The Southern Han army was defeated and many were killed. Li Cheng Wo had a very narrow escape. On that day the Song army took the city of Shaozhou. Xin Yan Wo, the governor of Shaozhou was captured.

Li Cheng Wo sent an envoy back to Guangzhou through small paths. When the envoy was received by Liu Chang, he conveyed Li Cheng Wo's suggestion that Liu Chang should surrender to the Song army. But Li Tuo, the officer in charge of weapon supplies, was strongly against this suggestion. All the people of the State of Southern Han were in great shock when they knew that the Song army was coming. Liu Chang ordered the soldiers to dig a big ditch around the city of Guangzhou to resist the Song army. At that time no more generals could be sent. Liang Ying Zhen, an old lady working in the palace, recommended her step son Guo Chong Yue. Then Liu Chang appointed Guo Chong Yue as the commander-in-chief of the Southern Han army defending Guangzhou. He also appointed Zhi Yan Xiao as general. Guo Chong Yue and Zhi Yan Xiao commanded sixty thousand soldiers to station in Majing (now Ma'anshan Mountain, which was situated five kilometers north to the city of Guangzhou). They built camps there to resist the advance of the Song army. Guo Chong Yue was not a brave man and was not good at strategic planning. What he was doing was to say prayers begging the gods and supernatural beings to protect him.

In this winter Lin Ren Zhao, a general of the State of Southern Tang, sent a secret letter to Li Yu, King of the State of Southern Tang. It read, "The Song troops stationed in the prefectures to the south of the Huaishui River were no more than a thousand men. The Song Dynasty conquered the State of Shu the year before last. Now the army of the Song Dynasty is attacking the State of Southern Han. The Song troops have to travel more than a thousand kilometers back and forth. The Song troops are now very tired. I hope Your Majesty might assign me several tens of thousands of troops. I will command this great army to cross the Yangtze River from Shouchun to the north of the river. I will command this army to march directly to Zhengyang and take it. The people there are longing for our army to come. In this way we will be able to recover the land ceded to the Song Dynasty. When the Song army comes to rescue these places, I can fight them with the protection of the

Huishui River. The Song army will not be able to defeat us. On the day when I command the army to march from Shouchun, Your Majesty may declare that I have held an armed rebellion and report this to the Emperor of the Song Dynasty. If it is successful, the nation will enjoy the benefit of the victory. If it fails, Your Majesty may kill all the members of my clan to show to the Emperor of the Song Dynasty that Your Majesty has not been involved in this and has been always devoted to the Emperor of the Song Dynasty."

But Li Yu did not dare to take his suggestion. A man named Lu Jiang wrote a letter to Chen Qiao, the head of the Privy Council of the State of Southern Tang, presenting him some other suggestions. Chen Qiao accepted his suggestions and promoted him to the position of the inspector along the Yangtze River. Lu Jiang recruited the runaways from the north of the Yangtze River and taught them how to fight on boats on the river. This naval force organized by Lu Jiang had several battles with the naval army of the State of Wuyue on the section of the Yangtze River in the area of Haimen (now Haimen, in the southeast part of Jiangsu Province). The navy of the State of Southern Tang under Lu Jiang captured several hundred warships of the State of Wuyue.

Lu Jiang went to see Li Yu, the King of the State of Southern Tang, and tried to persuade Li Yu to conquer the State of Wuyue. He said, "The State of Wuyue is our enemy. In the future the troops of the State of Wuyue will be the guides for the army of the Song Dynasty to attack our state and the army of the State of Wuyue will attack us from the southeast. Wu should destroy them first." Li Yu said, "The State of Wu Yue is a vassal state of the Song Dynasty. How dare I attack a vassal state of the Song Dynasty?" Lu Jiang said, "I may pretend that I have taken Xuanzhou and Shezhou and put up a rebellion against Your Majesty. Your Majesty may declare that you are going to carry out an expedition against me. Your Majesty may ask the King of the State of Wuyue to send troops to help Your Majesty. When the troops of the State of Wuyue arrive, Your Majesty may command your army to attack them. I will command the army under me to attack the Wuyue troops from behind. Then Your Majesty may surely conquer the State of Wuyue." But Li Yu refused to take his advice.

On 16 January 971 the Song armies under Pan Mei took Yingzhou (now Yingde, Guangdong Province) and Xiongzhou (now Nanxiong, Guangdong Province). On this day Pan Chong Che led the troops of the State of Southern Han, who had been waiting for the Song army along the He Jiang River, to surrender to the Song army. In this month Pan Mei commanded his armies to station themselves in Longtou, fifty kilometers north to Guangzhou.

Liu Chang, the King of the State of Southern Han, sent an envoy to Longtou to see Pan Mei and ask for peace. The envoy conveyed Liu Chang's request for the Song army to delay their march to Guangzhou. The mountains and rivers in the area of Longtou were dangerous. Pan Mei suspected that there were ambushes in this area. So he ordered the envoy to go with them. The Song army passed this dangerous area very quickly. On 28 January the

Song army under Pan Mei reached Majing where sixty thousand soldiers of the State of Southern Han under generals Guo Chong Yue and Zhi Yan Xiao had been stationed. Pan Mei stationed his army in Shuangnüshan Mountain, eight kilometers west of Guangzhou. From there the Song soldiers could see the camps of the army of the State of Southern Han. Pan Mei sent cavalrymen to those camps to challenge them to battle. But Guo Chong Yue refused to take up the challenge. He just ordered his soldiers to stay inside the camps and defend themselves.

Liu Chang, King of the State of Southern Han, knew that Guangzhou would fall very soon. He ordered the gold, silver, and all kinds of treasures to be loaded on board more than ten ships. He also let his concubines and maids embark. He intended to go out to sea with these treasures and concubines and maids. But before he could board, Yue Fan, a eunuch, and a thousand guards, stole the ships and sailed out to sea. Liu Chang was very afraid. Then he sent Xiao Cui, one of his chief advisers, and Zhuo Wei Xiu, the chief of the general secretariat, to the camps of the Song army to deliver a letter of surrender written by him to Pan Mei.

Pan Mei immediately sent a party of soldiers to escort Xiao Cui and Zhuo Wei Xiu to Daliang to the court of the Song Dynasty. When Liu Chang saw that Xiao Cui and Zhuo Wei Xiu did not come back, he was even more fearful. Then he ordered Guo Chong Yue to get ready for battle. On 1 February Liu Chang sent his younger brother Liu Bao Xing to command all the troops he could gather to go out of the city and put up a resistance to the Song army. Zhi Ting Xiao said to Guo Chong Yue, "Now the Song troops have defeated all the Southern Han troops resisting them. They are invincible. Although we still have many soldiers, they are all very afraid of the Song troops. Today if we don't force them to go out to fight, they will be killed tomorrow." On 4 February Zhi Ting Xiao arranged the vanguards of the Southern Han army in battle formation by the bank of a river. He asked Guo Chong Yue to command the main force as the rear of the battle formation. Then the Song army crossed the river to fight.

Zhi Ting Xiao fought very hard but he could not hold off the attackers. He was killed in battle. Guo Chong Yue commanded the troops under him to retreat into their camps. Pan Mei said to Wang Ming, "The Southern Han soldiers built the walls of their camps with bamboo. If we set fire to those walls, the soldiers will be in panic. Then we can attack from the front and from the rear. We will surely defeat them." Then Pan Mei sent out some able-bodied men to the camps of the Southern Han army. Each man had two torches in his hands. They hid themselves not far from the camps. At night, the men lit their torches and rushed to the walls of the camps. They threw the torches against the walls. Incidentally, the wind was blowing, too. The bamboo walls burst into flame. The fire and the smoke rose very high. The Southern Han troops were disastrously defeated.

Guo Chong Yue was killed in this great confusion. Liu Bao Xing ran back to Guangzhou. Gong Cheng Shu said to Li Tuo and Xue Chong Yu, "The northern army has come all this way in order to take all the treasures in the treasure houses of our state. If we burn all the treasure houses, they will only get an empty city and will not be able to get any of our treasures. Then they will not be able to stay here for long and they have to go back to the north." They set fire to the treasure houses, and in one night all the treasures were burn to ashes.

On 5 February the Song army reached the foot of the city wall of Guangzhou. Liu Chang, dressed in white, came out of the city to surrender. Pan Mei set him free, according to the order of Emperor Zhao Kuang Yin. Then he commanded the Song army to enter the city of Guangzhou. The Song troops captured ninety-seven officials and the members of the royal clan of the State of Southern Han. All these people and Liu Chang were kept in Longde Palace in Guangzhou. Liu Bao Xing, Liu Chang's younger brother, hid himself among the ordinary people. But later he was found out and was captured. More than a hundred eunuchs, all dressed in colorful clothes, went to see Pan Mei. Pan Mei said to the generals around him, "Look how many eunuchs there are. I am here to carry out a punitive expedition against the State of Southern Han on the order of the Emperor. One of the reasons for the punitive expedition is to punish these eunuchs." Then he issued an order to chop off all their heads.

Pan Mei sent envoys to report the great victory to Emperor Zhao Kuang Yin. On 23 February the report of this great victory reached Daliang, the capital. In this expedition the Song Dynasty won sixty prefectures, two hundred and fourteen counties, and one hundred and seventy thousand two hundred and sixty-three households. On 24 February all the ministers and generals went to court to see Emperor Zhao Kuang Yin to express their congratulations. To celebrate this great occasion, Emperor Zhao Kuang Yin held a grand banquet to entertain all the ministers and generals. On 25 February he issued an imperial order to let all the original local officials of the State of Southern Han remain in their positions and to abolish all the exorbitant taxes and excessive levies in the areas of the former State of Southern Han. On 8 March, Emperor Zhao Kuang Yin put Pan Mei and Yin Chong Ke in charge of the affairs in Guangzhou.

Pan Mei sent troops to escort Liu Chang, all the members of the royal clan, and all the officials of the court of the former State of Southern Han to Daliang, the capital of the Song Dynasty. When they reached Gong'an (now Gong'an, in the southern part of Hubei Province), they stayed in an official house of the former State of Southern Han. Pang Shi Jin, the man in charge of this house, went to see Liu Chang. At that time Huang De Zhao, a scholar of the former State of Southern Han, was in attendance, at the side of Liu Chang. Liu Chang asked Huang De Zhao, "Where is Pang Shi Jin from?" Huang De Zhao answered, "He is from our state." Liu Chang was surprised and asked, "Why is he here?" Huang De Zhao said, "When Liu Ren An, Emperor Gaozu of the Southern Han, was on the throne, he sent tribute to the big dynasty. All the carts carrying the heavy tribute had to go past the area of Jingzhou. So he ordered Pang Shi Jin to buy a house here. Carts were made here to carry heavy tribute payments to the big dynasty." Liu Chang said with a long sigh, "I have been on the throne for fourteen years. I have never heard about this. Today I have learned something about my ancestor, the land of my state, and the land of the Big Dynasty." Then he wept sorrowfully with tears in his eyes.

When Liu Chang, the members of the royal clan and the officials of the court of the former State of Southern Han reached Daliang, the capital of the Song Dynasty, they were put in Yujin Garden, the royal garden of the Emperor of the Song Dynasty. Emperor Zhao Kuang Yin sent Lü Yu Qing to interrogate Liu Chang. Lü Yu Qing asked him, "You already sent envoys with a letter of surrender to the Emperor, but later you went back on your own words and ordered your army to resist the Song army. Why have you done that? And you committed a serious crime by ordering persons to burn all the treasure houses in Guangzhou." Liu Chang said, "All these things were done by Gong Cheng Shu, Li Tuo and Xue Chong Yu." Then Emperor Zhao Kuang Yin sent officials to interrogate those three. All of them just bowed their heads and did not give any answer. Wang Gui, one of Liu Chang's advisers, said to Gong Cheng Shu, Li Tuo and Xue Chong Yu, "When you were in Guangzhou, you monopolized all the power to yourselves. You made all the military and political decisions. The fire was set from inside the treasure houses. Now you are trying to shift the responsibility onto others!" Wang Gui spat in their faces and slapped them in their faces.

On 1 May a ceremony was held, presenting the captives. The officials in charge of the ceremony tied Liu Chang and all the officials and generals of the former State of Southern Han with white silk, took them to the ancestral temple of the Song Dynasty and made a show of all these captives there. Then Liu Chang was brought to Mingde Gate (the southern gate of Daliang) where Emperor Zhao Kuang Yin was sitting on a chair. He sent Lu Duo Xun, the minister of law, to read out the imperial order to condemn Liu Chang for all his crimes. Liu Chang answered, "I ascended the throne of the State of Southern Han at the age of sixteen. Gong Cheng Shu and others were powerful officials when my father was on the throne. Actually I had no power to make decisions. At that time I was not the king. The actual king was Gong Cheng Shu. I was a figurehead." Having said that, Liu Chang just knelt down and touched his head to the ground and waited to hear the sentence pronounced by Emperor Zhao Kuang Yin. The Emperor ordered Gao Ji Shen, an official in the ministry of law, to take the three, Gong Cheng Shu, Li Tuo and Xue Chong Yu, to a place outside Qianqiu Gate (the middle gate of the west city wall of Daliang) and they were executed there. Then Emperor Zhao Kuang Yin set Liu Chang, his younger brother Liu Bao Xing, and all the officials and generals of the former State of Southern Han free. Emperor Zhao Kuang Yin presented them with fine clothes, horses and saddles, and money. Soon after, Emperor Zhao Kuang Yin appointed Liu Bao Xing as a commander of the royal guards guarding the gate of the palace.

On 18 June Emperor Zhao Kuang Yin made Liu Chang the Marquis of

Enshe and appointed him grand general of the royal guards. But it was not necessary for Liu Chang to perform any actual duty. The Emperor granted him fifty thousand coins of money and seventeen bushels of wheat every month beside his monthly salary. Liu Chang was a tall, fat man. He had dark, thick eyebrows and bright eyes. He was skillful with his hands. He once created a set of dragon-shaped horse reins decorated with strings of pearls and presented the reins to Emperor Zhao Kuang Yin. The Emperor appreciated the exquisite gift. He granted Liu Chang one million five hundred thousand coins of money for the total cost of the pearls and his hard work. Emperor Zhao Kuang Yin said to the officials attending around him, "Liu Chang is very skilful in making artifacts. If he had put all his efforts into ruling his state, his state would not have been destroyed."

In the past when Liu Chang was on the throne of the State of Southern Han, he often killed his officials by poisoned wine. One day Liu Chang followed Emperor Zhao Kuang Yin to visit the place where naval forces were trained. Before all the officials gathered together, Emperor Zhao Kuang Yin ordered the servants to present a cup of wine to Liu Chang. Liu Chang suspected that Emperor Zhao Kuang Yin would kill him with this cup of poisoned wine. He held the cup, wept bitterly and said to the Emperor, "I succeeded to the throne after my father. I opposed the orders of Your Majesty. Your Majesty sent a great army to carry out an expedition. I really committed a great crime which merited the death penalty. Your Majesty has spared me. I just want to be an ordinary person in Daliang and enjoy life in this flourishing age. I do not dare to drink this cup of wine." Emperor Zhao Kuang Yin smiled and said, "I treat you with sincerity. I have no intention to kill you." Then he ordered one of attendants to take the cup of wine from Liu Chang's hands and Emperor Zhao Kuang Yin drank it up. Then Emperor ordered his servants to take another cup of wine to Liu Chang. Liu Chang was ashamed. He knelt down, touched his head to the ground and expressed his heartfelt thanks to Emperor Zhao Kuang Yin.

21. The Relationship between Emperor Zhao Kuang Yin and His Premiers

When Emperor Zhao Kuang Yin had just ascended the throne of the Song Dynasty, he appointed Fan Zhi, Wang Pu and Wei Ren Pu, the three premiers of the Later Zhou Dynasty, as the premiers of the Song Dynasty. At that time Emperor Zhao Kuang did not make his brothers kings. Premier Fan Zhi wrote a memorandum to Emperor Zhao Kuang Yin which read, "Since ancient times, when an emperor established a new dynasty, it was a general practice for him to make his brothers and sons kings so as to consolidate the foundation of the new dynasty, so that the new dynasty would last. Zhao Guang Yi, the younger brother of Your Majesty, the Regional Military Governor of the army of Taining, is a man with military talent. He is now a regional governor in a big prefecture. He is respected by the people. Zhao

Guang Mei, another younger brother of Your Majesty, the Commander-in-chief of the army in Jiazhou, is an experienced man. I hope Your Majesty will make them kings. The sons and daughters of Your Majesty are still very young. I hope they may be given titles. As a premier it is one of my duties to recommend virtuous and capable persons to responsible positions to assist Your Majesty. As I see it, Lü Yu Qing, Your Majesty's scholar and adviser, and Zhao Pu, the Deputy Head of the Privy Council, are proficient in management of state affairs. They have served Your Majesty for a long time. They are devoted to Your Majesty. They should be given responsible positions." Emperor Zhao Kuang Yin happily accepted his suggestions.

During the period of the Tang Dynasty and the period of the Five Dynasties when the premiers saw the emperors and discussed political matters, they would sit face to face with the emperors. After discussion the emperors would give them tea and then they left. But now Emperor Zhao Kuang Yin was a wise and capable emperor. Fan Zhi, Wang Pu and Wei Ren Pu were in awe before Emperor Zhao Kuang Yin. So they just wrote down their opinions on official documents and present these documents to Emperor Zhao Kuang Yin. They said to Emperor Zhao Kuang Yin that they could express all their opinions in this way so as to avoid the embarrassment of making any mistakes when they discussed matters face to face; Emperor Zhao Kuang Yin agreed with them.

In September 964 Fan Zhi fell ill. Emperor Zhao Kuang Yin went to Fan Zhi's home several times to see him. Emperor Zhao Kuang Yin also sent his lady officials to enquire about Fan Zhi's health. There were no special cups and pots in Fan Zhi's home to serve tea and wine for Emperor Zhao Kuang Yin and the lady officials. One of the lady officials reported to Emperor Zhao Kuang Yin about this. The Emperor ordered the relevant department to send tables and drinking wares to Fan Zhi's home. Then Emperor went to visit Fan Zhi again. He asked Fan Zhi, "You are the premier. Why do you lead such a poor life?" Fan Zhi answered, "When I was still working in the secretariat, no person would visit me at my home. The persons with whom I drank wine were relatives and friends from when I was still an ordinary man. It was not necessary to use special wine or tea drinking wares. So I have never bought such things. It is not because I did not have the money to buy them." In the period of the Five Dynasties, the premiers often accepted presents from the local military governors. But Fan Zhi refused to accept such presents. All the emoluments he got as premier were given to the orphans of his clan. When Fan Zhi was seriously ill, he told his son Fan Wen not to ask the government to give him a posthumous title and not to carve a stone plaque for his grave. On 28 September 964 Fan Zhi died. Emperor Zhao Kuang Yin grieved over Fan Zhi and regretted his loss. One day when Emperor Zhao Kuang Yin was discussing with the ministers the qualities a premier should have, he said, "I hear that except for his residence Fan Zhi did not buy any other properties. He was really a true premier!"

After the State of Southern Han was conquered, Fan Zhi's son Fan Wen was appointed as governor of Yongzhou (now Nanning, Guangxi Zhuang Autonomous Region). At that time it was a custom of the local people not to treat illnesses. When they fell ill, they just killed chickens and pigs to offer them to supernatural beings and hoped that the supernatural being would protect them. Fan Wen issued an order to ban this practice. He used his own salary to buy medicines for people who fell ill. More than a thousand people were cured.

In October 971 Deng Cun Zhong, the former governor of Yongzhou appointed by the former king of the State of Southern Han, forced twenty thousand local people to lay siege to the city of Yongzhou for over seventy days. Fan Wen commanded the troops to go out of the city to fight the rebels. In the battle, Fan Wen was wounded by several arrows on his chest. But he still stood up to issue orders to the troops. The rebels had to retreat a bit. Fan Wen was seriously wounded, but he still defended the city heroically. He sent out envoys to Guangzhou to ask for relief. Fifteen envoys were sent. Only the last one successfully reached Guangzhou. When the rescuing army arrived, the siege was lifted. Fan Wen was still ailing from his wounds. Emperor Zhao Kuang Yin issued an order to carry Fan Wen back to Daliang on a stretcher. The government would repay all the cost to the people who carried Fan Wen back to the capital.

Wei Ren Pu, another former premier of the Later Zhou Dynasty, was appointed by Emperor Zhao Kuang Yin as a premier of the Song Dynasty. At that time Wei Ren Pu was ill and asked for leave and stayed at home. Emperor Zhao Kuang Yin went to his home to see him. Emperor Zhao Kuang Yin granted him two hundred ounces of gold and two million coins of money. Wei Ren Pu presented a letter of resignation to Emperor Zhao Kuang Yin, but Emperor Zhao Kuang Yin did not allow him to resign.

The Emperor decided to carry out an expedition against the State of Northern Han in the spring of 969. During a banquet, Wei Ren Pu went up to Emperor Zhao Kuang Yin with a cup of wine to drink a toast to the health of the Emperor. Emperor Zhao Kuang Yin secretly said to him, "I intend to command the northern expedition personally. What do you think?" Wei Rei Pu answered, "Haste does not bring success. I hope Your Majesty will think carefully about it." Emperor Zhao Kuang Yin praised him for his wise answer. After the banquet, Emperor Zhao Kuang Yin granted him one thousand liters of wine and one hundred goats and ordered servants to take these presents to Wei Ren Pu's home.

In February 969 Emperor Zhao Kuang Yin left Daliang on an expedition against the State of Northern Han. Wei Ren Pu accompanied the Emperor on the northern expedition. In March Emperor Zhao Kuang Yin reached the city of Taiyuan. In the second May of 969 (a leap year which had two months of May) Wei Ren Pu fell ill. Emperor Zhao Kuang Yin sent a party of soldiers to escort Wei Ren Pu back to Daliang. But when they reached Lianghouyi (a place to the south of Tuanbaigu Valley, Qixian, Shanxi Province), Wei Ren Pu died at the age of fifty-nine.

In January 964 Fan Zhi, Wei Ren Pu and Wang Pu resigned from their positions as premiers. Emperor Zhao Kuang Yin appointed Zhao Pu in charge of the state affairs. Zhao Pu became the actual premier although he did not have the title of the premier. Emperor Zhao Kuang Yin wanted to appoint officials as deputies of Zhao Pu. But he did not know what title should be given to these officials. He summoned Tao Gu, a scholar of Hanlin Academy, to discuss this matter. He asked Tao Gu, "What is the title for the official which is one rank lower than the position of the premier?" Tao Gu answered, "In the period of the Tang Dynasty, there was the official title of Assistant Administrator." So Emperor Zhao Kuang Yin appointed Xue Ju Zheng, the Minister of War, and Lü Yu Qing as Assistant Administrators to be deputies of Zhao Pu. They did not have the right to use the seal of the premier. They did not have the right to read out the imperial orders of the Emperor. When they were in court, they sat behind Zhao Pu. Their salary was half of that of Zhao Pu. This was because Emperor Zhao Kuang Yin did not want them to be equals of Zhao Pu.

Zhao Pu wanted to expand his house. So he sent his house keepers to go to the area of Qin Ling Mountains (in the southwest part of Shaanxi Province) to buy big logs of wood. They bound the big logs they had bought into rafts and transported them back to Daliang along the Yellow River. One of his housekeepers secretly resold the big logs in the market of the capital without Zhao Pu's permission. This was against the law. The government had issued an order to ban the reselling of big logs of wood. In March 971 Zhao Pin, a general of the guards of the palace gates, committed some crimes and was ordered to go back home and stay there. Zhao Pin was very angry. One day when Zhao Pu was riding a horse to the palace, Zhao Pin stood in front the horse and abused Zhao Pu loudly. Emperor Zhao Kuang Yin heard about this and summoned Zhao Pu and Zhao Pin to court and let them state their points. Zhao Pin said, "Zhao Pu has resold big logs of wood to gain interest. He has committed a serious crime." Emperor Zhao Kuang Yin was very angry with Zhao Pu. He summoned all the officials to court. He wanted to deprive Zhao Pu of all his titles and drive him away. He sent an envoy to ask Wang Pu, the Grand Tutor of the Crown Prince, what punishment should be given to Zhao Pu. Wang Pu asked the envoy to take a memorandum back to Emperor Zhao Kuang Yin. The memorandum read, "Zhao Pin, the general of the guards, has falsely accused Zhao Pu." Emperor Zhao Kuang Yin immediately realized the fact. Then Emperor Zhao Kuang Yin was very angry with Zhao Pin. He ordered a guard to hit the face of Zhao Pin with his weapon. Then he ordered the chief legal official to interrogate Zhao Pin in court. Zhao Pu did his best to save Zhao Pin. Then Emperor Zhao Kuang Yin spared Zhao Pin.

In 971, Li Yu, the King of the State of Southern Tang, sent an envoy to take eight hundred and fifty thousand ounces of silver to present to Zhao Pu, the Premier of the Song Dynasty. Zhao Pu reported this to Emperor Zhao Kuang Yin. Emperor Zhao Kuang Yin said, "You will have to accept these presents.

But you will have to write a reply letter to Li Yu to express your thanks to him. You may give a bribe to the envoy." Zhao Pu touched his head to the ground and said that he would not accept the silver. Emperor Zhao Kuang Yin said, "This has to do with the dignity of an important dynasty. You must not do anything to lessen the dignity of the Great Song Dynasty. You must let Li Yu know that you hold great power." On 1 September 971 Li Yu sent his younger brother Li Cong Shang to take tribute to present to Emperor Zhao Kuang Yin. Emperor Zhao Kuang Yin received Li Chong Shan. Li Chong Shan presented a letter written by Li Yu, King of the State of Southern Tang. In the letter Li Yu asked permission from Emperor Zhao Kuang Yin to change the name of the State of Southern Tang into the State of Jiangnan (meaning the State to the South of the Yangtze River), and to change his title of King of the Southern Tang to the Ruler of the State of Jiangnan and to change the seal for Li Yu to the seal of the Ruler of the State of Jiangnan. Emperor Zhao Kuang Yin gave his permission to these changes. Emperor Zhao Kuang Yin granted Li Cong Shan many gifts. Apart from the usual gifts granted to an envoy, Emperor Zhao Kuang Yin presented Li Cong Shan with quantities of silver, the value of the silver equal to that which Li Yu had presented to Zhao Pu. When Li Yu and his ministers learned about this, they were all shocked. They all admired the magnanimousness of Emperor Zhao Kuang Yin.

One day Emperor Zhao Kuang Yin went out of the palace and paid a sudden visit to Zhao Pu's home. At that time Qian Ti, the King of the State of Wuyue, had just sent an envoy to visit Zhao Pu. The envoy presented Zhao Pu a letter written by Qian Ti, and presented him ten jars of seafood. All these ten jars were put on the ground outside the house under the roof. When Emperor Zhao Kuang Yin arrived suddenly, Zhao Pu did not have the time to take the jars into the house. Zhao Pu came out of the house and greeted Emperor Zhao Kuang Yin. Emperor Zhao Kuang Yin pointed at the ten jars and asked, "What are these?" Zhao Pu answered, "Seafood presented by the King of the State of Wuyue." Emperor Zhao Kuang Yin said, "They must be seafood of good quality." Then he ordered servants to open the covers of these jars. To their great surprise theses ten jars were full of small pieces of gold in the shape of melon seeds. Zhao Pu was panic-stricken. Zhao Pu immediately knelt down to the ground, touched his head to the ground and said, "I have not yet opened the letter and the jars. If I had known that these jars had contained gold, I would have reported it to Your Majesty and refused to accept the gifts." Emperor Zhao Kuang Yin smiled and said, "You may just accept such gifts. The King of the State of Wuyue does this because he thinks that all the state affairs are decided by you scholars."

As the actual premier Zhao Pu arrogated all power to himself. The ministers in the court disliked him. Emperor Zhao Kuang Yin summoned Lu Duo Xun, a scholar of Hanlin Academy, to the palace and asked him about Zhao Pu. Lu Duo Xun said something against him. Lu Duo Xun told the Emperor that Zhao Pu had traded a narrow piece of land for a big tract of fertile land; he had unlawfully expanded his house; and he had leased out houses to earn money from the ordinary people. Emperor Zhao Kuang Yin asked Li Fang, a member of the Secretariat, for his opinion about Zhao Pu. Li Fang said, "I am a member of the Secretariat. My duty is to draw up imperial orders for Your Majesty. It is not my business to know what Zhao Pu has done." At his words Emperor Zhao Kuang Yin did not say anything more. But from then on Emperor Zhao Kuang Yin suspected Zhao Pu. In April 973 Emperor Zhao Kuang Yin ordered that Xue Ju Zheng and Lü Yu Qing had the right to use the seal of the premier and they had the right to stand side by side with Zhao Pu when they submitted a memorandum to the Emperor. Emperor Zhao Kuang Yin's purpose was to reduce the power of Zhao Pu and shift part of the power onto them.

In August 973 Emperor Zhao Kuang Yin dismissed Zhao Pu from the position of the premier and appointed him Regional Military Governor of the three cities in Heyang (now Mengxian, Henan Province).

22. The Situation in the State of Jiangnan (the State of Southern Tang)

After the State of Southern Han had been conquered by the Song Dynasty, Li Yu, King of the State of Southern Tang, was afraid. He knew that the State of Southern Tang would be the next target for the Emperor of the Song Dynasty. So he decided to degrade the name of the State of Southern Tang and his title of King of the State of Southern Tang so as to show his submission to the Emperor of the Song Dynasty. In September 971 he sent his younger brother Li Cong Shan to see Emperor Zhao Kuang Yin to ask permission to change the name of the State of Southern Tang into the State of Jiangnan, to change his tile of King of the State of Southern Tang into the Ruler of the State of Jiangnan, and to change the seal of the King of the State of Southern Tang into the seal of the Ruler of the State of Jiangnan. Emperor Zhao Kuang Yin gave permission to these changes.

But Emperor Zhao Kuang Yin did not let Li Cong Shan to go back to the State of Jiangnan. Emperor Zhao Kuang Yin appointed Li Cong Shan as the Regional Military Governor of the Army of Taining which was stationed in Yanzhou (now Yanzhou, Shandong Province). Emperor Zhao Kuang Yin granted Li Cong Shan a grand house in Daliang and Li Cong Shan just stayed in Daliang. This made Li Yu very afraid. Li Yu showed submission to the Emperor of the Song Dynasty and he did all he should do as the ruler of a vassal state of the Song Dynasty. But actually he was doing his best to recruit soldiers to expand his army and to improve the weapons of his army. He secretly made preparations to resist the attack of the Song army. Emperor Zhao Kuang Yin asked Li Cong Shan to write a letter to Li Yu to urge Li Yu to come to the court of the Song Dynasty. But Li Yu did not come. He just increased the amount of the yearly tribute to the Song Dynasty.

Lin Ren Zhao, a high ranking official of the State of Jiangnan, was a very capable man. The officials of the government department of the Song

Dynasty concerned saw him as an obstacle to the future attack of the State of Jiangnan. They decided to get rid of him. They sent secret agents who could draw portraits to steal into the State of Jiangnan. When they saw Lin Ren Zhao, they secretly drew a portrait of him. The secret agents went back to Daliang and presented Lin Ren Zhao's portrait to the officials concerned. They hung the portrait in a room. When the envoy sent by Li Yu came to court to see Emperor Zhao Kuang Yin, an official showed him to the room in which Lin Ren Zhao's portrait was hung. The official asked the envoy, "Who is this man?" The envoy answered, "This is Lin Ren Zhao." The official said to the envoy, "Lin Ren Zhao will come over to surrender to us. He sent this portrait to us as the evidence to show his determination to come over to us." Then the official pointed at a grand house and said to the envoy, "The Emperor will grant this house to Lin Ren Zhao when he comes." When the envoy went back to the State of Jiangnan, he told Li Yu of Lin Ren Zhao's intention to surrender to the Song Dynasty. Li Yu did not know that it was a scheme set up by the officials of the Song Dynasty. So he killed Lin Ren Zhao by forcing him to drink poison wine.

Lu Duo Xun, a scholar of the Hanlin Academy of the Song Dynasty, with other scholars, had finished compiling a book entitled "The General Rites of Kaibao" and presented the book to Emperor Zhao Kuang Yin. There were two hundred volumes in the work. This book set out all the regulations for all kinds of ceremonies and rites. Emperor Zhao Kuang Yin issued an order to carry out all ceremonies according to the regulations in this book.

In April 973 Emperor Zhao Kuang Yin appointed Lu Duo Xun as his envoy to carry out a mission to the State of Jiangnan. When Lu Duo Xun reached the State of Jiangnan, he was warmly welcomed by the Ruler and the ministers of the State of Jiangnan. They all liked him. When he completed his mission, Lu Duo Xun and his followers came back by ship. When the ship reached Xuanhuakou (the section of the Yangtze River in the area of Nanjing, Jiangsu Province), Lu Duo Xun sent one of his followers back to Jinling (now Nanjing, Jiangsu Province). The man sent by Lu Duo Xun said to Li Yu, the Ruler of the State of Jiangnan, "Now the court of the Song Dynasty has decided to recompile the map of the whole realm and history of different places of the realm. We have gathered all the materials for the book but we do not have the materials for the prefectures of the State of Jiangnan. Will you be so kind as to provide a copy of the geography and history of each prefecture of the State of Jiangnan?" Li Yu agreed readily. He ordered the officials concerned to work day and night to prepare the requisite geography and history of each of the prefectures of the State of Jiangnan. When the copies were made, Li Yu gave them to the man, who took them back to Xuanhuakou to Lu Duo Xun. From these copies Lu Duo Xun got to know the geography of all the nineteen prefectures of the State of Jiangnan, the armies stationed in each place, the number of households of each place and the roads and distances from place to place. When Lu Duo Xun went back to Daliang, he told Emperor Zhao Kuang Yin that the State of Jiangnan had become very weak and could be conquered. Emperor Zhao Kuang Yin highly praised what he had done in the State of Jiangnan.

Pan You, the minister in charge of agriculture of the State of Jiangnan, said to Li Yu, "For a ruler to make a state strong, the most important thing is to pay great attention to the development of agriculture." So he suggested to Li Yu that he should issued laws to prohibit rich people from annexing lands from the poor people, and to return lands which had been annexed by rich people to the peasants. He also suggested that undeveloped lands should be used to plant mulberry trees for the silk worms. He recommended Li Ping, an officer of the royal guards, as the official to carry out these policies. Li Yu accepted his suggestions and the recommendation.

Li Ping was anxious for success. He did not carry out the policies step by step. This damaged the interest of many people. Li Yu regretted appointing Li Ping as the official to carry out the policies. So he removed Li Ping from the position. At that time the State of Jiangnan was becoming weaker and weaker. The officials in power did nothing to save the state. Pan You was very angry. He presented a memorandum to Li Yu in which he used very harsh words to criticize all the officials who had done nothing to save the state from destruction; he only praised and recommended Li Ping. He suggested to Li Yu that Li Ping should be put in a more responsible position. Li Yu summoned all the ministers to discuss this matter. All the ministers rejected Pan You's suggestion. Pan You presented memorandums one after another to Li Yu. Li Yu removed him from his position and ordered him to concentrate his mind on compiling the history of the State of Jiangnan.

In October 973 Pan You again presented a memorandum to Li Yu which read, "I have presented several memorandums to Your Majesty. There are already over ten thousand words in all of my memorandums which have been presented to Your Majesty. I have discussed my points in great detail. I have done this out of my devotion to Your Majesty. But Your Majesty has been hoodwinked by treacherous court officials. They just flattered Your Majesty. This is the reason why our state has become weaker and weaker. Our State is like the sinking sun. In ancient times King Xia Jie of the Xia Dynasty, King Zhou of the Shang Dynasty and King Sun Hao of the State of Eastern Wu were kings who ruined their own states and their states were conquered and their royal clans were extinguished. And they have become a laughing stock in history. Now Your Majesty trusts wicked ministers and they have made the state a great mess. As a ruler Your Majesty is even worse than King Xia Jie of the Xia Dynasty, King Zhou of the Shang Dynasty and King Sun Hao of the State of Eastern Wu. I am not willing to serve a ruler of a fallen state together with those wicked ministers. I hope Your Majesty will grant me death so as to put down the anger of the people." After reading the memorandum Li Yu was furious. At that time Li Yu trusted Zhang Ji, the Head of the Secretariat, who was in charge of making policies and drawing up the imperial orders. They urged Li Yu to put Pan You and Li Ping into jail. As soon as Pan You was thrown into jail, he committed suicide. Li Ping was executed by hanging.

Since Li Cong Shan had been detained by Emperor Zhao Kuang Yin in Daliang, Li Yu missed Li Cong Shan very much. He sent Lu Zhao Fu, the Governor of Changzhou (now Changzhou, Jiangsu Province) to take tribute to present to Emperor Zhao Kuang Yin. Lu Zhao Fu brought a letter written by Li Yu to Emperor Zhao Kuang Yin begging Emperor Zhao Kuang Yin to let Li Cong Shan to go back to the State of Jiangnan. Emperor Zhao Kuang Yin refused. He showed Li Yu's letter to Li Cong Shan. He said some kind words to comfort Li Cong Shan and appointed Li Cong Shan as a member of the Secretariat. When Lu Zhao Fu had been in the State of Jiangnan, he had some grudges against Zhang Ji. When Emperor Zhao Kuang Yin learned about this, he said to Lu Zhao Fu, "Zhang Ji has held the greatest power of the government of the State of Jiangnan. I really want to know what he looks like. When you go back, you may ask him to come to Daliang on a mission so that I can see him with my own eyes." Lu Zhao Fu was afraid. So Lu Zhao Fu stayed in Daliang and never went back to the State of Jiangnan.

When Lu Duo Xun went back to Daliang, Li Yu understood that Emperor Zhao Kuang Yin was planning to attack the State of Jiangnan. Then he sent an envoy to see Emperor Zhao Kuang Yin to express his willingness to be made the king of a vassal state of the Song Dynasty. Emperor Zhao Kuang Yin refused his request. In July 973 Emperor Zhao Kuang Yin sent Liang Jiong, one of his attendants, as his envoy to Li Yu. When Liang Jiong saw Li Yu, he said, "This winter a grand ceremony making offers to Heaven by burning firewood will be held in Daliang. Will you come to Daliang to attend to the ceremony?" Li Yu stuttered something else but did not give any answer. Liang Jiong went back to Daliang and told Emperor Zhao Kuang Yin that Li Yu would not come. Then Emperor Zhao Kuang Yin made up his mind to carry out the expedition against the State of Jiangnan.

Fan Ruo Shui, a man in the State of Jiangnan, took part in the imperial examination for selecting candidates for civil posts, but he failed the examination. He presented memorandums to Li Yu, the Ruler of the State of Jiangnan, to put forward some suggestions. But Li Yu never gave a reply. So he decided to go to the north. He pretended that he was fishing, on a small boat on the Yangtze River, at the Caishi section (now Caishi, which is situated on the east bank of the Yangtze River five kilometers to the southwest of Ma'anshan, Anhui Province). He put a bundle of silk rope on the boat. He tied one end of the rope to a stone on the south bank of the Yangtze River. Then he rowed the small boat to the north bank of the river. He released the rope into the river while he was rowing the boat. When he reached the north bank, he measured the length of the rope. In this way he got to know the width of the Yangtze River at the Caishi section. He did this several times to make sure that the measurements were correct. Then he went to Daliang. He went to the palace and asked to see Emperor Zhao Kuang Yin, claiming that he had a good plan to take the State of Jiangnan. Emperor Zhao Kuang Yin was very glad to get a clear measurement of the width of the Yangtze River at the Caishi section; this enabled them to plan and build a floating bridge. Emperor Zhao Kuang Yin ordered he be sent to the Academy to take the exam for selecting officials. Fan Ruo Shi passed the exam and was appointed as an official under the commander-in-chief of the army stationed in Shuzhou (now Qianshan, Anhui Province).

Fan Ruo Shui sent a memorandum to Emperor Zhao Kuang Yin stating that his old mother and his kinfolks were still in the State of Jiangnan and that he was afraid that they would be killed by Li Yu, King of the State of Jiangnan. He hoped that his mother and his kinfolks would be sent to the Song Dynasty. Emperor Zhao Kuang Yin sent an envoy to the State of Jiangnan with a letter to Li Yu, ordering him to escort Fan Ruo Shui's mother and his kinfolks to Daliang. Emperor Zhao Kuang Yin also sent envoys to the area of Jingnan (now the area of Jiangling, Hubei Province) and the area of Dongting Lake (now Dongting Lake, in the north part of Hunan Province) to supervise the building of several thousand big warships and dragon boats of yellow and black for the building of the floating bridge across the Yangtze River according to the strategy presented by Fan Ruo Shui.

As early as in 960 Emperor Zhao Kuang Yin appointed Qian Ti, the King of the State of Wuyue, as the Great Marshal. In 973 Qian Ti sent Huang Yi Jian, an official of the Office of the Great Marshal in the State of Wuyue, to escort a caravan of tribute to Emperor Zhao Kuang Yin. Emperor Zhao Kuang Yin said to Huang Yi Jian, "Go back and tell the Great Marshal that he should train his troops well to prepare for war. The Ruler of the State of Jiangnan is very stubborn. He has refused to come to see me. I shall send my great armies to carry out an expedition against him. The Great Marshal should help me in this expedition." Emperor Zhao Kuang Yin had ordered the officials concerned to build a grand residence in the outskirts of Daliang. The residence was very big and occupied several streets. There was all the necessary furniture in the houses of this grand residence. Emperor Zhao Kuang Yin summoned Qian Wen Zhi, the official in charge of tributes of the State of Wuyue, to Daliang and said to him, "Several years ago I ordered Tao Gu to draft an imperial order to build a temporary abode for me to the south of the capital. Now I have given that place the name of Residence for Distinguished People. This residence has been built for Li Yu and your master. I will grant this residence to the one who comes to see me first."

Emperor Zhao Kuang Yin asked Qian Wen Zhi to convey what he had said to Qian Ti when he went back. On 3 August 973 Qian Ti sent Sun Cheng You, the Commander-in-chief of the army of the State of Wuyue, to escort more tribute to Emperor Zhao Kuang Yin. On 12 August, Sun Cheng You went to see Emperor Zhao Kuang Yin to take his leave. Emperor Zhao Kuang Yin secretly informed him of the timing of the expedition against the State of Jiangnan.

23. The Expedition against the State of Jiangnan

On 19 September Emperor Zhao Kuang Yin appointed Cao Bin, the Regional Military Governor of the Army of Yicheng stationed in Huazhou (now Huaxian, Henan Province), as the Commander-in-chief of all the infantry, cavalry and the naval armies of the Southwest Branch, Pan Mei, the Regional Military Governor of Shannandongdao (now Xiangyang, Hubei Province), as Supervisor of this branch of the army, and Cao Han, the Commander-in-chief of the army in Yingzhou (now Fuyang, Anhui Province), as the commander of the vanguard troops. Emperor Zhao Kuang Yin ordered them to lead their armies to Jingnan (now the area of Jiangling, in the south part of Hubei Province). There were over one hundred thousand men in this branch of the army. They would start from Jingnan and go along the Yangtze River to wage a campaign against the State of Jiangnan. Before they went to Jingnan, Emperor Zhao Kuang Yin summoned Cao Bin and Pan Mei to the court and said to them, "When the capital of the State of Jiangnan is taken, you must prohibit the soldiers from slaughtering the people. If the soldiers of Jiangnan put up a desperate fight, then the family members of Li Yu should be protected and not be harmed."

Emperor Zhao Kuang Yin had made all the arrangements for the expedition against the State of Jiangnan, but he needed to find a justification for sending out the army. He decided to send an envoy to summon Li Yu to the court of the Song Dynasty. On 23 September he sent Li Mu, a member of the Secretariat, as his envoy to the State of Jiangnan. When Li Mu reached Jinling, the capital of the State of Jiangnan, he conveyed the order of Emperor Zhao Kuang Yin to Li Yu. Li Yu was about to accept when Chen Qiao, one of his officials, said, "Your Majesty succeeded your father as the King of the State. I am also entrusted by your father to help you. If Your Majesty goes to the court of the Song Dynasty, there will be no hope of Your Majesty returning. Then the State will not go on. When I die, I will be too shameful to see your father in the nether world." Zhang Ji also tried to persuade Li Yu not to go the court of the Song Dynasty. So Li Yu refused to go on the excuse that he had been ill.

He said to Li Mu, "I will serve the Emperor of the big dynasty heart and soul. And I hope the Emperor will have mercy on me. If he forces me to go, I will have to die." Li Mu said, "It is for yourself to decide whether to go or not. But you must remember the troops of the Song Dynasty are all crack troops. The Song Dynasty has great material resources. It would be impossible for you to resist the attack of such a strong army. You must think about it carefully. There will be no time for regrets." Li Mu went back to Daliang to report his mission to Emperor Zhao Kuang Yin. The Emperor approved what Li Mu had said to Li Yu.

On 10 October Emperor Zhao Kuang Yin stood on the bank of the Bian Shui River to see the first batch of warships to sail along the Bian Shui River eastward. Bian Shui River was the upper section of the Tongji Canal dug in the period of the reing of Emperor Yang Guang (569-618) of the Sui Dynasty. On 12 October Emperor Zhao Kuang Yin again stood on the bank of the Bian Shui River to see the second batch of warships to sail to the east. These warships would sail from Bian Shui River into the Tongji Canal and then sail along the Tongji Canal to Songzhou (now Shangqiu, Henan Province), then to Shuzhou (now Shuzhou, Anhui Province) and then to Sizhou (now Xuyi, Jiangsu Province) Then the warships would sail along the Huai Shui River to Chŭzhou (now Huaiyin, Jiangsu Province). From Chŭzhou the warships would sail into Li Canal and along this canal to Changzhou (now Changzhou, Jiangsu Province) which was situated by the Yangtze River. They would attack Jinling along the Yangtze River.

The warships of the Song Dynasty on Bian Shui River

On 12 October Cao Bin with all the other generals went to the palace to bid farewell to Emperor Zhao Kuang Yin. The Emperor said to Cao Bin, "I shall entrust you with responsibility for all the matters of the southern expedition. Killing and looting ordinary people are strictly forbidden. You must show our great power and leniency so as to let Li Yu make his decision to surrender by himself. It is not necessary to attack very fiercely." Then Emperor Zhao Kuang Yin gave a sword to Cao Bin and said, "Kill anyone under you who dares to disobey your orders with this sword." Emperor Zhao Kuang Yin gave this strict order because when Wang Quan Bin conquered the State of Shu, he had allowed his soldiers to kill many ordinary people. Whenever Emperor Zhao Kuang Yin thought of this, he felt very regretful.

Cao Bin was a kind-hearted and benevolent man, so Emperor Zhao Kuang Yin entrusted him with the southern expedition.

On 23 October Emperor Zhao Kuang Yin appointed Qian Ti, the King of the State of Wuyue, as the Commander-in-chief of the army attacking Jinling from the southeast. Emperor Zhao Kuang Yin granted two hundred horses to Qian Ti, and he sent Ding De Yu, an official in charge of foreign affairs, to command one thousand infantry and cavalrymen to the State of Wuyue. Ding De Yu would be the supervisor of the army of the State of Wuyue attacking the State of Jiangnan.

In October Cao Bin commanded the army in Huazhou to march to Jingnan; Pan Mei commanded the army in Shannandongdao to march to Jingnan. Cao Han had already commanded the army in Yingzhou to march to Jiangling in September. When these armies met in Jiangling, Cao Bin and Pan Mei commanded the infantry, cavalry and naval armies to start their march from Jiangling eastward along the Yangtze River by boats and by land on 18 October. On 25 October the Song troops on board the ships attacked Xiakou Stronghold which was situated to the west of Chizhou (now Guichi, Anhui Province) on the southern bank of the Yangtze River. The Song troops took the stronghold. Then the Song army continued to go eastward. The troops of the State of Jiangnan stationed along the southern bank of the Yangtze River saw the warships of the Song army sailing eastward. They thought that these warships of the Song army were doing their routine cruise along the Yangtze River. So the troops of the State of Jiangnan just stayed inside their camps and did nothing against the warships of the Song army. On 5 of the second October (974 was an intercalary year which had two Octobers) the Song army under Cao Bin reached Chizhou (now Guichi, Anhui Province). Ge Yan, the general of the troops of the State of Jiangna defending Chizhou, gave up the city and ran away. Cao Bin commanded the Song troops entered Chizhou.

At the same time the big warships and one thousand black and yellow dragon boats which had been built in Jingnan and Dongting Lake according to the order of Emperor Zhao Kuang Yin also sailed eastward along the Yangtze River loaded with big bamboo woods and ropes. The dragon boats and these bamboo woods and ropes would be used to build a floating bridge over the section of the Yangtze River by Caishi. The warships and dragon boats first sailed to Shipaikou (now Shipai Town, Huaining, Anhui Province) where the Song troops successfully had a trial building of the floating bridge across that section of the Yangtze River. Emperor Zhao Kuang Yin ordered Lu Wan You, the commander of the Song army stationed in Ruzhou (now Ruzhou, Henan Province), to command the Song army to defend the floating bridge.

On 13 of the second October the Song army under Cao Bin and the army of the State of Jiangnan fought in the area of Tongling (now Tongling, Anhui Province). The Song army won the battle. The Song troops captured more than two hundred warships and more than eight hundred soldiers of the

State of Jiangnan. The Song army sailed down the Yangtze River. Then the Song troops took Wuhu (now Wuhu, Anhui Province). On 18 of the second October the Song army under Cao Bin reached Dangtu (now Dangtu, Anhui Province). Wei Yu, the general of the army of the State of Jiangnan defending the city of Dangtu, surrendered to the Song army and presented the city of Dangtu to Cao Bin. On 23 of the second October the Song army reached Caishi. Twenty thousand soldiers of the State of Jiangnan stationed in Caishi came to fight the Song army. The Jiangnan troops were defeated. Their generals Yang Xiu and Sun Zhen were captured.

After Caishi was taken, Emperor Zhao Kuang Yin ordered them to move the floating bridge from Shipaikou to Caishi. The building of the floating bridge over the section of the Yangtze River by Caishi was completed within three days. The Song troops under Pan Mei who marched along the northern bank of the Yangtze River crossed the Yangtze River using the floating bridge. They marched on it just as if they were marching on flat land.

At first, when Li Yu heard that the Song troops were planning to build a floating bridge over the Yangtze River, he told Zhang Ji about this. Zhang Ji said, "No bridge has ever been built across the Yangtze River according to all the descriptions in the history books. Their attempt will certainly fail." Li Yu said, "I also think that they are attempting the impossible." Then he sent General Zheng Yan Hua to command ten thousand naval troops to sail up the Yangtze River on warships and General Du Zhen to command ten thousand foot soldiers to march along the bank of the Yangtze River to beat back the approaching Song troops. Before they left, Li Yu said to them, "The naval troops and the foot soldiers should help each other. In this way you will surely win." On 20 November the naval army of the State of Jiangnan under Zheng Yan Hua met with the naval army of the Song Dynasty under Cao Bin on the Yangtze River. A naval battle broke out. The foot soldiers of the State of Jiangnan under Du Zhen just watched the fight and did not give any help. The naval army of the State of Jiangnan was totally defeated. On 6 December the Song army under Cao Bin defeated the army of Jiangnan in Bailuzhou (which was situated in the Yangtze River, 2.5 kilometers west to the city of Nanjing, Jiangsu Province). On 23 December the Song army under Cao Bin defeated the army of the State of Jiangnan in Xinlingang (which was situated ten kilometer southwest to the city of Nanjing, Jiangsu Province).

When Li Yu found out that Emperor Zhao Kuang Yin had appointed Qian Ti, the King of the State of Wuyue, as the commander-in-chief of the army attacking the State of Jiangnan from the southeast, he wrote a letter to Qian Ti. The letter read, "If I perish today, you will become extinct tomorrow. When the Emperor of the Song Dynasty takes away your land and rewards you handsomely for your contributions, you will become an ordinary man in Daliang." On 14 November Qian Ti sent an envoy to see Emperor Zhao Kuang Yin with two purposes: to express his thanks to the Emperor for appointing him as the commander-in-chief of the army attacking the State of Jiangnan from the southeast, and to show the Emperor the letter which Li

Yu had sent to him.

In December Qian Ti commanded the army of the State of Wuyue to lay siege to Changzhou (now Changzhou, Jiangsu Province). On 20 December the army of the State of Wuyue took Licheng stronghold. On 28 December the army of the State of Wuyue defeated the troops of the State of Jiangnan in the area north to Changzhou.

As early as in September 974, Emperor Zhao Kuang Yin appointed Wang Ming, an official in charge of transportation of military supplies, as the Governor of Huangzhou (now Xinzhou, Hubei Province). Before Wang Ming left for Huangzhou, Emperor Zhao Kuang Yin gave him secret instructions. When Wang Ming arrived at Huangzhou to take up the position of the Governor of Huangzhou, he was ordered to repair and strengthen the city. Wang Ming paid great attention to the training of officers and soldiers in Huangzhou. In January 975 Emperor Zhao Kuang Yin appointed Wang Ming as the commander-in-chief of the naval troops patrolling the section of the Yangtze River from Chizhou (now Guichi, Anhui Province) to Yuezhou (now Yueyang, in the northeast part of Hunan Province). On 8 January 975 Wang Ming sent Wu Shou Qian, the supervisor of the naval army, to command the army to cross the Yangtze River. The Song army under Wu Shou Qian defeated the army of Jiangnan in Wuchang (now Wuchang, Hubei Province).

On 17 January 975 the Song army under Cao Bin and Pan Mei started their action to attack Jinling, the capital of the State of Jiangnan. The Song troops advanced to Qinhuai He River which flowed from west to east in the area south to the city of Jinling. More than a hundred thousand naval and foot soldiers of the State of Jiangnan were deployed in battle formation outside the city. On that day there were no boats or ships to carry the Song troops across Qinhuai He River. General Pan Mei shouted to the troops under him, "I have been ordered by the Emperor to command tens of thousands of elite troops to attack the State of Jiangnan. The Emperor expects that we will surely win. We shall not be stopped by this little river. Now let's cross this river without boats and ships!" After saying that, he jumped into the river together with his horse. The soldiers followed his example and jumped into the river and crossed it. The troops of the State of Jiangnan were defeated and ran into the city. Several days later more than twenty warships of the State of Jiangnan sailed up the Yangtze River trying to destroy the floating bridge over the Yangtze River. Pan Mei commanded the Song troops to fight the troops of Jiangnan. The Song troops captured all these warships and Sheng Bin, the commanding officer of the troops of Jiangnan in this action.

On 11 April 975 Qian Ti, King of the State of Wuyue commanded his army to lay siege to the city of Changzhou. Yu Wan Cheng, the Governor of Changzhou intended to defend the city resolutely. But Jin Cheng Li, the commanding general of the army of the State of Jiangnan defending Changzhou, abducted Yu Wan Cheng and opened the city gates to surrender to Qian Ti. On 1 May 975 Emperor Zhao Kuang Yin appointed Qian Ti as the

Grang Tutor and Head of the Secretariat of the court of the Song Dynasty. On 13 May Qian Ti reported to Emperor Zhao Kuang Yin that the army of the State of Jiangnan defending Jiangyin (now Jiangyin, Jiangsu Province) and the army of the State of Jiangnan along the southern bank of the Yangtze River had surrendered.

Before the Song army reached Jingling, Chen Qiao and Zhang Ji said to Li Yu, "We shall fortify the defense works of our capital and leave nothing usable to the coming Song army. In this way we shall stop the advancing Song army in front of the strongly defended city and they cannot get food from the area around the capital. The Song troops will be exhausted and have to leave. Your Majesty has nothing to be worried about." Li Yu was very glad to hear that. He entrusted the defense of the capital to Huangpu Ji Xun, a young and inexperienced general. He entrusted all the important political affairs to Chen Qiao and Zhang Ji. He did not attend to the military and political affairs of the State of Jiangnan. He just stayed in the royal garden in the palace to listen to the Buddhist monks to chant the Buddhist scriptures.

Huangpu Ji Xun did not have the determination to defend the city. He just hoped Li Yu would surrender as soon as possible. He did not send any situation reports to Li Yu. Chen Qiao and Zhang Ji did not inform Li Yu about the attack. One day in May, Li Yu went up to the top of the city wall. He was greatly surprised to see that the Song troops had already built camps around the city and had their flags flying all around the city. He realized that he had been hoodwinked by his subordinates. He ordered Huangpu Ji Xun arrested and had him executed. Then he sent an envoy to Hukou (now Hukou, in the north part of Jiangxi Province) to ask Zhu Wen Yun, the supervisor of the army of the Royal Guard Army of the State of Jiangnan, to bring his army to rescue the capital. Zhu Wen Yun had a great army of over one hundred thousand men stationed in Hukou. When the envoy reached Hukou and conveyed Li Yu's order, the generals under him all asked Zhu Wen Yun to command the naval army to sail to Jinling while the Yangtze River was at high tide. But Zhu Wen Yun said, "If we now go forward Huangpu Ji Xun to rescue Jinling, our enemies will certainly cut us off from behind. If we successfully rescue the capital, it will be all right. If we are not successful, our supply line will be cut. Then what shall we do?" Zhu Wen Yun sent a letter to Chai Ke Zhen, the commander of the army in Nandu (now Nanchang, Jiangxi Province) to come to Hukou to defend Hukou for him. Chai Ke Zhen would not go on the excuse that he was ill. Zhu Wen Yun did not dare to leave Hukou to rescue Jinling. Li Yu sent envoys one after another to urge him to come to the rescue Jinling, but Zhu Wen Yun still would not go.

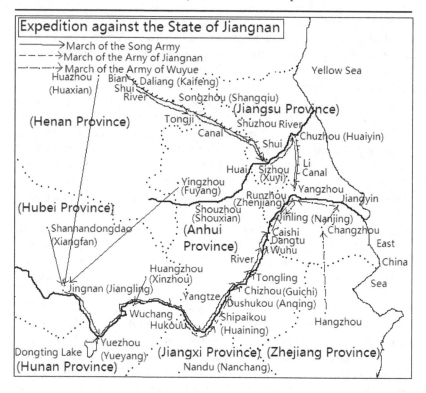

Expedition against the State of Jiangnan

————→ March of the Song Army
– – – –→ March of the Army of Jiangnan
—·—·→ March of the Army of Wuyue

Before the Song army laid siege to Jinling, Li Yu thought that Runzhou (now Zhenjiang, Jiangsu Province) was an important place because it was situated to the east of Jinling, and Qian Ti, the King of Wuyue, might take Runzhou and attack Jinling from the east. He decided to send Liu Cheng, the Supervisor of his bodyguards, as the commander-in-chief of the army of the State of Jiangnan to defend Runzhou. Before Liu Cheng left, Li Yu said to him, "You have never parted with me and I am not willing to part with you. But only you will be able to complete this task." Liu Cheng said good-bye to Li Yu with tears in his eyes. When he went back home, he packed all the gold, silver and jade and brought all these valuable things with him to Runzhou. He said to others, "These things were given to me by His Majesty. I shall bring these things with me to do mighty deeds."

When Li Yu heard about this, he was very glad. In September when the troops of the State of Wuyue reached Runzhou and they had not built their camps, the general under Liu Cheng wanted to go out of the city to start and attack the army of the State of Wuyue. But Liu Cheng refused to let them go out to fight. When Li Yu understood that the army of Wuyue had come to attack Runzhou, he sent Lu Jiang to command eight thousand naval troops to rescue Runzhou. At that time Liu Cheng had informed the commanding general of the army of the State of Wuyue that he would surrender. When Lu

Jiang arrived, Liu Cheng said to him, "I hear that the capital has been under siege for a very long time. If the capital falls, it is not necessary to defend this city." Lu Jiang knew that the city of Runzhou would fall sooner or later. So he commanded his soldiers to make a breakthrough and ran away. On 10 September Liu Cheng led all his subordinates to open the city gate and surrender to the army of Wuyue.

In September Emperor Zhao Kuang Yin again sent Li Mu to Jinling to see Li Yu. Li Mu conveyed Emperor Zhao Kuang Yin's order demanding Li Yu to surrender. Li Yu was about to accept the order to surrender when Chen Qiao and Zhang Ji said that the defense of Jinling was very strong and the Song troops surrounding Jinling would retreat very soon. Then Li Yu refused to surrender. Li Mu went back to report to Emperor Zhao Kuang Yin that Li Yu had refused to surrender. Then Emperor Zhao Kuang Yin issued the order to Cao Bin to step up the attack on Jinling.

After Runzhou had fallen into the hands of Qian Ti, the King of the State of Wuyue, and the Song army had stepped up the attack on Jinling, Li Yu considered sending envoys to Daliang to beg Emperor Zhao Kuang Yin to slow down his attack. Li Yu appointed Xu Xuan, a scholar in the Literature Center, and Zhou Wei Jian, a Taoist priest who often gave lessons on Taoist doctrines to Li Yu, as envoys. Before Xu Xuan and Zhou Wei Jian left Jinling on their mission, Li Yu said to them, "I have ordered Zhu Quan Yun to command all the troops under him to come to rescue the capital. Since you are going on a mission to Daliang to ask the Emperor of the Song Dynasty to slow down the attack, I will order Zhu Quan Yun not to come to rescue the capital." Xu Xuan said, "Our mission may not be successful. The defense of the capital depends on the rescuing army. Why should Your Majesty stop the rescuing army from coming?" Li Yu said, "Now I am asking for peace from the Emperor of the Song Dynasty. But at the same time I am ordering an army to come. This will put you in a very dangerous situation." Xu Xuan said, "Your Majesty should not consider our safety. Your Majesty, just does what Your Majesty thinks fit." Li Yu shed tears when he heard Xu Xuan's words. Then Li Yu wrote down more than ten pages outlining his conditions for peace. He gave these pages to Zhou Wei Jian and asked him to show these pages to Emperor Zhao Kuang Yin when the chance came.

On 1 October Cao Bin sent a party of soldiers to escort Xu Xuan and Zhou Wei Jian, the envoys sent by Li Yu, to Daliang. Xu Xuan had been famous as a virtuous and capable official in the State of Jiangnan. He wanted to preserve the State of Jiangnan by using his tongue. Before the envoys reached Daliang, some officials said to Emperor Zhao Kuang Yin, "Xu Xuan is a learned man. He is very good at debating. Your Majesty should be well prepared." Emperor Zhao Kuang Yin laughed and said, "You just stand aside and look on. This is not your business." When Xu Xuan and Zhou Wei Jian went into the court and saw Emperor Zhao Kuang Yin, Xu Xuan said bluntly to Emperor Zhao Kuang Yin, "Li Yu is innocent. Your Majesty has sent out an army to attack our state without a justifiable reason."

Then Emperor Zhao Kuang Yin asked Xu Xuan to go up the steps of the court and let him finish what he wanted to say. Xu Xuan went several steps forward, then he continued, "Li Yu has served Your Majesty as a son would serve his father. He has never made any mistakes. I can't see the reason why Your Majesty has sent an army against him." Emperor Zhao Kuang Yin asked Xu Xuan, "Now you tell me. Can father and son be considered as two different families?" Xu Xuan was at a total loss as to what to say. Zhou Wei Jian presented the pages outlining Li Yu's conditions to Emperor Zhao Kuang Yin. Having read the terms requested, Emperor Zhao Kuan Yin said, "I can't make out what your master is telling me." Although Emperor Zhao Kuang Yin did not give any permission to slow down the attack, he treated Xu Xuan and Zhou Wei Jian with due courtesy as if there had been no war goping on. On 4 October Xu Xuan and Zhou Wei Jian left Daliang to go back to the State of Jiangnan.

In October Zhu Quan Yun commanded the army of one hundred and fifty thousand men under him to rescue Jinling from Hukou (now Hukou, in the north part of Jiangxi Province). The soldiers of the State of Jiangnan under Zhu Quan Yun bound big logs of wood to make rafts of about three hundred meters long. They had many big warships. The biggest ones could carry one thousand soldiers each. Zhu Quan Yun intended to sail down the Yangtze River to destroy the floating bridge by Caishi. But by that time the water in the Yangtze River was comparably shallow, and the big ships could not sail very fast. At that time Wang Ming, the commander-in-chief of the naval troops patrolling the section of the Yangtze River from Chizhou (now Guichi, Anhui Province) to Yuezhou (now Yueyang, in the northeast part of Hunan Province), stationed the troops under him in Dushukou (which is situated to the southwest of Anqing, Anhui Province). He sent his son to ride very quickly to Daliang to report to Emperor Zhao Kuang Yin that Zhu Quan Yun was coming with a great army along the Yangtze River. Wang Ming hoped that Emperor Zhao Kuang Yin would order three hundred warships be built so that he could resist the naval troops under Zhu Quan Yun. Emperor Zhao Kuang Yin said, "This is not a good way to meet an urgent need. Zhu Quan Yun will arrive very soon. If Zhu Quan Yun's army reaches Jinling, the siege of Jinling will have to be lifted."

Emperor Zhao Kuang Yin sent an envoy to convey his instruction that the Song troops under Wang Ming should erect tall poles of wood in the sandy islands in the Yangtze River so that they looked like masts of ships. Wang Ming ordered the soldiers under him to erect such poles as instructed. When Zhu Quan Yun arrived with his great army, he was convinced that there were many warships in this area. So he hesitated and ordered his troops to station in Wuankou (the place where Wan He River joins the Yangtze River, ten kilometers southwest to Anqing, Anhui Province). Cao Bin sent Liu Yu, the supervisor of the Song army, to command an army to sail up the Yangtze River on boats to fight the army under Zhu Quan Yun. On 21 October Liu Yu commanded his army to attack the biggest warship, on which the flag of the commanding general was flying, from the north. Zhu Quan Yun ordered the soldiers to pour petroleum on the river and set fire to it. At that time a southern wind was blowing. The fire threatened the warships of the Song army. Liu Yu had to order the warships to retreat. But suddenly the direction of the wind changed to the north. The northern wind blew the fire to the warships of the State of Jiangnan, and they caught fire. The troops of the State of Jiangnan were defeated. Zhu Quan Yun was captured. The army under Zhu Quan Yun was the only hope for Li Yu to rescue Jinling. Now that the army under Zhu Quan Yun had been totally destroyed, no army could come to rescue the besieged city of Jinling.

Xu Xuan and Zhou Wei Jian went back to Jinling. Not long later Li Yu sent Xu Xuan and Zhou Wei Jian as his envoys to Daliang again. On 3 November Emperor Zhao Kuang Yin received Xu Xuan and Zhou Wei Jian. Xu Xuan said in a stern voice, "Li Yu has fallen ill. He cannot attend to state affairs. He cannot travel such a long way to come to see Your Majesty. He does not dare to go against the order of Your Majesty. I hope Your Majesty will hold back on the attack against our state so as to preserve the lives of the people." Emperor Zhao Kuang Yin explained to him that if Li Yu came to Daliang, the Song army would stop attacking Jinling. But Xu Xuan ignored what Emperor Zhao Kuang Yin had said and repeated his words three more times, even more sternly. This made Emperor Zhao Kuang Yin very angry. He stood up, put his hand on the handle of his sword and said to Xu Xuan, "Say no more! Li Yu has not committed any crime. But the whole realm is one family. It is like my bed room. The bed room is mine and for me only. I will not allow another man to sleep on a bed beside mine and snoring loudly!" Xu Xuan was scared and shut up.

Then Emperor Zhao Kuang Yin reproached Zhou Wei Jian for coming as a mouthpiece for Li Yu. Zhou Wei Jian was very afraid and said, "I was a Taoist priest living in the mountains. I did not intend to become an official. But Li Yu has forced me to come. I hear that there are many kinds of medical herbs in Zhongnanshan Mountains. In the future if I get a chance to withdraw from the official position and live in a secluded place, may I go and live there?" Emperor Zhao Kuang Yin had pity on him and gave his permission. Emperor Zhao Kuang Yin granted Xu Xuan and Zhou Wei Jian generous sums money and sent them back.

When Cao Bin laid siege to the city of Jinling, he divided the Song troops in three groups and established three camps. Pan Mei was in charge of the group of the Song army camped in the place north to the city of Jinling. After the deployment, Cao Bin drew a map of the deployment of the Song army and sent an envoy to take the map to Emperor Zhao Kuang Yin. After Emperor Zhao Kuang Yin had read the map, he pointed at the camp situated to the north of Jinling and said to the envoy, "A deep trench should be dug here to strengthen the defense of the camp. I am sure that the troops of the State of Jiangnan will come to attack this camp at night. Go back quickly to tell Cao Bin that he should get the trench dug as soon as possible. Otherwise the State of Jiangnan will attack our army north of the city." He gave food to the envoy. The envoy hurried back as soon as he finished eating. The envoy conveyed the Emperor's order to Cao Bin, who immediately supervised his sturdiest men in digging a trench. Very soon the trench was dug. And like clockwork, on 18 November, 975, five thousand soldiers of the State of Jiangnan came out of the city of Jinling and launched a surprise attack on the northern camp at night. Each of the soldiers of the State of Jiangnan held a torch and made very loud war cry as he dashed forward. Cao Bin and Pan Mei let the Jiangnan troops come to the northern camp. The Jiangnan troops had great difficulty in going over the ditch. The Song troops took the chance to kill the enemies. The Jiangnan troops were defeated and many of them were captured.

Jinling had been under siege from spring to winter. The people could not leave the city to get firewood. Cao Bin hoped that Li Yu would surrender. He sent envoys to say to Li Yu, "The city will surely be taken. You should make your decision to surrender as early as possible." Li Yu promised to send his son Li Zhong Yu to the court of the Song Dynasty. But Li Zhong Yu did not come out of the city. Cao Bin sent an envoy to the city to say to Li Yu, "Your son does not need to go all the way to Daliang. If he comes to my army's camp, our attack on the city will stop." The ministers and officials of the State of Jiangnan did their best to persuade Li Yu not to send his son out. So Li Yu let the envoy tell Cao Bin that Li Zhong Yu had not yet got his luggage ready and could not go out right away. Cao Bin again sent an envoy to say to Li Yu, "If you still delay your surrender, it will be too late for regrets." But Li Yu still refused to surrender.

Since the siege of the city of Jinling Emperor Zhao Kuang Yin had sent several envoys to instruct Cao Bin not to harm the innocent people in Jinling and to protect the royal clan of Li Yu if the troops of the State of Jiangnan put up a desperate fight. Cao Bin was determined to carry out Emperor Zhao Kuang Yin's instructions, but it was hard to see how he could do it. On 25 November Cao Bin suddenly declared that he was ill and could not attend to the daily affairs in the army. All the generals came to see him. Cao Bin said to the generals, "My illness cannot be cured by any medicine. I hope you will all make a vow not to kill a single innocent person when the city of Jinling is taken. Then my illness will be cured." All the generals promised to make that vow. They held a ceremony in which they burned incense and made their solemn vow not to kill any innocent persons. The next day Cao Bin declared that he had recovered from his illness.

On 27 November 975 the Song troops under Cao Bin started a general attack and broke into the city of Jinling. The troops of the State of Jiangnan put up a desperate fight. They fought bravely till they were all killed in the street battles. Chen Qiao and Zhang Ji had expressed their determination not to surrender and they planned to die together when the city fell. But actually Zhang Ji did not have the guts to face death. So when the city fell, Zhang Ji went into the palace with his wife and children. Zhang Ji and Chen

Qiao went to see Li Yu. Chen Qiao said to Li Yu, "I have failed to live up to the expectations of Your Majesty. Your Majesty may kill me. If the Emperor of the Song Dynasty reproaches Your Majesty, Your Majesty may put all the blames on me." Li Yu said, "The nation is doomed to fall. Your death will not do much help." Chen Qiao said, "Even if Your Majesty does not kill me, I will be too ashamed to face the people of the state." So he went out of the palace and killed himself. Zhang Ji said to Li Yu, "Chen Qiao and I were in charge of the most important state affairs together. Now that the nation has been fallen, I should die together with Chen Qiao. But when Your Majesty goes to the court of the Song Dynasty, who will explain all the responsibilities to the Emperor of the Song Dynasty? This is the reason why I have decided not to die now."

Cao Bin marched his army in great discipline to the palace city. Li Yu led all the ministers and officials of the State of Jiangnan to stand at the gate of the palace city. Li Yu stood there with a petition of surrender in his hands. When Pan Mei arrived, Li Yu bowed to him. Pan Mei bowed to Li Yu in return. When Cao Bin arrived, Li Yu bowed to him. Cao Bin sent an officer to tell Li Yu that he could not make a bow to Li Yu because he was wearing armor. Then Cao Bin selected one thousand elite troops to guard the gate of the palace city. He ordered the guards not to let anyone to go into the palace. Li Yu had ordered his servants to put a lot of firewood inside the palace. He intended to set fire to it so that he and all the members of the royal clan would go up in flames. When Cao Bin came, he comforted Li Yu. Cao Bin said to Li Yu, "You will be escorted to Daliang. The Emperor will pay you. But the amount is limited. The government treasure houses of your state have been sealed. You will not be able to take anything from the treasure houses. You'd better go back into your palace and take as much gold as you want." Li Yu went back into the palace. The generals under Cao Bin said to him, "If Li Yu commits suicide inside the palace, who will be responsible for it?" Cao Bin smiled but did not answer them. They continued to argue. Then Cao Bin said, "Li Yu has never been a decisive man. Now that he has surrendered, he will surely not commit suicide. Don't worry about it." Cao Bin sent a hundred soldiers to prepared carriages to carry the things which Li Yu would take to Daliang. But since the State of Jiangnan had been destroyed, Li Yu was disheartened. He was not interested in valuable things. And he had distributed all he had to his subordinates. So he did not bring much with him to Daliang.

On 1 December 975 Cao Bin's report of victory was delivered to Emperor Zhao Kuang Yin. The State of Jiangnan had been conquered. There were nineteen prefectures, one hundred and eight counties and six hundred and fifty-five thousand and sixty-five households. All the ministers came to the palace to express their congratulations to Emperor Zhao Kuang Yin. But the Emperor wept and said, "When the city of Jinling was under siege, the people suffered greatly. When the city was taken by storm, some people must have been killed in the confusion. This makes me grieved." Then he issued an imperial ordered to send two hundred and seventy thousand bushels of rice to Jinling to provide relief to the hungry people.

By the end of December 975 Cao Bin sent Guo Shou Wen, a scholar in Hanlin Academy, to escort Li Yu, Li Yu's sons and brothers, and officials, forty-five in all, to Daliang. Li Yu was a poet. He wrote a poem to commemorate the day when he left Jinling:

> The state established by my grandfather has lasted for forty years,
> It has an area of over one thousand square kilometers with beautiful
> mountains and rivers.
> The grand palace buildings spread so wide that they connect with the sky,
> Thick mist hangs among the big trees in the gardens of the palace.
> I have never experienced any wars.
>
> Since I became a captive,
> I have become thin and my hair has turned white.
> The most heart-breaking moment is
> When I said good-bye to my ancestors in the ancestral temple,
> The band was playing the song of farewell.
> I stood there face to face with the palace maids with tears in my eyes.

Portrait of Li Yu, Master of the State of Jiangnan

On the way to Daliang, Li Yu was very worried because he had refused to accept the order of Emperor Zhao Kuang Yin demanding that he to go to the court, and he came to the court very late. He expressed his worry to

Guo Shou Wen. Guo Shou Wen comforted him by saying, "The Emperor's purpose is to unify the whole realm and maintain peace in the whole realm. He will not punish you for coming late." At these words Li Yu felt at ease. On 3 January 976 Li Yu arrived at Daliang. Emperor Zhao Kuang Yin sat at the top of Mingde Gate (the gate of the south city wall of Daliang) to receive the captives. Li Yu and all the other captives were dressed in white. They were waiting for Emperor Zhao Kuang Yin to declare the punishment he would give them. But Emperor Zhao Kuang Yin set them free and granted them clothes, horses and saddles, money, and other things. Xu Xuan was one of captives who followed Li Yu to Daliang. Emperor Zhao Kuang Yin asked him very sternly, "Why didn't you persuade Li Yu to come to my court earlier?" Xu Xuan answered, "I am a minister in the State of Jiangnan. Now that the State of Jiangnan has been destroyed, this is reason enough for me to deserve the death penalty. It is not necessary to ask any other questions." Emperor Zhao Kuang Yin said, "You are a devoted minister. You should serve me as devotedly as you have served Li Yu." Then he granted a seat to Xu Xuan and comforted him.

Then he summoned Zhang Ji. He asked Zhang Ji sternly, "You persuaded Li Yu not to surrender. This is the reason why Li Yu has come to the court so late." The Emperor showed a secret letter written by Zhang Ji to call for a rescuing army. Zhang Ji knelt down, touched his head to the ground and said calmly voice, "This letter was indeed written by me. This is only one of the many letters of the kind that I wrote. The dog barks at the man who is not his master. If I shall be executed today, it will be a worthy death. This shows that I have done my duty." At first Emperor Zhao Kuang Yin had really wanted to kill Zhang Ji. But having heard these words, he changed his mind. He said to Zhang Ji, "You are a man of courage and vision. I shall not punish you. From now on you should serve me as devotedly as you have served Li Yu."

On 7 January 976 Emperor Zhao Kuang Yin appointed Li Yu as the Great General of the Royal Guard army. He made Li Yu Marquis of Weiming (meaning the marquis who goes against the order of the emperor). He appointed Li Yu as the Minister of Works. He appointed Xu Xuan as an official under the Crown Prince in charge of the gate guards of the palace, and Zhang Ji as an official under the Crown Prince in charge of ceremonies.

On 12 February 976 Emperor Zhao Kuang Yin appointed Cao Bin as the Head of the Privy Council and concurrently Regional Military Governor of Zhongwu (in Xuzhou, now Xuzhou, Henan Province); he appointed Pan Mei as the Director of the Northern Court Affairs and concurrently Regional Military Governor of Shannandongdao (in Xiangfan, Hubei Province). Emperor Zhao Kuang Yin granted them these promotions in order to reward them for their great contributions in the conquering of the State of Jiangnan. Emperor Zhao Kuang Yin also granted Cao Bin five hundred thousand coins of money.

24. Qian Ti, King of the State of Wuyue, Goes to the Court of the
    Song Dynasty

When the war against the State of Jiangnan was still going on, Emperor
Zhao Kuang Yin summoned Ren Zhi Guo, the envoy sent by Qian Ti, to
the court of the Song Dynasty, and asked him to tell Qian Ti, "The Marshal
has made great military contributions in the expedition against the State
of Jiangnan. When the State of Jiangnan is conquered, he may come to see
me. I really want to meet with him. He does not need to stay here for a long
time. He will go back to his state after we meet with each other. This is an
earnest promise. I will not go back on my own words." When Ren Zhi Guo
went back to the State of Wuyue, he conveyed Emperor Zhao Kuang Yin's
intention to Qian Ti. Cui Ren Ji, an official in the State of Wuyue, said to
Qian Ti, "The Emperor of the Song Dynasty is a wise and mighty emperor. He
is invincible. He will unify the whole realm. In order to preserve the state and
protect the people, Your Majesty should go." Then Qian Ti made up his mind
to go to the court of the Song Dynasty. On 29 December 975 Qian Ti sent an
envoy to take a petition to Emperor Zhao Kuang Yin to ask permission to
have an audience with Emperor Zhao Kuang Yin during the period of the
Long Spring Festival (on 16 February) which was the birthday of Emperor
Zhao Kuang Yin. Emperor Zhao Kuang Yin gave his permission.

In February Qian Ti, his wife Lady Sun, his son Qian Wei Xun and Sun
Cheng You, the Regional Military Governor of the army of Pingjiang, started
their journey to Daliang. Emperor Zhao Kuang Yin sent his son Zhao De
Zhao to welcome Qian Ti and his party in Songzhou (now Shangqiu, Henan
Province). Before Qian Ti arrived, Emperor Zhao Kuang Yin personally made
an inspection to the Residence for Distinguished People to make sure that
everything had been ready for Qian Ti and his party. When Qian Ti and his
party came, they were invited to live in this grand residence. On 21 February
Qian Ti, Qian Wei Xun and Sun Cheng You went to Chongde Hall of the
palace to have an audience with Emperor Zhao Kuang Yin. Qian Ti presented
forty thousand ounces of silver and fifty thousand bolts of silk to Emperor
Zhao Kuang Yin as tribute. Emperor Zhao Kuang Yin granted Qian Ti grand
clothes and jade belts, one thousand ounces of gold wares and three thousand
ounces of silverwares. Then a grand banquet was held in Changchun Hall of
the palace. On 3 March Emperor Zhao Kuang Yin issued an imperial order
which read, "In ancient times, an Emperor showed the greatest grace to a
king or a minister who had made great contributions by allowing him to go
to the court to see the Emperor wearing a sword, or his name would not be
mentioned but only his title would be mentioned in an imperial order issued
to him. The King of Wuyue has made great contributions in the expedition
against the State of Jiangnan. I will allow the King of Wuyue to come to the
court to see me wearing a sword and only his title will be mentioned in my
imperial orders issued to him."

On 4 March Emperor Zhao Kuang Yin created Lady Sun, Qian Ti's wife,

Queen of the State of Wuyue. At that time the Premier said to Emperor Zhao Kuang Yin, "There is no precedent in history for creating the wife of a king as the queen when she has a family name other than the family name of the emperor." Emperor Zhao Kuang Yin said, "I will create this precedent. I do this in order to show my grace on Qian Ti."

Emperor Zhao Kuang Yin was going to make a trip to Louyang (now Luoyang, Henan Province), the Western Capital. Qian Ti wanted to follow Emperor Zhao Kuang Yin to Luoyang. But Emperor Zhao Kuang Yin did not agree. He let Qian Ti to go back to the State of Wuyue. Emperor Zhao Kuang Yin held a banquet in Jiangwu Hall of the palace to see him off. During the banquet, Emperor Zhao Kuang Yin said to Qian Ti, "The weather in the north and the weather in the south are different. It is now getting hot in this place. You'd better go back sooner." Qian Ti was moved to tears. He asked permission to come to the court to see Emperor Zhao Kuang Yin every three years. Emperor Zhao Kuang Yin said, "The way from the State of Wuyue to Daliang is very far. You may come when I issue an imperial order to summon you."

Before Qian Ti left, Emperor Zhao Kuang Yin gave him a yellow bag which was tightly sealed. Emperor Zhao Kuang Yin said to Qiang Ti, "You may secretly open the bag and read the things inside it on your way home." On his way back to the State of Wuyue, Qian Ti opened the bag. To his great surprise there were many petitions written by the ministers asking the Emperor to detain Qian Ti and not allow him to go back to the State of Wuyue. This made Qian Ti very afraid. When he got back home, he was very careful in everything he did. When he attended state affairs in Gongchen Hall in the palace of the State of Wuyue, he sat in the east corner of the hall. He said to his subordinates, "The capital of the Song Dynasty is on the northwest. That is where the Emperor is. I dare not go against his intention. I dare not do anything by my own will." So he contributed all the precious things in the palace of the State of Wuyue to Emperor Zhao Kuang Yin. And every time he sent tribute to Emperor Zhao Kuang Yin, he would display all the things in the court and burn incense and then send them to Emperor Zhao Kuang Yin.

25. Emperor Zhao Kuang Yin Makes a Trip to Luoyang, the Western Capital

On 9 March 976 Emperor Zhao Kuang Yin started his journey to Luoyang (now Luoyang, Henan Province) from Daliang. On 12 Mach Emperor Zhao Kuang Yin reached Gongxian (now Gongyi, Henan Province) where Anling Mausoleum, that is, his father Zhao Hong Yin and his mother Lady Du's tomb, was situated. Emperor Zhao Kuang Yin went to Anling Mausoleum to perform a memorial service for his father and mother. During the ceremony Emperor Zhao Kuang Yin cried bitterly. All the people attending the ceremony cried. After the ceremony, Emperor Zhao Kuang Yin went up a platform by the tomb. He asked his followers to give him a bow and a whistling arrow. Then he drew the bow in full and shot the whistling arrow in the direction of northwest. The whistling arrow flew through the air making its shrill sound, and then landed. Emperor Zhao Kuang Yin pointed at the place where the whistling arrow landed and said, "After I die, I will be buried there."

On 14 March Emperor Zhao Kuang Yin reached Luoyang. Emperor Zhao Kuang Yin was very happy to see the grand palaces in Luoyang. On 3 April Emperor Zhao Kuang Yin held a grand ceremony to offer sacrifices to Heaven and to the Earth in the south skirt of Luoyang. The old people of Luoyang were very happy to see Emperor Zhao Kuang Yin. They said, "We have experienced a very chaotic period and suffered so much. Now at last we have a chance to see the Emperor who has brought peace to the whole realm."

Emperor Zhao Kuang Yin was born in Luoyang. He liked the natural conditions and social customs of Luoyang. He intended to move the capital from Daliang to Luoyang. After the ceremony of offering sacrifices to Heaven and the Earth, it was time for him to go back to Daliang. But Emperor Zhao Kuang Yin lingered in Luoyang and did not want to go back. None of the officials dared to persuade him to go back.

Then Li Huai Zhong, the Commander-in-chief of the cavalry of the Royal Guards, went to see Emperor Zhao Kuang Yin and said to him, "Let's think about the Bian Canal leading to the Eastern Capital. Every year over a million bushels of rice are transported from the areas of the Yangtze River and the Huai River to Daliang through this canal. There are several hundred thousand soldiers in the capital area. The food supplies for these soldiers depend on this canal. If Your Majesty lives in Luoyang, how can so much food be obtained? And all the treasure houses and great armies are in Daliang. Our foundation has been laid solidly in Daliang. We should not do anything to harm this foundation." But Emperor Zhao Kuang Yin refused to take his advice. Zhao Guang Yi, King of Jin, tried his best to explain to Emperor Zhao Kuang Yin that moving the capital to Luoyang was not a proper step. Emperor Zhao Kuang Yin said, "Moving the capital to Luoyang is not my last step. Later I will move the capital from Luoyang to Chang'an." Zhao Guang Yi touched his head to the ground and still tried to persuade Emperor Zhao Kuang Yin to give up the idea of moving the capital to Luoyang. Emperor Zhao Kuang Yin said, "The purpose of moving the capital to the west is to make use of the natural barriers to protect the capital so as to reduce the number of the soldiers defending the capital. Emperor Gaozu of the Han Dynasty moved the capital from Luoyang to Chang'an. I will follow his example. My purpose is to bring peace to the whole realm." Zhao Guang Yi said, "The most important thing is to practice measures and polices beneficial to the well-being of the people. Protection by natural barriers is only secondary." Then Emperor Zhao Kuang Yin did not say anything more. After Zhao Guang Yi had gone out of the hall, Emperor Zhao Kuang Yin said to the officials attending him, "What the King of Jin said is correct. But within one hundred years the financial resources of the people will be exhausted."

On 7 April Emperor Zhao Kuang Yin informed the ministers that he would go back to the east. On 9 April the procession started from the palace of Luoyang. On 14 April Emperor Zhao Kuang Yin reached Daliang.

26. Emperor Zhao Kuang Yin and His Brothers and Sons

Emperor Zhao Kuang Yin had two younger brothers: Zhao Guang Yi and Zhao Guang Mei. In June 961, before Empress Dowager Du died, she had ordered Emperor Zhao Kuang Yin to pass the throne of the Song Dynasty to his younger brother Zhao Guang Yi when his turn came. Emperor Zhapo Kuang Yin had to accept her order and promised to pass the throne to Zhao Guang Yi after he died. Empress Dowager Du had asked Zhao Pu to write down Emperor Zhao Kuang Yin's vow to this effect, and as you may recall, the vow was kept in a gold safe in the palace.

In September 974, Emperor Zhao Kuang Yin created Zhao Guang Yi King of Jin. Zhao Guang Yi's residence was built on high ground. Water could not reach his residence. One day in June 976 Emperor Zhao Kuang Yin walked to Zhao Guang Yi's residence. He ordered craftsmen to build a big wheel to lift water to Zhao Guang Yi's residence. He personally supervised the progress of the project. Zhao Guang Yi had served in the position of the Governor of Kaifeng Area for fifteen years. He had done a very good job in the management of the capital area. Emperor Zhao Kuang Yin often visited Zhao Guang Yi after his daily work.

One day Zhao Guang Yi, King of Jin, was ill. He was so ill that he fainted away. When Emperor Zhao Kuang Yin heard about this, he hurried to Zhao Guang Yi's residence. Emperor Zhao Kuang Yin carried out moxibustion therapy by burning moxa for Zhao Guang Yi. Zhao Guang Yi felt painful when the burning moxa was put close to his skin. The Emperor also put the burning moxa close to his own skin. The treatment was carried out from eight in the morning. In three o'clock in the afternoon Zhao Guang Yi regained consciousness. Then Emperor Zhao Kuang Yin went back to the palace.

One night Emperor Zhao Kuang Yin held a banquet in the palace. Zhao Guang Yi drank a lot of wine and got drunk. When the banquet was over, he was so drunk that he could not mount his horse to go back. Emperor Zhao Kuan Yin personally supported King Zhao Guang Yi by the arm and walked down the steps of the hall. Then the guards helped Zhao Guang Yi to mount the horse and carefully supported Zhao Guang Yi on the horse. Emperor Zhao Kuang Yin saw this. He rewarded the guards handsomely. He said to the officials attending him, "The King of Jin walks like a dragon and a tiger. He will surely become the emperor who will unify the whole realm and bring peace to the people. He will enjoy greater fortune than mine."

Zhao Guang Mei was his second younger brother. In 960 Emperor Zhao Kuang Yin appointed him Commander-in-chief of the army in Jiazhou (now Leshan, Sichuan Province). In 961 Emperor Zhao Kuang Yin appointed him

Governor of Xingyuan (now Hanzhong, Shaanxi Province) and Regional Military Governor of Shannanxidao (also in the area of Hanzhong, Shaanxi Province). In 964 Emperor Zhao Kuang Yin made him Jointly Manager of Affairs with the Secretariat-Chancellery. In 973 Emperor Zhao Kuang Yin appointed him Grand Guardian and the Regional Military Governor of the Army of Yongxing (in Xi'an, Shaanxi Province). Zhao Guang Mei was never created a king during the reign of Emperor Zhao Kuang Yin although he gained much experience.

Emperor Zhao Kuang Yin had two sons: Zhao De Zhao and Zhao De Fang. In 964, Zhao De Zhao reached the age of six. According to the usual practice, when the son of an emperor reached the age of six he would be made king. But Emperor Zhao Kuang Yin did not made him a king. He just appointed Zhao De Zhao Commander-in-chief of the army in Guizhou (now Guixian, Guangxi Zhuang Autonomous Region). Since Emperor Zhao Kuang Yin had made a vow before his mother Empress Dowager Du to pass the throne to his younger brother Zhao Guang Yi, he did not make Zhao De Zhao crown prince although he was his eldest son. In 971 Emperor Zhao Kuang Yin appointed him Governor of Xingyuan (now Hanzhong, Shaanxi Province) and Regional Military Governor of Shannanxidao (also in the area of Hanzhong, Shaanxi Province), and Jointly Manager of Affairs with the Secretariat-Chancellery. During the reign of Emperor Zhao Kuang Yin, Zhao De Zhao was not made a king.

Emperor Zhao Kuang Yin's second son was Zhao De Fang. In 976 Zhao De Fang reached the age of six. But Zhao De Fang was not made king either. Emperor Zhao Kuang Yin appointed him Commander-in-chief of the army in Guizhou (now Guixian, Guangxi Zhuang Autonomous Region). During the reign of Emperor Zhao Kuang Yin Zhao De Fang was not made a king.

27. Emperor Zhao Kuang Yin's Last Effort to Conquer the State of Northern Han

On 13 August 976 Emperor Zhao Kuang Yin appointed Dang Jin, the Commander-in-chief of the cavalry of the Royal Guard Army, as the Commander-in-chief of the Cavalry and Infantry of the Hedong branch of the Army; he appointed Pan Mei, the Director of the Northern Court Affairs, as its Supervisor and the Commander-in-chief of its Right Branch; he appointed Yang Guang Mei as the Chief Supervisor. Niu Si Jin and Mi Wen Yi were commanders in this branch of the army. On 22 August they reached the area of Taiyuan. On 1 September the Song army under Dang Jin defeated the army of the State of Northern Han outside the city of Taiyuan. Liu Ji Yuan, King of the State of Northern Han, sent envoys to the State of Liao asking Yelu Xian, the Emperor of the State of Liao, to send an army to rescue Taiyuan. The Emperor of the State of Liao accordingly sent Yelu Sha, the Premier of the state of Liao, and Ta'er, King of Ji, to head an army and go to the rescue Taiyuan. But in October Emperor Zhao Kuang Yin passed away and Zhao Guang Yi ascended the throne of the Song Dynasty. Then Emperor Zhao Guang Yi ordered the generals to withdraw from Taiyuan back to Daliang.

28. Emperor Zhao Kuang Yin Passes Away

In October 976, Emperor Zhao Kuang Yin fell ill. On 19 October Emperor Zhao Kuang Yin ordered Wang Ji En, an attendant of the Emperor, to go to Jianlong Taoist Temple to prepare the settings for the ceremony to pray for good fortune. That night Emperor Zhao Kuang Yin summoned his brother Zhao Guang Yi to his bed chamber to have a long talk. When Zhao Guang Yi left the palace, it was already midnight.

In early morning of 20 October Emperor Zhao Kuang Yin passed away at the age of fifty. Empress Song was at his side. When she found that Emperor Zhao Kuang Yin had passed away, she sent Wang Ji En to summon Zhao De Fang, the second son of Emperor Zhao Kuang Yin, to the palace to ascend the throne. But Wang Ji En knew very well that Emperor Zhao Kuang Yin had been determined to pass the throne to Zhao Guang Yi. So he did not go to the residence of Zhao De Fang, but he went directly to the residence of the Governor of Kaifeng Area to summon Zhao Guang Yi. When he reached the residence, he saw Cheng De Yuan, an official of the Office of the Governor of Kaifeng Area, sitting by the gate of the residence. Then they both knocked at the gate of the residence. A servant opened the gate and let them in. When they met Zhao Guang Yi in the hall, Wang Ji En told Zhao Guang Yi that Emperor Zhao Kuang Yin had passed away and that Zhao Guang Yi should go to the palace immediately to ascend the throne.

Zhao Guang Yi was shocked when he learned that Emperor Zhao Kuang Yin had passed away. But as for ascending the throne, he hesitated and said, "I should discuss this matter with my family members." Then he left the hall and went into the inner room. He stayed in the inner room for a long time. Wang Ji En went into the inner room and said to Zhao Guang Yi, "If you hesitate for long, the throne will be taken by another person." Then Zhao Guang Yi decided to go to the palace immediately. At that time it was snowing hard. They walked against the snow to the palace. When they reached the palace, Wang Ji En asked Zhao Guang Yi to stay in the room for the attendants on duty outside the bed chamber of the palace and said to Zhao Guang Yi, "Will you wait here? I will go into the bed chamber to report to the Empress first." But Cheng De Yuan said to Zhao Guang Yi, "Your Highness should go into the bed chamber directly. It is not necessary to wait outside." Then Zhao Guang Yi, Cheng De Yuan and Wang Ji En went directly to the bed chamber of Emperor Zhao Kuang Yin.

Wang Ji En entered the bed chamber first. Empress Song asked him, "Has De Fang come?" Wang Ji En answered, "the King of Jin has come." Empress Song was very surprised to see Zhao Guang Yi. She said to Zhao Guang Yi, "King of Jin, we shall entrust our lives to your protection." Zhao Guang Yi wept and said, "Don't worry. I guarantee that you and my nephews will enjoy high status and wealth."

Emperor Zhao Kuang Yin was buried in Yongchangling Mausoleum in Gongxian (now Gongyi, Henan Province). His temple title was Taizu (supreme ancestor, founder of the dynasty).

In the period of Five Dynasties and Ten States, the whole realm of China had been was in chaos. Zhao Kuang Yin rose from the ranks of the army and became Emperor. All the powerful local magnates submitted to him. He conquered the states one by one. He tried his best to unify the whole realm of China and bring peace and better living conditions to the people. He was on the throne for seventeen years. He established the Song Dynasty which lasted for more than three hundred years. He is regarded by the historians as one of the greatest emperors in Chinese history.

1. Zhao Guang Yi Ascends the Throne of the Song Dynasty

On 21 October 976 Zhao Guang Yi ascended the throne of the Song Dynasty. On 26 October Emperor Zhao Guang Yi appointed his younger brother as the Governor of Kaifeng Area (the area of Daliang, the capital) and Head of the Secretariat. This brother was called Zhao Ting Mei (his original name was Zhao Guang Mei; in order to avoid the second word "Guang" in his name, being the same in the name of Emperor Zhao Guang Yi, his name was changed into Zhao Ting Mei). Emperor Zhao Guang Yi made Zhao Ting Mei King of Qi. Emperor Zhao Guang Yi appointed Zhao De Zhao, the late Emperor's elder son, as the Regional Military Governor of Yongxing (in Chang'an, now Xi'an, Shaanxi Province) and a Manager of Governmental Affairs. Emperor Zhao Guang Yi made Zhao De Zhao King of Wugong Prefecture. He appointed Zhao De Fang, the second son of the late Emperor, Regional Military Governor of Shannanxidao (in Xingyuanfu, now Hanzhong, Shaanxi Province) and a Manager of Governmental Affairs. He appointed Xue Ju Zheng, the Premier, as the Head of the Executive Bureau; he appointed Shen Lun another Head of the Executive Bureau. He appointed Lu Duo Xun as the Head of the Secretariat and a Manager of Governmental Affairs. He appointed Cao Bin, the Head of Chancellery Council, to be a Manager of Governmental Affairs.

In March 977, Zhao Pu, the Regional Military Governor of Heyang (now Mengxian, Henan Province), came to have an audience with Emperor Zhao Guang Yi. He asked Emperor Zhao Guang Yi's permission to let him go to visit the Mausoleum of the late Emperor. Emperor Zhao Guang Yi gave the permission. After visiting the late Emperor's mausoleum, he came back to Daliang. On 18

March, Emperor Zhao Guang Yi appointed Zhao Pu as the Protector of the Crown Prince and Zhao Pu would stay in Daliang.

Statue of Zhao Guang Yi, Emperor Taizong of the Song Dynasty

2. Qian Ti, the King of the State of Wuyue, Hands over the State of Wuyue to Emperor Zhao Guang Yi

In March 978, Qian Ti, the King of the State of Wuyue, started his journey to Daliang to have an audience with Emperor Zhao Guang Yi. When he left Hangzhou (now Hangzhou, Zhejiang Province), the capital of the State of Wuyue, he brought with him fifty thousand ounces of silver, a million coins of money, a hundred thousand bolts of silk and ten thousand catties of tea. He would present these things as tribute to Emperor Zhao Guang Yi so that the Emperor would let him go back to the State of Wuyue after his visit to Daliang. On 25 March, Qian Ti reached Daliang. He went into the palace to have an audience with Emperor Zhao Guang Yi in Chongde Hall of the Palace. On that day Emperor Zhao Guang Yi held a grand banquet in Changchun Hall of the Palace. Cui Ren Ji, a minister of the State of Wuyue, who had followed Qian Ti to Daliang, was also present at the banquet.

On 25 April Chen Hong Jin, the Regional Military Governor of Pinghai and the actual ruler of the area of Zhangzhou and Quanzhou, presented a memorandum to Emperor Zhao Guang Yi to announce that he would hand over Zhangzhou Prefecture (now Zhangzhou, Fujian Province) and Quanzhou Prefecture (now Quanzhou, Fujian Province) which were under his jurisdiction to the Song Dynasty, and these two prefectures were added to the territory of the Song Dynasty. There were fourteen counties and one hundred and fifty thousand households in these two prefectures. On 29 April Emperor Zhao Guang Yi appointed Chen Hong Jin as the Regional Military Governor of Wuning (in Xuzhou, now Xuzhou, Jiangsu Province) and concurrently as a Manager of Governmental Affairs; he appointed Chen Hong Jin's son Chen Wen Xian as the Governor of Quanzhou and he appointed Chen Wen Yi, Chen Hong Jin's another son, as the Governor of Zhangzhou.

Premier Lu Duo Xun succeeded in persuading Emperor Zhao Guang Yi not to let Qian Ti to go back to the State of Wuyue but to detain Qian Ti in Daliang. At that time Chen Hon Jin handed over the prefectures of Zhangzhou and Quanzhou. This made Qian Ti very afraid. Then he offered to hand over the whole army in the State of Wuyue to Emperor Zhao Guang Yi and asked the Emperor to let him go back to the State of Wuyue. But still Emperor Zhao Guang Yi refused to let him go. Qian Ti was at a total loss as to what he should do. Cui Ren Ji said to Qian Ti, "The intention of the Emperor is very clear. If Your Highness does not hand over the whole State of Wuyue to the Emperor, great trouble will come." All the other officials of Wuyue who had followed Qian Ti to Daliang were strongly against Cui Ren Ji's suggestion. But Cui Ren Ji said in a very firm voice, "We are under the control of the Emperor. We are more than five hundred kilometers way from our home state. We could only leave here if we had wings to fly with." So Qian Ti made up his mind to hand over the State of Wuyue to Emperor Zhao Guang Yi, and he presented a memorandum. On 1 May Emperor Zhao Guang

Yi held a ceremony in Qianyuan Hall of the palace to accept Qian Ti's offer to hand over the State of Wuyue. There were thirteen prefectures, eighty-six counties and five hundred and fifteen thousand and six hundred and eighty households in the State of Wuyue. When the news that Qian Ti had handed over the State of Wuyue to the Emperor of the Song Dynasty, all the officials in the State of Wuyue cried and said, "Our King will never come back again!"

On 3 May Emperor Zhao Guang Yi made Qian Ti King of the State of Huaihai; he appointed Qian Wei Xun, Qian Ti's elder son, as the Regional Military Governor of Huainan (in Yangzhou, now Yangzhou, Jiangsu Province); he appointed Qian Wei Zhi, Qian Ti's younger son, as the Regional Military Governor of Zhenguo (in Shaanzhou, now Sanmenxia, in the west part of Henan Province).

3. The Death of Li Yu

When Zhao Guang Yi ascended the throne, he issued an order to remove Li Yu's title of Marquis of Weiming (meaning the marquis who goes against the order of the emperor) and made Li Yu Duke of Longxi Prefecture. In 977 Li Yu told Emperor Zhao Guang Yi that he was in poverty. Emperor Zhao Guang Yi increased his monthly provision and granted him three million coins of money. One day Emperor Zhao Guang Yi paid a visit to Chongwenyuan Library. He sent his attendants to ask Li Yu and Liu Chang to come to the library. When Li Yu came, Emperor Zhao Guang Yi said to him, "I hear that when you were in the State of Jiangnan, you liked reading books very much. Many of the books in this library originally belonged to you. After you have come to court, do you still read books?" Li Yu nodded and expressed his thanks to the Emperor.

Since Li Yu was captured and escorted to Daliang, he had lived in sadness. He often thought of his fallen state and the life as a king in the palace in Jinling of the State of Jiangnan. He wrote many poems to express his feelings. The most famous one was as the follows:

> Flowers are in bloom every spring
> The full moon is bright every autumn
> My sad days as a captured king seem to have no end
> I had many happy days in the past
> Last night when I was sitting in the small house
> I heard the east wind blowing again
> Under the bright moon I thought of my fallen state
>
> The grand palace buildings should still be there
> Only the color of the faces of the palace maids has changed
> If I am asked, How much sadness are you holding?
> It is as much as the water in the Yangtze River flowing east in springtime.

On 7 July 978 Li Yu died at the age of forty-two. To mourn his death, Emperor Zhao Guang Yi held no court for three days. He granted Li Yu posthumously the title of Grand Tutor and conferred him posthumously the King of Wu.

4. Expedition against the State of Northern Han

One day in January 979 Emperor Zhao Guang Yi summoned Cao Bin, the Head of the Privy Council, to the palace and asked him, "Emperor Shizong of the Zhou Dynasty and Emperor Taizu of our Dynasty both personally carried out campaigns against Taiyuan but could not take it. Is the city of Taiyuan so strong that it cannot be taken?" Cao Bin Answered, "During the expedition commanded by Emperor Zhizong of the Zhou Dynasty his general Shi Chao was defeated in Shilingguan Pass. The soldiers of the Zhou Dynasty were shocked. This is the reason why Emperor Shizong of the Zhou Dynasty had to withdraw his army back to his capital. During the expedition commanded by Emperor Taizu the Song army camped in the grasslands. Many soldiers contracted diarrhea. Then Emperor Taizu had to halt the attack of Taiyuan and withdraw the army back to Daliang. It is not because the city of Taiyuan is very strong and cannot be taken." Emperor Zhao Guang Yi said, "Well, I plan to raise a great army to attack Taiyuan. What do you think?" Cao Bin said, "Now our troops are well-equipped and highly combat effective. And they are keen on taking Taiyuan. If Your Majesty commands these troops to carry out such an expedition, it will be as easy as crushing dry weeds and smashing rotten wood." Then Emperor Zhao Guang Yi made up his mind to carry out the expedition against the State of Northern Han and take Taiyuan.

Premier Due Ju Zheng said to Emperor Zhao Guang Yi, "In the past Emperor Shizong of the Zhou Dynasty raised an army to attack Taiyuan. The King of the State of Northern Han depended on the army from the State of Khitan to come and support him and would not go out of the city of Taiyuan to fight the army of the Zhou Dynasty. Then the troops of the army of the Zhou Dynasty were exhausted and had to withdraw from Taiyuan. Emperor Taizu of our dynasty defeated the Khitan army in the area to the south of Yanmenguan Pass. Emperor Taizu ordered all the people in the area of Taiyuan to move to the area south of the Yellow River. Although Taiyuan was left untaken, it is already in a very difficult situation. If we take it, our territory would not be expanded very much. If we leave it untaken, it will not cause much trouble. I hope Your Majesty will think it over carefully before Your Majesty makes a decision." Emperor Zhao Guang Yi said, "Although we are planning to do the same thing, the situation has changed greatly. When the late Emperor defeated the Khitan army and moved the people around Taiyuan to the south of the Yellow River, he was exactly making preparations for our action today. Say no more. I have made up my mind."

On 8 January 979 Emperor Zhao Guang Yi appointed Pan Mei, the Director of the Northern Court Affairs, as the Commander-in-chief of the army of the North Branch; he ordered Generals Cui Yan Jin, Li Han Qiong,

Cao Han and Liu Yu each to command his army to attack one side of the city of Taiyuan. According the order, Liu Yu should be in charge of attacking the west side of the city of Taiyuan. The west side of the city of Taiyuan was the place where the palace of the State of Northern Han was situated. The topography there was perilous and very difficult to attack. General Liu Yu wanted to change places with General Cao Han. But General Cao Han refused. General Liu Yu insisted. This matter was discussed for a long time and no decision was made. Emperor Zhao Guang Yi worried that the generals could not coordinated their actions properly. So he said to General Cao Han, "You are both intelligent and courageous. Nobody but you can be in charge of attacking the west side of the city of Taiyuan." Then Cao Han accepted the order of the Emperor.

On 9 January Emperor Zhao Guang Yi appointed Guo Jin as the Commander-in-chief of the Song army in the Shilingguan Pass (in Yangqu, Shanxi Province) which was an important pass leading to Taiyuan from north. His task was to prevent the army of the State of Liao from coming to rescue Taiyuan. Guo Jin was a brave general. He was given the title of the field commander of Yunzhou (now Datong, Shanxi Province), but he was actually appointed as the commander-in-chief of the army stationed in Xingzhou (now Xingtai, Hebei Province). He had followed Emperor Zhao Kuang Yin to attack the State of Northern Han. He was the most proper person to guard Shilingguan Pass.

As early as in March 974 Emperor Zhao Kuang Yin had sent envoys to hold a peace talk with the Emperor of the State of Liao. The Emperor of the State of Liao sent Yelu Chang Zhu, the Governor of Zhuozhou of the State of Liao, to Daliang and a peace agreement between the Song Dynasty and the State of Liao was made. When Yelu Xian, the Emperor of the State of Liao, heard that Emperor Zhao Guang Yi was making preparation to attack Taiyuan, he sent Daima Chang Shou to Daliang to see Emperor Zhao Guang Yi. When he was received by Emperor Zhao Gaung Yi, he asked the Emperor, "On what basis are you preparing to attack the State of Northern Han?" Emperor Zhao Guang Yi said, "The King of the State of Northern Han has gone against my order. I will raise an army to punish him. If the Emperor of your state does not send any army to help the State of Northern Han, the peace agreement is still in effect. If he sends armies to rescue the State of Northern Han, then we will have to fight each other in the battle field."

On 13 January Emperor Zhao Guang Yi held a banquet in Changchun Hall of the palace to entertain Pan Mei and the other generals who were going to carry out the expedition. During the banquet Emperor Zhao Guang Yi gave instructions to Pan Mei and the other generals on strategy and tactics of the expedition against the State of Northern Han. Liu Chang, the captured King of the State of Southern Han, Qian Ti, the former King of the State of Wuyue who had been detained in Daliang, and Chen Hong Jin who had handed over Quanzhou and Zhangzhou which had been under his jurisdiction to Emperor Zhao Guang Yi, were present at the banquet. Liu Chang said to Emperor Zhao Guang Yi, "Your Majesty's resounding fame is heard afar. All the former kings who had occupied a part of the realm are now present at this banquet. When the State of Northern Han is conquered and Li Ji Yuan is captured and is brought here, I hope Your Majesty will make me the head of the captured kings because I am the first one who was captured and brought here!" When Emperor Zhao Guang Yi heard his words, he burst out laughing. Emperor Zhao Guang Yi awarded Liu Chang handsomely for his words.

On 6 February Emperor Zhao Guang Yi appointed Premier Shen Lun as the Commander-in-chief of the army defending Daliang, the capital, and concurrently in charge of the affairs in the capital area; he appointed Wang Ren Zhan, the Head of the Office in charge of the General Affairs of the Palace, as the Commander-in-chief of the Army Defending the Palace. Emperor Zhao Guang Yi intended to appoint Zhao Ting Mei, King of Qi, to stay behind and take charge of the affairs in the capital. Lü Duan, an official in the Office of the Governor of Kaifeng Area, said to Zhao Ting Mei, "His Majesty is going on an expedition in the face of all kinds of danger. You are His Majesty's closest relative. You should go with His Majesty on the expedition. It is not proper for you to stay behind." So Zhao Ting Mei asked permission from Emperor Zhao Guang Yi to go on the expedition with the Emperor. The Emperor gave permission.

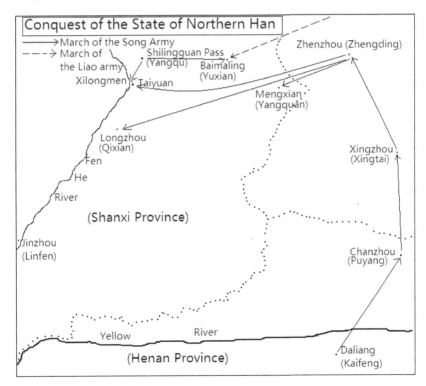

Conquest of the State of Northern Han

On 15 February Liu Ji Yuan, the King of the State of Northern Han, sent an envoy to the State of Liao to ask the Emperor of the State of Liao to send armies to relieve Taiyuan. The Emperor of the State of Liao appointed Yelu Sha, the premier of the State of Liao, as the Commander-in-chief of the army sent to Taiyuan; he appointed Ta'er, King of Yi, as the Supervisor of this army. He also ordered Yelu Sezhen, the King of the South Court of the State of Liao, to command the troops under him to rescue Taiyuan.

On 14 February Emperor Zhao Guang Yi started out from Daliang. On 18 February he reached Chanzhou (now Puyang, Henan Province). Song Jie, an official from a place by the Yellow River presented a memorandum to Emperor Zhao Guang Yi by the roadside. When Emperor Zhao Guang Yi had read the memorandum and knew his name, he shouted with great joy, "Our army will be victorious!" Because in the name of Song Jie, the first word "Song" means "the Song Dynasty" or "the Song army", the second word "Jie" means "victorious." The two words "Song" and "Jie" put together means "The Song army will be victorious." Emperor Zhao Guang Yi thought it was a good omen for the Song Dynasty. So he promoted Song Jie to a high ranking position.

On 24 February Emperor Zhao Guang Yi reached Xingzhou (now Xingtai, Hebei Province). On 1 March Emperor Zhao Guang Yi reached Zhenzhou (now Zhengding, Hebei Province). Emperor Zhao Guang Yi ordered Yin Xun, the Governor of Yingzhou, to command an army to lay siege to the city of Longzhou (now Qixian, Shanxi Province) because Longzhou was a stronghold that prevented the Song army from attacking the city of Taiyuan from the south. On 2 March, Emperor Zhao Guang Yi ordered Qi Ting Chen, the Commander-in-chief of the infantry and cavalry stationed in Zhenzhou, to command his army to attack Mengxian (now Yangquan, Shanxi Province).

General Guo Jin went to Shilingguan Pass to take up his position as the commander-in-chief of the Song army stationed in Shilingguan Pass. Tian Qin Zuo was the supervisor of the army stationed in Shilingguan Pass. Tian Qin Zuo did not get along well with General Guo Jin, the commander-in-chief of the army stationed in Shilingguan Pass. On 8 March the Song army under General Guo Jin defeated the Northern Han army in the stronghold of Xilongmen (now a place 15 kilometers north to Taiyuan, Shanxi Province). Yelu Sha, the Premier of the State of Liao, and Ta'er, King of Ji of the State of Liao, commanded their armies to rescue Taiyuan. On 16 March the Liao army under Yelu Sha and Ta'er reached Baimaling (in Yuxian, Shanxi Province). A wide brook lay before the Liao army. The Song army under General Guo Jin had been deployed on the southern bank of the brook. Yelu Sha and his generals wanted to wait for the rear army. But Ta'er and Muji insisted that they should attack the Song army immediately. Yelu Sha could not convince them. Then Ta'er commanded the vanguards to cross the brook. When half of the Liao army had crossed the Brook, General Guo Ji●n commanded the cavalrymen to ride forward to attack the Liao troops. The Liao army was defeated. Ta'er and his son Huage, Yelu Sha's sons Yelu Delin and Yelu Lingguen, Yelu Tumin and Yelu Tanggu were all killed in battle. It happened that Yelu Sezhen, the King of the South Court of the State of Liao, had arrived with the rescuing army. He ordered his troops to shoot arrows at the Song troops. Then the Song troops had to retreat. Yelu Sha and Muji had a narrow escape.

Liu Ji Yuan, the King of the State of Northern Han, sent an envoy to go through side roads to take a letter to the State of Liao to ask the Emperor of the State of Liao to rescue Taiyuan. But the envoy was captured by the Song soldiers under General Guo Jin. The General ordered his soldiers to escort the envoy to the city of Taiyuan and showed him to the Northern Han troops on the top of the city of Taiyuan. The troops of the State of Northern Han were disheartened.

On 3 April Lu Jun, Liu Ji Yuan's son-in-law, rode to the State of Liao from Daizhou (now Daixian, Shanxi Province) to ask the Emperor of the State of Liao to send armies to rescue Taiyuan. But the Emperor of the State of Liao would not send any rescuing army because the rescuing army formerly sent had been defeated and no more army could be sent.

On 14 April Emperor Zhao Guang Yi started from Zhenzhou for Taiyuan. On 22 April Emperor Zhao Guang Yi reached Taiyuan. He camped on the east bank of Fenshui River. On 23 April Emperor Zhao Guang Yi made an inspection on the camps of the Song army and the city attacking equipments such as stone launchers and ladders on the west side of Taiyuan. He brought gifts to the generals and soldiers who were attacking this side of the city. He sent an envoy to take a letter written by him to the gate of the city of Taiyuan demanding Liu Ji Yuan, King of the State of Northern Han, to surrender. But the gate guards did not dare to accept the letter.

On the early morning of 24 April Emperor Zhao Guang Yi personally supervised the generals and men to attack the west side of the city of Taiyuan. Jing Si, an officer, commanded the soldiers under him to climb up to the top of the city wall by ladders. Jing Si was the first one who got to the top of the city wall. He fought very bravely and killed several Northern Han soldiers. But he was hit by two arrows in the leg and his face was hit by a stone — two of his teeth were broken. But still he fought on bravely. Emperor Zhao Guang Yi saw this, and he ordered soldiers to carry him down. He granted Jing Si a silk robe and a silver belt. Emperor Zhao Guang Yi wore armor and commanded the generals and men to attack the city against arrows and stones. The ministers attending him tried to persuade him to stay in a safe place. But Emperor Zhao Guang Yi said, "The generals and men are fighting in the rain of arrows at the risk of their lives. How can I just sit and watch?" When the generals and men heard of this, they fought all the more bravely and tried to get to the top of the city wall at the risk of their lives. More than ten thousand soldiers were deployed in battle formations in front of the Emperor. They shot arrows to the city of Taiyuan. The arrows struck on the city of Taiyuan like the spines of hedgehogs. The soldiers of the Song army captured a Northern Han soldier. This soldier told the soldiers of the Song army that the King of the State of Northern Han had bought each arrow collected by the people in the city for ten coins. He had collected a million of them and stored them in a store house. When Emperor Zhao Guang Yi heard of this, he laughed and said, "He has stored these arrows for me!"

On 27 April Emperor Zhao Guang Yi went to the south side of the city of Taiyuan. The soldiers of the Song army had built shelters against the hail of arrows and stones that assailed them from the top of the city wall by erecting wooden poles and stretching leather skins between the tops of the poles. On that day, General Li Han Qiong commanded his troops to climb the city wall with ladders. General Li Han Qiong was the first to reach the top. He was hit by arrows in his head and his hand. He fought on valiantly, despite being seriously wounded. Emperor Zhao Guang Yi sent an envoy to bring Li Han Qiong to his tent and personally examined his wounds. He treated Li Han Qiong with very good medicine. Emperor Zhao Guang Yi wanted to go out to the shelters to extend his regards to the soldiers. Li Han Qiong wept and said, "It's far too dangerous, with arrows and stones flying everywhere. The shelters are no place for our Emperor. Why should Your Majesty ignore your own safety when we are fighting to protect you and the realm? If Your Majesty does not listen to me, I will die first." So Emperor Zhao Guang Yi gave up the idea of visiting the soldiers in the field.

On 1 May Emperor Zhao Guang Yi went to the southwest corner of the city wall of Taiyuan to supervise the Song army's night attack on the city. In the early morning the Song troops took the outer wall of Taiyuan. Fan Chao, the head of the Office of Palace Affairs of the State of Northern Han, exited the city to surrender. But the Song soldiers thought that he was coming out to fight. So they captured him and presented him to Emperor Zhao Guang Yi. The Emperor ordered him to be executed under the great banner of the Emperor. But on the next day Fan Chao's wife and sons were all executed by the officials of the State of Northern Han and their heads were flung down from of the city wall. On 3 May, Emperor Zhao Guang Yi went to the northwest corner of the city wall of Taiyuan. Guo Wan Chao, the Commander-in-chief of the infantry and cavalry of the Northern Han army, came out of the city to surrender.

The next day, Emperor Zhao Guang Yi went to the south side of the city wall. He said to the generals in charge of attacking this side of the city, "Tomorrow will be May 5. It is an important festival. We shall hold a banquet to celebrate this festival inside the city of Taiyuan." Then he personally wrote an imperial order demanding Liu Ji Yuan, the King of the State of Northern Han, to surrender. That evening there was a big white cloud in the shape of a man hanging in the sky over the city of Taiyuan.

On 5 May the Emperor went back to the south side of the city wall to supervise his Generals and men. The Song army fought very bravely and they all vied to be the first to the top of the city wall. Emperor Zhao Guang Yi worried that the Song troops would start slaughtering the people when they got into the city. So he ordered the Song troops to back off a little bit. The Northern Han soldiers still wanted to defend the city. Ma Feng, one of the premiers of the State of Northern Han, was ill and had stayed home. He went to see Liu Ji Yuan, the King of the State of Northern Han. He told Liu Ji Yuan that the State of Northern Han was doomed to fall and he succeeded in persuading Liu Ji Yuan to surrender. At night, Liu Ji Yuan sent Li Xun, the official in charge of foreign relations, to take a letter to Emperor Zhao Guang Yi offering his surrender.

Emperor Zhao Guang Yi was very glad. He immediately sent Xue Wen Bao, an official in the department of Foreign Affairs, to take a letter into the city of Taiyuan to console Liu Ji Yuan and the officials of the State of Northern Han. At midnight Emperor Zhao Guang Yi went up to the platform at the top of the Southern part of the city wall of Taiyuan. He held a grand banquet to entertain all the ministers and generals who had followed him to attack the city. And in that place Emperor Zhao Guang Yi accepted the surrender of Liu Ji Yu, the King of the State of Northern Han.

In the early morning of 6 May, Liu Ji Yuan and his officials, all dressed in white and wearing white caps, knelt down on the platform a top the southern part of the city wall and waited to hear their sentences. Emperor Zhao Guang Yi issued an imperial order to set all of them free. Then he consoled them. Liu Ji Yuan touched his head to the ground and said, "When I heard that Your Majesty would personally come to Taiyuan, I wanted to surrender to Your Majesty. But some of the officials abducted me to prevent me from doing it." Emperor Zhao Guang Yi ordered to find those who had abducted Liu Ji Yu and put them all to death. Emperor Zhao Guang Yi turned to Qian Ti, the former King of the State of Wuyue, and said, "You handed over the State of Wuyue to me and you have come over to me. This was done peacefully without a battle. This was a major contribution to the people and the realm."

The State of Northern Han was conquered, with its ten prefectures, forty-one counties and thirty-five thousand two hundred and twenty households in this state. Emperor Zhao Guang Yi appointed Liu Bao Xun, a high ranking official in the Ministry of Rituals, as the Governor of the Taiyuan Area.

On 11 May Emperor Zhao Guang Yi appointed Liu Ji Yuan as the Grand General of the Royal Guards and made him Duke of Pengcheng Prefecture. On 17 May Emperor Zhao Guang Yi ordered that Liu Ji Yuan and all his relatives be escorted to Daliang, the capital of the Song Dynasty.

5. Emperor Zhao Guang Yi's Expedition against the State of Liao and His Efforts to Take Back the Territory of Youzhou and Jizhou

Emperor Zhao Guang Yi decided it was time for a campaign against the State of Liao to take back the territory of Youzhou (now the area of Beijing) and Jizhou (now the area around Jixian, Hebei Province) which had been ceded to the State of Khitan by Shi Jing Tang, the Emperor of the Later Jin Dynasty, in 938. On 22 May, Emperor Zhao Guang Yi and his army started out from Taiyuan. On 29 May Emperor Zhao Guang Yi arrived at Zhenzhou (now Zhengding, Hebei Province). The generals were not actually willing to go along with this, because they had fought in the area of Taiyuan for more than three months and they were very tired. But none of them said anything against the Emperor's decision. Hou Cui Han, the Supervisor of the Royal Guards, said to the Emperor, "We must seize the momentum brought by our victory over the State of Northern Han and carry out the expedition against the State of Liao now, so that we do not need to go to the north again. If we exploit the favorable situation, we are sure to defeat the State of Liao. This is a rare chance that we cannot afford to lose." Emperor Zhao Guang Yi was pleased to hear these words, and he sent a secret envoy to go back to Daliang to ask Cao Bin, the Head of Privy Council, to send armies to the north.

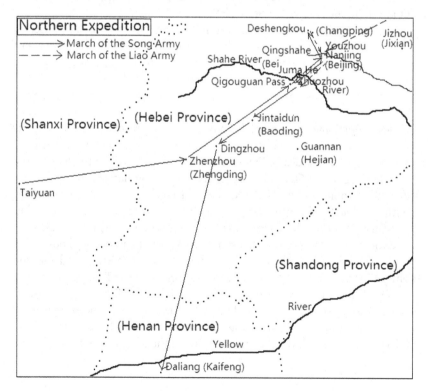

On 12 June, Emperor Zhao Guang Yi left Zhenzhou to start his northern expedition against the State of Liao. Six armies had followed Emperor Zhao Guang Yi to Zhenzhou. Some of the armies did not come along immediately. Emperor Zhao Guang Yi was enraged. He wanted to punish the generals and officers of these armies according to military law. Zhao Yan Pu, an officer, said to Emperor Zhao Guang Yi, "Our task is to carry out an expedition against the State of Liao. Our enemies are the generals and officers of the State of Liao. Now our enemies have not been defeated but our generals and officers are being punished. Who will be willing to render their services for Your Majesty in the future?" Emperor Zhao Guang Yi accepted his advice.

On 18 June Emperor Zhao Guang Yi reached Qigouguan Pass, 20 kilometers southwest of Zhuozhou (now Zhuozhou, Hebei Province) in the territory of the State of Liao. Emperor Zhao Guang Yi wore armor and personally commanded the Song troops to prepare to attack the Pass. Liu Yu, the Governor of Qigouguan Pass of the State of Liao, surrendered. Emperor Zhao Guang Yi left one thousand troops to defend Qigouguan Pass.

Yelu Xida, a king of the State of Liao, deployed the soldiers under him along the east bank of Shahe River (now Bei Juma He River, which is situated to the north of the city of Zhuozhou) to wait for the Song army to come. Kong Shou Zhen, a general of the Song army, commanded the troops under him to reach there first. He commanded the Song troops under him to attack the battle formation of the army of the State of Liao. Then the main force of the Song army arrived. They defeated Liao troops under Yelu Xida and captured more than five hundred Liao soldiers. On 20 June Emperor Zhao Guang Yi and his armies reached Zhuozhou. Liu Yuan Hou, the Governor of Zhuozhou of the State of Liao, surrendered.

On 22 June Emperor Zhao Guang Yi and his armies reached south to Nanjing (meaning Southern Capital) (formerly Youzhou, now Beijing) of the State of Liao. Yelu Sezhen, the King of the South Court of the State of Liao, knew very well that the coming Song armies were too strong to fight. He thought of a way to deal with them. He knew that the Song armies had recently defeated the troops of the State of Liao under Yelu Xida and had no respect for such troops. So he ordered his troops to take the green banners from the troops under Yelu Xida and pretend that they were also Yelu Xida's troops. They were deployed in Deshengkou (to the northwest of Changping, Hebei Province) to lure the Song army. Emperor Zho Guang Yi sent troops to attack the Liao troops in Deshengkou. The Song troops fought hard and killed more than one thousand Liao soldiers. But suddenly Yelu Sezhen commanded the Liao troops under him to launch a surprise attack on the rear of the Song troops. The Song troops had to retreat. Then Yelu Sezhen commanded his troops to march forward and stationed his troops on the north bank of Qingshahe River (which ran through the south of Qinghe ten kilometers north to Beijing). These Liao troops under Yelu Sezhen were ready to rescue Nanjing.

On 24 June, Emperor Zhao Guang Yi ordered his generals to attack the city of Nanjing. Song Wo, the Regional Military Governor of Dingguo, commanded his troops to attack from the south; Cui Yan Jin, the Regional Military Governor of Heyang, commanded his troops to attack from the north; Liu Yu, the Regional Military Governor of Zhangxin, commanded his troops to attack from the east; Meng Yuan Zhe, the Regional Military Governor of Dingwu, commanded his troops to attack from the west. Emperor Zhao Guang Yi appointed Pan Mei, the Director of the Northern Court Affairs, to take charge of the affairs of Youzhou. Han De Rang, the Commander-in-chief of the Liao army defending Nanjing, was very afraid. He went up to the top of the city wall and supervised the defense of Nanjing day and night. Song troops surrounding the city and shouted loud threats. Yelu Xuegu, a general of the State of Liao, had commanded an army to station outside the city of Nanjing. When he saw that the Song army had surrounded the city of Nanjing, he ordered the soldiers to dig a tunnel into the city of Nanjing. Then he led his troops into the city of Nanjing through the tunnel and joined forces with the Liao army under Han De Rang. Yelu Xuegu and Han De Rang ordered the soldiers to repair the city defense equipment and inspired the soldiers to defend the city resolutely. At night three hundred Song troops climbed up the city wall by ladders. Yelu Xuegu led his troops in beating them back.

On 29 June, Yelu Xian, the Emperor of the State Liao, knew that Nanjing had been surrounded. He order Yelu Sha, the Premier of Nanjing, to command a great army to rescue Nanjing. Yelu Xiuge, the official in charge of the affairs of the royal clan of the State of Liao, understood that the situation was critical. He went to ask permission from Emperor Yelu Xian to command an army to rescue Nanjing. Then Emperor Yelu Xian ordered Yelu Xiuge to replace Yelu Xida.

On 2 July Liu Yan Su, the Regional Military Governor of Jianxiong of the State of Liao came to surrender. On 4 July Liu Shou En, the Governor of Jizhou (now Jixian, Hebei Province) of the State of Liao, also surrendered.

Emperor Zhao Guang Yi supervised the generals and men in an attack on Nanjing, but the generals and men did not put their hearts into it. General Cao Han and General Mi Xin stationed their troops at the southeast corner outside the city. One day when the soldiers were digging in the soil, they caught a big crab. Cao Han said to the generals under him, "Crabs live in water, but this crab lives on land. That means it has lost the place it should live. The crab has many legs. This predicts that the enemy rescuing armies are coming. Crabs are called 'Xie' which sounds like 'Jie,' which means to raise the siege. I predict that we shall withdraw very soon."

On 5 July Yelu Sha of the State of Liao came with a great army to relieve the city. The Liao army under Yelu Sha and the Song armies fought by

Gaolinghe River (now in Xizhimen, Beijing). The Liao army was defeated and withdrew. At night they came back using a side road. Each of the soldiers of the Liao troops held two torches. The Song soldiers did not know how many soldiers had come, so the Song soldiers were in a great panic. The troops under Yelu Xiuge and the Liao troops under Yelu Sezhen joined forces. Then they were divided into the left wing and the right wing. They fought very bravely. Yelu Xiuge was wounded three times but he still fought on. When Yelu Xuegu saw that these armies had come to the rescue, he opened the city gate and deployed his troops into battle formations. The Liao soldiers beat their drums loudly and they shouted out. The sound of the drums and the war cries of the Liao troops shook the sky. Yelu Xiuge took this chance and ordered his troops to attack. The Song armies were disastrously defeated. Emperor Zhao Guang Yi took a cart drawn by a donkey to escape to the south. Yelu Xiuge was badly wounded. He was not able to ride a horse, so he took a light chariot to pursue the Song troops. The Liao army chased the Song troops to Zhuozhou. They captured innumerable weapons, food supplies and money.

On 8 July Emperor Zhao Guang Yi reached Jintaiyi (also called Jintaidun, now Baoding, Hebei Province). On 10 July Emperor Zhao Guang Yi reached Dingzhou (now Dingzhou, Hebei Province). On 12 July Emperor Zhao Guang Yi ordered Meng Yuan Zhe, the Regional Military Governor of Dingwu, and Cui Han, the Supervisor of the Royal Guard Army, to station the troops under them in Dingzhou (now Dingzhou, Hebei Province). He ordered Li Han Qiong, the Regional Military Governor of Zhangde, to station the troops under him in Zhenzhou (now Zhengding). He ordered Cui Yan Jin, the Regional Military Governor of Heyang, to station the troops under him in Guannan (the area around Hejian, Hebei Province). Emperor Zhao Guang Yi said to these generals, "I am sure that the troops of the State of Liao will come to invade the border areas. When they come, you may join forces with each other and lay ambushes. Then we will surely defeat the invaders." On 27 July Emperor Zhao Guang Yi made it back to Daliang, the capital.

6. The Death of Zhao De Zhao, the Elder Son of the Late Emperor Zhao Kuang Yin

Zhao De Zhao, King of Wugong Prefecture, took part in the expeditions against the State of Northern Han and the State of Liao commanded by Emperor Zhao Guang Yi. He commanded the generals and men under him to fight in the area of Nanjing of the State of Liao. Then, one night Emperor Zhao Guang Yi disappeared.

The generals and men under Zhao De Zhao did not know the whereabouts of the Emperor. They were in great panic. Since the Emperor was not found, the generals under Zhao De Zhao planned to make Zhao De Zhao emperor. But very soon they found out where Emperor Zhao Guang Yi was, and they had to give up the plan. When Emperor Zhao Guang Yi got wind of the generals' plan to make Zhao De Zhao emperor, he was outraged.

After Emperor Zhao Guang Yi and his armies retreated back to Daliang, the Emperor Zhao Guang Yi held off on rewarding the generals who had fought valiantly because he was disappointed in the overall failure of the expedition against the State of Liao. The generals began to complain. On 26 August Zhao De Zhao went to the palace to see Emperor Zhao Guang Yi. He said that the generals hoped that the Emperor would reward them for their contributions in conquering the State of Northern Han. Emperor Zhao Guang Yi became furious and said, "You may do it yourself after you have ascended the throne. There's still time for that!" Zhao De Zho left the hall with a heavy heart. He asked the guards who had followed him into the palace, "Do you have a sword?" They answered, "No. We are not allowed to bring swords into the palace." Zhao De Zhao went into a room in which tea and wine were stored. He found a paring knife in a closet and killed himself with it.

When Emperor Zhao Guang Yi heard that Zhao De Zhao had committed suicide, he was shocked and regretted having said those words. He ran to that room and held Zhao De Zhao's dead body, crying bitterly. He said, "You silly boy. I did not expect that you would kill yourself!" Emperor Zhao Guang Yi made him King of Wei posthumously.

In March 981 Zhao De Fang, the younger son of the late Emperor Zhao Kuang Yin, died at the age of twenty-six. Emperor Zhao Guang Yi made Zhao De Fang King of Chu posthumously.

7. The Death of Zhao Ting Mei, Emperor Zhao Guang Yi's Younger Brother

When Emperor Zhao Guang Yi first ascended the throne, he had appointed his younger brother Zhao Ting Mei as the Governor of Kaifeng Area and made him King of Qi. He also ordered that Zhao De Zhao, the late Emperor Zhao Kuang Yin's elder son, and Zhao De Gong, Zhao Ting Mei's elder son, both be called princes. This gave the people the impression that Emperor Zhao Guang Yi would pass the throne to his younger brother Zhao Ting Mei when he died. And then Zhao Ting Mei should pass the throne to Zhao De Zhao when Zhao Ting Mei died. Then when Zhao De Zhao died, he should pass the throne to Zhao De Gong.

After the expedition of the State of Northern Han, Emperor Zhao Guang Yi promoted Zhao Ting Mei to King of Qin. But Zhao De Zhao committed suicide and Zhao De Fang died not long after. When Zhao Ting Mei thought about this, he felt threatened.

At that time Lu Duo Xun, the Head of the Secretariat and concurrently the Minister of War, was in power. Zhao Pu had been transferred back from Heyang to Daliang in March 977 and Emperor Zhao Guang Yi appointed him as the Protector of the Crown Prince. Zhao Pu had been back at the capital for several years, but Lu Duo Xun said bad words against him in front of Emperor Zhao Guang Yi. Zhao Pu felt very depressed. Zhao Pu's son Zhao Cheng Zong was the Governor of Tanzhou (now Changsha, Hunan Province). He was engaged to the daughter of Princess of Yanguo, sister of Emperor Zhao Guang Yi. In September 981, Emperor Zhao Guang Yi issued an imperial order to let Zhao Cheng Zong come back to the capital from Tanzhou to marry, but in less than a month, Lu Duo Xun ordered that Zhao Cheng Zong should go back to Tanzhou. Zhao Pu was very angry.

It happened that Chai Yu Xi, an official in the capital, reported to Emperor Zhao Guang Yi that Zhao Ting Mei was arrogant and willful and that he was likely to carry out a conspiracy. Emperor Zhao Guang Yi summoned Zhao Pu and asked him whether this would happen. Zhao Pu said that he would investigate. Then Zhao Pu secretly presented a memorandum to the Emperor. The memorandum read, "I am one of the persons who have helped to establish this dynasty. But I have been wrongly accused by certain powerful officials. I was the person who witnessed the order of Empress Dowager Du that Emperor Taizu should pass the throne to Your Majesty. But a powerful official accused me to Emperor Taizu of having said something against Your Majesty. At that time I wrote a memorandum to Emperor Taizu to clarify this matter." Emperor Zhao Guang Yi looked for the memorandum presented by Zhao Pu to Emperor Zhao Kuang Yin. He found it. The memorandum read, "Some officials have accused me of saying something against the Governor of Kaifeng Area, the younger brother of Your Majesty. This is a false accusation. The younger brother of Your Majesty is a person of devotion and filial piety. I would not have said anything against him. I actually witnessed the order of Empress Dowager Du. Your Majesty knows very well that I would not have said anything like that." Having read the memorandum, Emperor Zhao Guang Yi realized that Zhao Pu had been wronged and that the charges were fabricated. And Emperor Zhao Guang Yi opened the gold safe and read the vow of Emperor Zhao Kuang Yin, written by Zhao Pu. Then he issued an imperial order to allow Zhao Cheng Zong to stay in the capital.

On 17 September, Emperor Zhao Guang Yi appointed Zhao Pu as the premier and concurrently Director of the Chancellery. On 18 September Zhao Ting Mei asked permission from Emperor Zhao Guang Yi to be given a rank lower than that of Zhao Pu. Emperor Zhao Guang Yi gave the permission.

One day Emperor Zhao Guang Yi summoned Zhao Pu to the palace and told him that he intended to pass the throne to Zhao Ting Mei when he died. Zhao Pu said, "Emperor Taizu lost the chance to pass the throne to his son. Your Majesty should not lose the chance to pass the throne to the son of Your Majesty." So Emperor Zhao Guang Yi decided not to pass the throne to Zhao Ting Mei.

On 3 March 982 a hall built on the middle of Jinming Lake was completed.

At that time there was no bridge leading to that hall. Emperor Zhao Guang Yi planned to use a boat to get there. But suddenly an official came to report to the Emperor that Zhao Ting Mei was about to start an attack on Emperor Zhao Guang Yi and take the throne. Emperor Zhao Guang Yi cancelled the boat trip.

Zhao Ting Mei had to give up his scheme. Then he feigned illness. He planned that when Emperor Zhao Guang Yi came to his residence to visit him, he would attack the Emperor. But Emperor Zhao Guang Yi saw through his evil plot. On 11 March Emperor Zhao Guang Yi dismissed Zhao Ting Mei as Governor of Kaifeng Area and appointed him as the Commander-in-chief of the army stationed in Luoyang, the Western Capital.

After Zhao Pu had been appointed premier, Lu Duo Xun felt worried. Zhao Pu tried to persuade him to resign many times, but Lu Duo Xin would not give up his power. The investigation carried by Zhao Pu showed that Lu Duo Xun had colluded with Zhao Ting Mei. Zhao Pu reported the result of the investigation to Emperor Zhao Guang Yi. Emperor Zhao Guang Yi issued an order on 6 April to deprive Lu Duo Xun of his position of the Head of the Secretariat and Minister of War and to arrest him and put him in jail. Zhao Bai, an official under Lu Duo Xun, and Yan Mi and Fan De Ming, officials under Zhao Ting Mei, were also arrested. Emperor Zhao Guang Yi ordered Li Fang, a scholar of Hanlin Academy, He Meng, also a scholar of Hanlin Academy, and Cui Ren Ji, the Head of the Royal Guards, to hear the case. In the trial Lu Duo Xun made the following confession: "I sent Zhao Bai to tell Zhao Ting Mei about state secrets several times. In mid September last year I sent Zhao Bai to convey the following words to Zhao Ting Mei, 'I wish that the Emperor would die right away so that I could serve Your Highness heart and soul.' Zhao Ting Mei sent Fan De Ming to tell me, 'What you have said is exactly what I hope for. I also hope that the Emperor dies soon.'" Zhao Bai and Fan De Ming admitted their crimes.

On 14 April Emperor Zhao Guang Yi summoned his civil and military officials to court to discuss what punishment should be given to Zhao Ting Mei, Lu Duo Xun and the other persons involved. All the officials, seventy-four in all, agreed that Lu Duo Xun and Zhao Ting Mei had cursed the Emperor and had committed a capital offense; Zhao Bai and Fan De Ming should be executed. On 15 April Emperor Zhao Guang Yi issued an imperial order to take away all Lu Duo Xun's titles and to send him into exile to Yazhou (now Yacheng Town, Sanya, Hainnan Province); he ordered Zhao Ting Mei to be removed from his position as Commander-in-chief of the army stationed in Luoyang, the Western Capital, and put him under house arrest in Luoyang. Zhao Bai, Yan Mi and Fan De Ming were executed outside the city gate of Daliang.

In May, Zhao Pu began thinking that it was not proper for Zhao Ting Mei to stay in Luoyang, the western capital. So he instigated Li Fu, an official in the Office of the Capital Areas, to tell Emperor Zhao Guang Yi, "the King of Qin is unrepentant. He resents Your Majesty's punishments. Perhaps Your Majesty should send him to a remote place so as to take precautions against any possible actions he might take." On 24 May Emperor Zhao Guang Yi ordered that Zhao Ting Mei be demoted from King of Qin to Duke of Fuling County and sent him to Fangzhou (now Fangxian, Hubei Province). After Zhao Ting Mei arrived at Fangzhou, he was so distressed that he took ill. In January 984, Zhao Ting Mei died at the age of thirty-eight.

When news of this death reached the Emperor, he was extremely sad. He said to the premier, "Ting Mei had been headstrong since he was young. When he grew up he became even more ferocious. I was not hardhearted enough to punish him according to laws. I sent him to Fangzhou because I hoped that he would be repentant. I just wanted to let him come back, but he died. I am really very sorry for his death." Then he made Zhao Ting Mei King of Fangling posthumously. Emperor Zhao Guang Yi ordered that a mourning ceremony be held for the death of Zhao Ting Mei, and he put on the white clothes of mourning. After the ceremony, Emperor Zhao Guang Yi said to the officials standing around him, "I ordered the digging of the West Pond. When the pond was ready, I wanted to go boating in the pond. Ting Mei used this information to secretly plan an attack on me. If I had ordered the officials of the Law Department to investigate this case, Ting Mei would surely have been sentenced to death. But I only sent him to Luoyang. Even so, he was extremely dissatisfied and spoke out against me. I did not punish him for that. I just ordered him to move to Fangzhou. I tried to protect him. I have done my best for Ting Mei. My conscience is clear."

8. Emperor Zhao Guang Yi Makes His Third Son Zhao Yuan Kan Crown Prince

Emperor Zhao Guang Yi had nine sons. The eldest was Zhao Yuan Zuo, who was made King of Chu. When his uncle Zhao Ting Mei was sent into exile to Fangzhou in May 982, Zhao Yuan Zuo tried his best to save him. When Zhao Ting Mei died, Zhao Yuan Zuo suddenly became mad.

The second son was Zhao Yuan Xi, who was made King of Guangping Prefecture in 982. In September 992 he fell seriously ill and then died. Emperor Zhao Guang Yi was very sad. He made Zhao Yuan Xi Crown Prince of Zhaocheng posthumously.

The third son was Zhao De Chang. He was very clever even as a little boy. When he played with his brothers, he named himself marshal of the army. His uncle, then Emperor Zhao Kuang Yin, liked this nephew very much and let him stay in the palace. One day Zhao De Chang went into the Hall of Long Life and sat on the bed of Emperor Zhao Kuang Yin. Emperor Zhao Kuang Yin was greatly surprised. He touched Zhao De Chang's back gently and asked him, "Is it good to be an emperor?" Zhao De Chang answered, "It depends on the will of Heaven." He was made King of Hanin 983, and his name was changed into Zhao Yuan Xiu. He was made King of Xiang in 988 and his name was changed into Zhaoi Yuan Kan. In September 994 he was made King of Shou and was appointed as the Governor of Kaifeng Area.

The fourth son was Zhao Yuan Fen, who was made King of Ji in 983. He was promoted as King of Yue in 986.

The fifth son was Zhao Yuan Jie, who was made King of Yi in 983.

The sixth son was Zhao Yuan Wo, who was made Duke of Xuguo in 988.

The seventh son was Zhao Yuan Cheng, who was made Duke of Jingguo at the age of seven.

The eighth son was Zhao Yuan Yan. He was very clever. Emperor Zhao Guang Yi loved him very much and did not want him to leave the palace. So he was not made king or duke until he was twenty.

The ninth son was Zhao Yuan Yi, who died when he was very young.

Kou Zhun was Emperor Zhao Guang Yi's advisor and Deputy Head of the Privy Council. He was a capable and upright person. He had a quarrel with Zhang Xun, another high ranking official. Emperor Zhao Guang Yi was angry with Kou Zhen and demoted him to Governor of Qingzhou (now Qingzhou, Shandong Province). In September 994, Emperor Zhao Guang Yi summoned Kou Zhun to Daliang from Qingzhou. Kou Zhun went into the palace to see the Emperor. Emperor Zhao Guang Yi asked him, "Why have you come so late?" Kou Zhun said, "I am not allowed to come to the capital without an order from Your Majesty." Emperor Zhao Guang Yi asked him, "Of all my sons, to whom do you think I can pass the throne?" Kou Zhun said, "Your Majesty is choosing the emperor for the people of the whole realm. Your Majesty should not discuss this important matter with women and with the eunuchs around Your Majesty. Your Majesty should not discuss this matter with the favorite ministers of Your Majesty, either. Your Majesty should choose the emperor by yourself, so that the Emperor's choice will satisfy the people of the whole realm." Emperor Zho Guang Yi lowered his head and thought for a long moment. Then he asked the other officials to leave the hall. After all the other officials had left the hall, Emperor Zhao Guang Yi said to Kou Zhun, "Can Yuan Kan be chosen as the emperor?" Kou Zhun answered, "Your Majesty knows your sons best. If Your Majesty thinks that Yuan Kan serve as the future emperor, I hope Your Majesty will make the decision."

Then Emperor Zhao Guang Yi moved to appoint Zhao Yuan Kan as the Governor of Kaifeng Area and made him King of Shou. On 18 August, 995, the Emperor made Zhao Yuan Kan Crown Prince, and Zhao Yuan Kan's name was changed into Zhao Heng. A ceremony to make Zhao Heng the Crown Prince was held in the Ancestral Temple. When the ceremony was over, the people in the capital were all very happy and celebrated in the street. They all praised the Crown Prince, "What a bright young emperor!" When Emperor Zhao Guang Yi heard about this, he was not happy at all. He summoned

Kou Zhun into the palace and said to him, "Now the Crown Prince is very popular among the people. Then what will the people think of me?" Kou Zhun knelt down and touched his head to the ground and said, "This is the blessing for the whole realm!" Emperor Zhao Guang Yi cheered up and went into the imperial harem and told the Empress and the concubines of this. All of them expressed their congratulations to Emperor Zhao Guang Yi.

9. Emperor Zhao Guang Yi Passes Away and Zhao Heng Succeeds to the Throne

On 6 February 997 Emperor Zhao Guang Yi fell ill. Wang Ji En, a eunuch who took care of the Emperor's daily life, disliked Crown Prince Zhao Heng because he was such a brilliant man. He colluded with Li Chang Ling and Hu Dan, officials attending Emperor Zhao Guang Yi, and plotted to put Zhao Yuan Zuo, Emperor Zhao Guang Yi's eldest son, on the throne after Emperor Zhao Guang Yi died.

Lü Duan, the Premier, went into the palace to visit Emperor Zhao Guang Yi who was lying in bed. Lü Duan found that Crown Prince Zhao Heng was not there. This aroused great suspicion in him. He rapidly wrote a secret letter and asked an attendant whom he trusted to get the letter to Crown Prince Zhao Heng, asking him to go to the Emperor's bed chamber and look after Emperor Zhao Guang Yi. When Crown Prince Zhao Heng came, Lü Duan was relieved.

On 29 March 997 Emperor Zhao Guang Yi passed away at the age of fifty-nine. Emperor Zhao Guang Yi had sat on the throne for twenty-two years. After he passed away, the officials suggested that his temple title be Taizong (meaning "Supreme Ancestor").

On the day when the Emperor passed away, Empress Li sent Wang Ji En to summon Lü Duan to the palace to discuss the succession. Lü Duan knew that there had been a great change in the plans for the succession. When Lü Duan and Wang Ji En stepped into the palace, Lü Duan said to Wang Ji En, "Let's go to the study to find out whether the Emperor has left any imperial order about this." Then they went to the study room. Lü Duan pushed Wang Ji En into the Study and locked him in, and asked the guards to guard the door.

Then Lü Duan went to see Empress Li. The Empress said to Lü Duan, "The Emperor has passed away. General practice is to let the eldest son of the Emperor succeed to the throne. What shall we do?" Lü Duan said, "The late Emperor named a Crown Prince just for this occasion. Now, the Emperor has just passed away. Why should you go against his imperial order and put another son on the throne?" Empress Li did not dare to say anything more and kept silent. Then Lü Duan accompanied Crown Prince Zhao Heng into the palace, where Crown Prince Zhao Heng ascended the throne.

Emperor Zhao Heng held the throne for 25 years, further contributing to the stability of the realm. After he died, he was given the temple title of Zhenzong (meaning "True Ancestor").

Statue of Zhao Heng, Emperor Zhenzong of the Song Dynasty

BIBLIOGRAPHY

In writing this book the following original sources were indispensable. For each chapter of the book, I have indicated the specific volumes I drew upon in presenting distant history as it has come to us down through the ages.

Old Book of Tang (Chinese: 舊唐書 or jiutangshu) by Liu Xu (劉煦: 887-946) of the Later Jin Dynasty (936-947)

Old History of the Five Dynasties (Chinese: 舊五代史 or jiuwudaishi) by Xue Ju Zheng (薛居正: 912-981) of the Song Dynasty (960-1279)

New History of the Five Dynasties (Chinese: 新五代史or xinwudaishi) by Ouyang Xiu (歐陽修: 1007-1072) of the Song Dynasty (960-1279)

History of Liao (Chinese: 遼史 or liaoshi) by Tortox (脫脫: 1314-1355) of the Yuan Dynasty (1279-1368)

New Book of Tang (Chinese: 新唐書 or xintangshu) by Ouyang Xiu (歐陽修: 1007-1072) of the Song Dynasty (960-1279)

A Comprehensive Mirror for the Aid of Government (Chinese: 資治通鑒 or zizhitongjian) by Sima Guang (司馬光: 1019-1086) of the Song Dynasty (960-1279)

History of the Song Dynasty (Chinese: 宋史 or songshi) by Tortox (脫脫: 1314-1355) of the Yuan Dynasty (1279-1368)

Continuation of A Comprehensive Mirror for the Aid of Government (Chinese: 續資治通鑒 or xuzizhitongjian) by Bi Yuan (畢沅: 1730-1797) of the Qing Dynasty (1644-1912).

Abbreviations:
    Old Five (Old History of the Five Dynasties)
    New Five (New History of the Five Dynasties)
    Mirror (A Comprehensive Mirror for the Aid of Government)
    Continuation of Mirror (Continuation of A Comprehensive Mirror
    for the Aid of Government)

Chapter One: The Background. The Chaotic Period of Five Dynasties and Ten States (907-979)

The Five Dynasties

Annals of Xizong, Part Two of Vol. 19, *Old Book of Tang*

Annals of Aidi, Part Two of Vol. 20, *Old Book of Tang*

Part One, Annals of Taizu, Part 1 of the Book of the Liang Dynasty, Vol. 1, *Old History of the Five Dynasties* (henceforth, *Old Five*)

Part Two, Annals of Taizu, Part 2 of the Book of the Liang Dynasty, Vol. 2, *Old Five*

Part Three, Annals of Taizu, Part 3 of the Book of the Liang Dynasty, Vol. 3, *Old Five*

Part One, Annals of Modi, Part 8 of the Book of the Liang Dynasty, Vol. 8, *Old Five*

Part Three, Annals of Modi, Part 10 of the Book of the Liang Dyn., Vol. 10 of the *New History of the Five Dynasties* (henceforth, *New Five*)

Part One, Annals of Wuhuang, Part 1 of the Book of the Tang Dynasty, Vol. 25, *Old Five*

Part Two, Annals of Wuhuang, Part 2 of the Book of the Tang Dyn., Vol. 26, *Old Five*

Part One, Annals of Zhuangzong, Part 3 of the Book of the Tang Dyn., Vol. 27, *Old Five*

Part Two, Annals of Zhuangzong, Part 4 of the Book of the Tang Dyn., Vol. 28, *Old Five*

Part Three, Annals of Zhuangzong, Part 5 of the Book of the Tang Dyn., Vol. 29, *Old Five*

Part Four, Annals of Zhuangzong, Part 6 of the Book of the Tang Dyn., Vol. 30, *Old Five*

Part Eight, Annals of Zhuangzong, Part 10 of the Book of the Tang Dyn., Vol. 34, *Old Five*

Part One, Annals of Mingzong, Part 11 of the Book of the Tang Dyn., Vol. 35, *Old Five*

Part Two, Annals of Mingzong, Part 12 of the Book of the Tang Dyn., Vol. 36, *Old Five*

Part Ten, Annals of Mingzong, Part 20 of the Book of the Tang Dyn., Vol. 44, *Old Five*

Annals of Mindi, Part 21 of the Book of the Tang Dyn., Vol. 45, *Old Five*

Part One of Modi, Part 22 of the Book the Tang Dyn., Vol. 46, *Old Five*

Part One, Annals of Taizu, Part 1 of the Book of the Jin Dyn., Vol. 75, *Old Five*

Part Two, Annals of Taizu, Part 2 of the Book of the Jin Dyn., Vol. 76, *Old Five*

Part Six, Annals of Taizu, Part 6 of the Book of the Jin Dyn., Vol. 78, *Old Five*

Part One, Annals of Shaodi, Part 7 of the Book of the Jin Dyn., Vol. 81, *Old Five*

Part Five, Annals of Shaodi, Part 11 of the Book of the Jin Dyn., Vol. 85, *Old Five*

Part One, Annals of Gaozu, Part 1 of the Book of the Han Dyn., Vol. 99, *Old Five*

Part Two, Annals of Gaozu, Part 2 of the Book of the Han Dyn., Vol. 100, *Old Five*

Part One, Annals of Yindi, Part 3 of the Book of the Han Dyn., Vol. 101, *Old Five*

Part Three, Annals of Yindi, Part 5 of the Book of the Han Dyn., Vol. 103, *Old Five*

Part One, Annals of Taizu, Part 1 of the Book of the Zhou Dyn., Vol. 110, *Old Five*

Part One, Annals of Taizu, Part One of Annals, Vol. 1, *History of Liao*

Part Two, Annals of Taizu, Part Two of Annals, Vol. 2, *History of Liao*

Part One, Annals of Taizong, Part Three of Annals, Vol. 3, *History of Liao*

Annals of Shizong, Part Five of Annals, Vol. 5, *History of Liao*.

Part One, Annals of Muzong, Part Six of Annals, Vol. 6, *History of Liao*

Part Two, Annals of Taizong, Part Four of Annals, Vol. 4, *History of Liao*

The Ten States

Biographies of Yang Xing Mi (including Yang Wo, Yang Wei, Yang Pu), Li Sheng (including Li Jing), Wang Shen Zhi (including Wang Yan Jun, Wang Chang, Wang Yan Xi), Part One of Biographies of Bogus Emperors and Kings, Vol. 134, *Old Five*

Biographies of Liu Shou Guang, Liu Zhi (including Liu Fen, Liu Cheng, Liu Chang), Liu Chong, Part Two of Biographies of Bogus Emperors and Kings, Vol. 135, *Old Five*

Biographies of Wang Jian (including Wang Yan), Meng Zhi Xiang (including Meng Chang), Part Three of Biographies of Bogus Emperors and Kings, Vol. 136, *Old Five*

Biographies of Gao Ji Xing (including Gao Cong Hui, Gao Bao Xu), Ma Yin (including Ma Xi Fan extra, Liu Yan), Qian Liu (including Qian Yuan Guan, Qian Zuo, Qian Zong, Qian Ti), Part Two of Biographies of Hereditary Houses, Vol. 133, *Old Five*.

House of King of Chu, Part Six of Houses of Kings, Vol. 66, *New Five*

House of King of Southern Han, Part Five of Houses of Kings, Vol. 65, *New Five*

House of Liu, Kings of Southern Han, Part Four of Houses of Kings, Vol. 481, *History of the Song Dynasty*

House of King of Nanping, Part Nine of Houses of Kings, Vol. 69, *New Five*

Biographies of Huang Chao, Qin Zong Quan and Dong Chang, Part Three of Rebels, Part Three of Vol. 225, *New Book of Tang*

Vol. 252, *A Comprehensive Mirror for the Aid of Government* (henceforth, Mirror)

Vol. 254–258 *Mirror*

Vol. 260, 262–269, 271–272, 274, *Mirror*

Chapter Two: In the Period of the (Later) Zhou Dynasty

The Birth of Zhou Kuang Yin

Part One, Annals of Taizu, Part One of Annals, Vol. 1, *History of the Song Dynasty*

Part One, Annals of Taizu, Part 1 of the Book of the Zhou Dynasty, Vol. 110, *Old Five*

Part Four, Annals of Taizu, Part 4 of the Book of the Zhou Dyn., Vol. 113, *Old Five*

Part One, Annals of Shizong, Part 5 of the Book of the Zhou Dyn., Vol. 114, *Old Five*

Vol. 291, *Mirror*

Under the Reign of Emperor Guo Wei of the (Later) Zhou Dyn.

Part Four, Annals of Taizu, Part 4 of the Book of the Zhou Dyn., Vol. 113, *Old Five*

Part One Annals of Shizong, Part 5 of the Book of the Zhou Dyn., Vol. 114, *Old Five*

Vol. 291, *Mirror*

Under the Reign of Emperor Guo Wei of the (Later) Zhou Dynasty

Part Four, Annals of Taizu, Part 4 of the Book of the Zhou Dynasty, Vol. 113, *Old Five*

Part One, Annals of Shizong, Part 5 of the Book of the Zhou Dyn., Vol. 114, *Old Five*

Volume 290, *Mirror*

Under the Reign of Emperor Guo Rong of the (Later) Zhou Dynasty

3.1 The Great Battle of Gaopin

Part One, Annals of Taizu, Part 1 of Annals, Vol. 1, *History of the Song Dynasty*

Part One, Annals of Shizong, Part 5 of the Book of the Zhou Dyn., Vol. 114, *Old Five*

Biographies of Liu Shou Guang, Liu Zhi (including Liu Fen, Liu Cheng, Liu Chang), Liu Chong, Part Two of Biographies of Bogus Emperors and Kings, Vol. 135, *Old Five*

Vol. 291, *Mirror*

Vol. 292, *Mirror*

3.2 Emperor Guo Rong of the (Later) Zhou Dynasty

Part One, Annals of Shizong, Part 5 of the Book of the Zhou Dyn., Vol. 114, *Old Five*

Vol. 299, *Mirror*

3.3 The Death of Liu Chong; Liu Cheng Jun Is Made Emperor of the State of Northern Han

Biographies of Liu Shou Guang, Liu Zhi (including Liu Fen, Liu Cheng, Liu Chang), Liu Chong, Part Two of Biographies of Bogus Emperors and Kings, Vol. 135, *Old Five*

Vol. 292, *Mirror*

3.4 The War against the State of Southern Tang

Part One, Annals of Taizu, Part 1 of Annals, Vol. 1, *History of the Song Dynasty*

Part Two, Annals of Shizong, Part 6 of the Book of the Zhou Dyn., Vol. 115, *Old Five*

Part Three, Annals of Shizong, Part 7 of the Book of the Zhou Dyn., Vol. 116, *Old Five*

Part Four, Annals of Shizong, Part 8 of the Book of the Zhou Dyn., Vol. 117, *Old Five*

Part Five, Annals of Shizong, Part 9 of the Book of the Zhou Dyn., Vol. 118, *Old Five*

Biographies of Yang Xing Mi (including Yang Wo, Yang Wei, Yang Pu), Li Sheng (including Li Jing), Wang Shen Zhi (including Wang Yan Jun, Wang Chang, Wang Yan Xi), Part One of Biographies of Bogus Emperors and Kings, Vol. 134, *Old Five*

House of King of Southern Tang, Part Two of Houses of Kings, Vol. 62, *New Five*

Biography of Zhao Pu (including his younger brother Zhao An Yi), Vol. 206, *History of the Song Dynasty*

Biographies of Han Ling Kun (including his father Han Lun), Murong Yan Zhao (including his son Murong De Feng, his nephew Murong De Chen), and Fu Yan Qing (including his sons Fu Zhao Yuan and Fu Zhao Shou), Vol. 251 *History of the Song Dynasty*

Vol. 293–294, *Mirror*

3.5 Northern Expedition

Part One, Annals of Taizu, Part One of Annals, Vol. 1, *History of the Song Dynasty*

Part Six, Annals of Shizong, Part 10 of the Book of the Zhou Dynasty, Vol. 119, *Old Five*

Vol. 294, *Mirror*

3.6 *Emperor Guo Rong is Succeeded by Seven-Year-Old Guo Zong Xun*

Part One, Annals of Taizu, Part One of Annals, Vol. 1, *History of the Song Dynasty*

Part Six, Annals of Shizong, Part 10 of the Book of the Zhou Dyn., Vol. 119, *Old Five*

Annals of Gongdi, Part 11 of the Book of the Zhou Dyn., Vol. 120, *Old Five*

Vol. 294, *Mirror*

Chapter Three: The Establishment of the Song Dynasty and the Reign of Emperor Zhao Kuang Yin

Zhao Kuang Yin Is Draped with a Yellow Robe

Part One, Annals of Taizu, Part One of Annals, Vol. 1, *History of the Song Dynasty*

Annals of Gongdi, Part 11 of the Book of the Zhou Dynasty, Vol. 120, *Old Five*

Biographies of Fan Zhi (including his son Fan Min, the son of elder brother Fan Gao), Wang Pu (including his father Wang Zuo), Wei Ren Pu (including his son Wei Xian Xin, his grandson Wei Zhao Liang), Vol. 249, *History of the Song Dynasty*

Biography of Zhao Pu, Vol. 256, *History of the Song Dynasty*

Biographies of Zhao Xiu Yi, Wang Chu Na, Miao Xun, Ma Shao, Chu Zhi Lan, Han
Xian Fu, Shi Xu, Zhou Ke Ming, Liu Han, Wang Huai Yin, Zhao Zi Hua, Feng
Wen Zhi, Shamen Hong Yun, Su Cheng Yin, Ding Shao Wei, Zhao Zi Ran, Vol.
461, *History of the Song Dynasty*

Biographies of Shi Shou Xin (including his sons Shi Bao Xing and Shi Bao Ji, his
grandson Shi Yun Sun), Wang Shen Qi (including his sons Wang Chen Yan
and Wang Cheng Kan, his great grandson Wang Ke Chen, the son of his great
grandson Wand Shi Yue), Gao huai De, Han Chong Yun (including his sons Han
Chon Xun and Han Chong Ye), Zhang Ling Duo, Wang Yan Sheng, Vol. 250,
History of the Song Dynasty

Biographies of the Three Ministers of the Zhou Dynasty: Han Tong, Li Jun, Li Chong
Jin, Vol. 484, *History of the Song Dynasty*

Part One of the Song Dynasty, Vol. 1, *Continuation of Mirror* (henceforth, *Continuation
of Mirror*)

Zhao Kuang Yin Becomes Emperor

Part One, Annals of Taizu, Part One of Annals, Vol. 1, *History of the Song Dynasty*

Biographies of Fan Zhi (including his son Fan Min, the son of elder brother Fan Gao),
Wang Pu (including his father Wang Zuo), Wei Ren Pu (including his son Wei
Xian Xin, his grandson Wei Zhao Liang), Vol. 249, *History of the Song Dynasty*

Annals of Gongdi, Part 11 of the Book of the Zhou Dynasty, Vol. 120, *Old Five*

Part One of the Song Dynasty, Vol. 1, *Continuation of Mirror*

Emperor Zhao Kuang Yin Grants Rewards

Part One, Annals of Taizu, Part One of Annals, Vol. 1, *History of the Song Dynasty*

Part One, Annals of Taizong, Part Four of Annals, Vol. 4, *History of the Song Dynasty*

Part One of the Song Dynasty, Vol. 1, *Continuation of Mirror*

Emperor Zhao Kuang Yin Makes Lady Du Empress Dowager

Part One, Annals of Taizu, Part One of Annals, Vol. 1, *History of the Song Dynasty*

Biographies of Empress Dowager Du, Emperor Taizu's Mother; Empress He, Empr.
of Emperor Taizu; Empress Wang, Empress of Taizu; Empress Song, Empr. of
Emperor Taizu; Empress Yin, Empr. of Emperor Taizong; Empress Fu, Empr. of
Emperor Taizong; Empress Li, Empr. of Emperor Taizong; Empress Li, Empr.
of Emperor Taizong; Empress Pan, Empr. of Emperor Zhenzong; Empress
Guo, Empr. of Emperor Zhenzong; Empress Liu, Empr. of Emperor Zhenzong;
Empress Guo, Empr. of Emperor Zhenzong; Concubine Li, Conc. of Emperor
Zhenzong; Concubine Yang, Conc. of Emperor Zhenzong; Concubine Shen,
Conc. of Emperor Zhenzong; Empress Guo, Empr. of Emperor Renzong;
Empress Cao, Empr. of Emperor Renzong; Concubine Zhang, Conc. of Emperor
Renzong; Concubine Miao, Conc. of Emperor Renzong; Concubine Zhou, Conc.
of Emperor Renzong; Concubine Yang, Conc. of Emperor Renzong; Concubine
Feng, Conc. of Emperor Renzong; Empress Gao, Empr. of Emperor Yingzong;
Part One of Empresses and Concubines, Vol. 242, *History of the Song Dynasty*

Part One of the Song Dynasty, Vol. 1, *Continuation of Mirror*

Appointments of Officials of the Government

Part One, Annals of Taizu, Part One of Annals, Vol. 1, *History of the Song Dynasty*

Biographies of Fan Zhi (including his son Fan Min, his nephew Fan Gao), Wang Pu (including his father Wang Zuo), Wei Ren Fu (including his son Wei Xian Xin, his grandson Wei Zhao Liang), Vol. 249, *History of the Song Dynasty*

Biographies of Wu Ting Zuo (including his sons Wu Yuan Fu, Wu Yuan Zai, Wu Yuan Yi), Li Chong Ju (including his son Li Ji Chang), Wang Ren Shan, Chu Zhao Fu, Li Chu Yun (including his sons Li Ji Long, Li Ji He), Vol. 257, *History of the Song Dynasty*

Part One of the Song Dynasty, Vol. 1, *Continuation of Mirror*

Suppression of Li Jun's Rebellion

Part One, Annals of Taizu, Part One of Annals, Vol. 1, *History of the Song Dynasty*

Biographies of the Three Ministers of the Zhou Dynasty: Han Tong, Li Jun, Li Chong Jin, Vol. 484, *History of the Song Dynasty*

Biographies of Wu Ting Zuo (including his sons Wu Yuan Fu, Wu Yuan Zai, Wu Yuan Yi), Li Chong Ju (including his son Li Ji Chang), Wang Ren Shan, Chu Zhao Fu, Li Chu Yun (including his sons Li Ji Long, Li Ji He), Vol. 257, *History of the Song Dynasty*

Biographies of Shi Shou Xin (including his sons Shi Bao Xing and Shi Bao Ji, his grandson Shi Yun Sun), Wang Shen Qi (including his sons Wang Chen Yan and Wang Cheng Kan, his great grandson Wang Ke Chen, the son of his great grandson Wand Shi Yue), Gao huai De, Han Chong Yun (including his sons Han Chon Xun and Han Chong Ye), Zhang Ling Duo, Wang Yan Sheng, Vol. 250, *History of the Song Dynasty*

Biographies of Guo Chong, Yang Ting Zhang, Song Wo, Xiang Gong, Wang Yan Chao, Zhang Yong De, Wang Quan Bin (including his son Wang Kai), Kang Yan Ze (including Wang Ji Tao, Gao Yan Hui), Vol. 255, *History of the Song Dynasty*

Biography of Zhao Pu (including his younger brother Zhao An Yi), Vol. 256, *History of the Song Dynasty*

Part One of the Song Dynasty, Vol. 1, *Continuation of Mirror*

Suppression of Li Chong Jin's Rebellion

Part One, Annals of Taizu, Part One of Annals, Vol. 1, *History of the Song Dynasty*

Biographies of the Three Ministers of the Zhou Dynasty: Han Tong, Li Jun, Li Chong Jin, Vol. 484, *History of the Song Dynasty*

Biographies of Shi Shou Xin (including his sons Shi Bao Xing and Shi Bao Ji, his grandson Shi Yun Sun), Wang Shen Qi (including his sons Wang Chen Yan and Wang Cheng Kan, his great grandson Wang Ke Chen, the son of his great grandson Wand Shi Yue), Gao huai De, Han Chong Yun (including his sons Han Chon Xun and Han Chong Ye), Zhang Ling Duo, Wang Yan Sheng, Vol. 250, *History of the Song Dynasty*

Biographies of Wu Ting Zuo (including his sons Wu Yuan Fu, Wu Yuan Zai, Wu Yuan Yi), Li Chong Ju (including his son Li Ji Chang), Wang Ren Shan, Chu Zhao Fu, Li Chu Yun (including his sons Li Ji Long, Li Ji He), Vol. 257, *History of the Song Dynasty*

House of Li, Kings of Southern Tang, Part One of Houses of Kings, Vol. 478, *History of the Song Dynasty*

Part One of the Song Dynasty, Vol. 1, *Continuation of Mirror*

Li Jing, King of the State of Southern Tang, Moves His Capital from Jinling to Nanchang

House of King of Southern Tang, Part Two of Houses of Kings, Vol. 62, *New Five*

House of Li, Kings of Southern Tang, Part One of Houses of Kings, Vol. 478, *History of the Song Dynasty*

Part One of the Song Dynasty, Vol. 1, *Continuation of Mirror*

The Death of Empress Dowager Du

Part One, Annals of Taizu, Part One of Annals, Vol. 1, *History of the Song Dynasty*

Biographies of Empress Dowager Du, Emperor Taizu's Mother; Empress He, Empress of Emperor Taizu; Empress Wang, Empress of Taizu; Empress Song, Empr. of Emperor Taizu; Empress Yin, Empr. of Emperor Taizong; Empress Fu, Empr. of Emperor Taizong; Empress Li, Empr. of Emperor Taizong; Empress Li, Empr. of Emperor Taizong; Empress Pan, Empr. of Emperor Zhenzong; Empress Guo, Empr. of Emperor Zhenzong; Empress Liu, Empr. of Emperor Zhenzong; Empress Guo, Empr. of Emperor Zhenzong; Concubine Li, Conc. of Emperor Zhenzong; Concubine Yang, Conc. of Emperor Zhenzong; Concubine Shen, Conc. of Emperor Zhenzong; Empress Guo, Empr. of Emperor Renzong; Empress Cao, Empr. of Emperor Renzong; Concubine Zhang, Conc. of Emperor Renzong; Concubine Miao, Conc. of Emperor Renzong; Concubine Zhou, Conc. of Emperor Renzong; Concubine Yang, Conc. of Emperor Renzong; Concubine Feng, Conc. of Emperor Renzong; Empress Gao, Empr. of Emperor Yingzong; Part One of Empresses and Concubines, Vol. 242 *History of the Song Dynasty*

Part Two of the Song Dynasty, Vol. 2, *Continuation of Mirror*

The Death of Li Jing, King of the State of Southern Tang; Li Yu Ascends the Throne of the State of Southern Tang

Part One, Annals of Taizu, Part One of Annals, Vol. 1, *History of the Song Dynasty*

House of King of Southern Tang, Part Two of Houses of Kings, Vol. 62, *New Five*

House of Li, Kings of Southern Tang, Part One of Houses of Kings, Vol. 478, *History of the Song Dynasty*

Part Two of the Song Dynasty, Vol. 2, *Continuation of Mirror*

Emperor Zhao Kuang Yin Relieves the Great Generals of their Military Power

Biographies of Shi Shou Xin (including his sons Shi Bao Xing and Shi Bao Ji, his grandson Shi Yun Sun), Wang Shen Qi (including his sons Wang Chen Yan and Wang Cheng Kan, his great grandson Wang Ke Chen, the son of his great grandson Wand Shi Yue), Gao huai De, Han Chong Yun (including his sons Han Chon Xun and Han Chong Ye), Zhang Ling Duo, Wang Yan Sheng, Vol. 250, *History of the Song Dynasty*

Part Two of the Song Dynasty, Vol. 2, *Continuation of Mirror*

The Conquest of the Area of Jingnan (the State of Nanping) and the Area of Hunan (the State of Chu)

Part One, Annals of Taizu, Part One of Annals, Vol. 1, *History of the Song Dynasty*

Biographies of Han Ling Kun (including his father Han Lun), Murong Yan Zhao (including his son Murong De Feng, his nephew Murong De Chen), and Fu Yan Qing (including his sons Fu Zhao Yuan and Fu Zhao Shou), Vol. 251, *History of the Song Dynasty*

Biographies of Wu Ting Zuo (including his sons Wu Yuan Fu, Wu Yuan Zai, Wu Yuan Yi), Li Chong Ju (including his son Li Ji Chang), Wang Ren Shan, Chu Zhao Fu, Li Chu Yun (including his sons Li Ji Long, Li Ji He), Vol. 257, *History of the Song Dynasty*

Biographies of Wang Zan, Zhang Bao Xu, Zhao Pi, Lu Huai Zhong, Wang Ji Xun, Ding De Yu, Zhang Yan Tong, Liang Jiong, Shi Gui, Tian Qin Zuo, Hou Yun, Wang Wen Bao, Zhai Shou Su, Wang Shen, Liu Shen Qiong, Vol. 274, *History of the Song Dynasty*

House of Zhou, Kings of Hunan, House of Gao, Kings of Jingnan, House of Liu, Kings of Zhangquan, House of Chen, Part Six of Houses of Kings, Vol. 483, *History of the Song Dynasty*

Part Three of the Song Dynasty, Vol. 3, *Continuation of Mirror*

Zhao Pu Becomes the Manager of the Governmental affairs

Part One, Annals of Taizu, Part One of Annals, Vol. 1, *History of the Song Dynasty*

Biography of Zhao Pu (including his younger brother Zhao An Yi), Vol. 206, *History of the Song Dynasty*

Biographies of Wu Ting Zuo (including his sons Wu Yuan Fu, Wu Yuan Zai, Wu Yuan Yi), Li Chong Ju (including his son Li Ji Chang), Wang Ren Shan, Chu Zhao Fu, Li Chu Yun (including his sons Li Ji Long, Li Ji He), Vol. 257, *History of the Song Dynasty*

Biographies of Fan Zhi (including his son Fan Min, the son of elder brother Fan Gao), Wang Pu (including his father Wang Zuo), Wei Ren Pu (including his son Wei Xian Xin, his grandson Wei Zhao Liang), Vol. 249, *History of the Song Dynasty*

Part Three of the Song Dynasty, Vol. 3, *Continuation of Mirror*

The Expedition against the State of Shu

Part One, Annals of Taizu, Part One of Annals, Vol. 1, *History of the Song Dynasty*

House of Meng, Kings of Western Shu, Part Two of Houses of Kings, Vol. 479, *History of the Song Dynasty*

Biographies of Guo Chong, Yang Ting Zhang, Song Wo, Xiang Gong, Wang Yan Chao, Zhang Yong De, Wang Quan Bin (including his son Wang Kai), Kang Yan Ze (including Wang Ji Tao, Gao Yan Hui), Vol. 255, *History of the Song Dynasty*

Biographies of Wu Ting Zuo (including his sons Wu Yuan Fu, Wu Yuan Zai, Wu Yuan Yi), Li Chong Ju (including his son Li Ji Chang), Wang Ren Shan, Chu Zhao Fu, Li Chu Yun (including his sons Li Ji Long, Li Ji He), Vol. 257, *History of the Song Dynasty*

Biographies of Zhang Mei, Guo Shou Yi, Yin Chong Ke, Liu Ting Rang, Yuan Ji Zhong, Cui Yan Jin, Zhang Ting Han, Huangfu Ji Ming, Zhang Qiong, Vol. 259, *History of the Song Dynasty*

Biographies of Cao Bin (including his sons Cao Can, Cao Wei, Cao Cong), Pan Mei (including Li Chao), Vol. 258, *History of the Song Dynasty*

Part Four of the Song Dynasty, Vol. 4, *Continuation of Mirror*

Part Five of the Song Dynasty, Vol. 5, *Continuation of Mirror*

Emperor Zhao Kuang Yin Visits Zhao Pu in a Snowy Night

Biography of Zhao Pu (including his younger brother Zhao An Yi), Vol. 206, *History of the Song Dynasty*

Part Five of the Song Dynasty, Vol. 5, *Continuation of Mirror*

The Situation in the State of Northern Han

House of Liu, Kings of Northern Han, Part Five of Houses of Kings, Vol. 482, *History of the Song Dynasty*

Part Five of the Song Dynasty, Vol. 5, *Continuation of Mirror*

The Situation in the State of Liao

Part Two, Annals of Muzong, Part Seven of Annals, Vol. 7, *History of Liao*

Part One, Annals of Jingzong, Part Eight of Annals, Vol. 8, *History of Liao*

Part Five of the Song Dynasty, Vol. 5, *Continuation of Mirror*

Expedition against the State of Northern Han

Part Two, Annals of Taizu, Part Two of Annals, Vol. 2, *History of the Song Dynasty*

Biographies of Hou Yi (including his sons Hou Ren Ju and Hou Ren Bao, his grandson Hou Yan Guang), Zhang Cong En, Hu Yan Ke, Xue Huai Rang, Zhao Zan, Li Ji Xun, Yao Yuan Fu, Zhao Chao, Vol. 254, *History of the Song Dynasty*

Biographies of Cao Bin (including his sons Cao Can, Cao Wei, Cao Cong), Pan Mei (including Li Chao), Vol. 258, *History of the Song Dynasty*

Biographies of Shi Shou Xin (including his sons Shi Bao Xing and Shi Bao Ji, his grandson Shi Yun Sun), Wang Shen Qi (including his sons Wang Chen Yan and Wang Cheng Kan, his great grandson Wang Ke Chen, the son of his great grandson Wand Shi Yue), Gao huai De, Han Chong Yun (including his sons Han Chon Xun and Han Chong Ye), Zhang Ling Duo, Wang Yan Sheng, Vol. 250, *History of the Song Dynasty*

Biographies of Cao Han, Yang Xin (including his younger brother Yang Si Zan), Dang Jin, Li Han Qiong, Liu Yu, Li Huai Zhong, Mi Xin, Tian Chong Jin, Liu Ting Han, Cui Han, Vol. 260, *History of the Song Dynasty*

House of Liu, Kings of Northern Han, Part Five of Houses of Kings, Vol. 482, *History of the Song Dynasty*

Part Five of the Song Dynasty, Vol. 5, *Continuation of Mirror*

The Situation in the State of Southern Han

House of Liu, Kings of Southern Han, Part Four of Houses of Kings, Vol. 481, *History of the Song Dynasty*

Biographies of Liu Shou Guang, Liu Zhi (incl. Liu Fen, Liu Cheng, Liu Chang), Liu Chong, Part Two of Biographies of Bogus Emperors and Kings, Vol. 135, *Old Five*

House of King of Southern Han, Part Five of Houses of Kings, Vol. 65, *New Five*

The Expedition against the State of Southern Han

Part Two, Annals of Taizu, Part Two of Annals, Vol. 2, *History of the Song Dynasty*

Biographies of Cao Bin (including his sons Cao Can, Cao Wei, Cao Cong), Pan Mei (including Li Chao), Vol. 258, *History of the Song Dynasty*

House of Liu, Kings of Southern Han, Part Four of Houses of Kings, Vol. 481, *History of the Song Dynasty*

Biographies of Liu Shou Guang, Liu Zhi (including Liu Fen, Liu Cheng, Liu Chang), Liu Chong, Part Two of Biographies of Bogus Emperors and Kings, Vol. 135, *Old Five*

House of King of Southern Han, Part Five of Houses of Kings, Vol. 65, *New Five*

Part Five of the Song Dynasty, Vol. 5, *Continuation of Mirror*

Part Six of the Song Dynasty, Vol. 6, *Continuation of Mirror*

The Relationship between Emperor Zhao Kuang Yin and His Premiers

Biographies of Fan Zhi (including his son Fan Min, the son of elder brother Fan Gao), Wang Pu (including his father Wang Zuo), Wei Ren Pu (including his son Wei Xian Xin, his grandson Wei Zhao Liang), Vol. 249, *History of the Song Dynasty*

Biography of Zhao Pu (including his younger brother Zhao An Yi), Vol. 206, *History of the Song Dynasty*

Part Four of the Song Dynasty, Vol. 4, *Continuation of Mirror*

Part Six of the Song Dynasty, Vol. 6, *Continuation of Mirror*

The Situation in the State of Jiangnan

Part Three, Annals of Taizu, Part Three of Annals, Vol. 3, *History of the Song Dynasty*

House of Li, Kings of Southern Tang, Part One of Houses of Kings, Vol. 478, *History of the Song Dynasty*

House of Qian, Kings of Wuyue, Part Three of Houses of Kings, Vol. 480, *History of the Song Dynasty*

Biographies of Xue Ju Zheng (including his son Xue Wei Ji), Shen Lun (including his son Shen Ji Zhong), Lu Duo Xun (including his father Lu Yi), Song Qi (including Song Xiong), Vol. 264, *History of the Song Dynasty*

Part Seven of the Song Dynasty, Vol. 7, *Continuation of Mirror*

The Expedition against the State of Jiangnan

Part Three, Annals of Taizu, Part Three of Annals, Vol. 3, *History of the Song Dynasty*

House of Li, Kings of Southern Tang, Part One of Houses of Kings, Vol. 478, *History of the Song Dynasty*

House of Qian, Kings of Wuyue, Part Three of Houses of Kings, Vol. 480, *History of*

Qian Ti, King of the State of Wuyue, Goes to the Court of the Song Dynasty

Emperor Zhao Kuang Yin Makes a Trip to Luoyang, the Western Capital

Emperor Zhao Kuang Yin and His Brothers and Sons

Emperor Zhao Kuang Yin's Last Effort to Conquer the State of Northern Han

Emperor Zhao Kuang Yin Passes Away

Part Three, Annals of Taizu, Part Three of Annals, Vol. 3, *History of the Song Dynasty*

Part Eight of the Song Dynasty, Vol. 8, *Continuation of Mirror*

Chapter Four: The Reign of Emperor Zhao Guang Yi

Zhao Guang Yi Ascends the Throne of the Song Dynasty

Part One, Annals of Taizong, Part Four of Annals, Vol. 4, *History of the Song Dynasty*

Biographies of Zhao Ting Mei, King of Wei, Zhao De Zhao, King Of Yan, and Zhao De Fang, King of Qin (including Zhao Zi Cheng, the Descendent of Zhao De Fang), Part One of the Royal Clan, Vol. 244, *History of the Song Dynasty*

Biography of Zhao Pu (including his younger brother Zhao An Yi), Vol. 206, *History of the Song Dynasty*

Part Nine of the Song Dynasty, Vol. 9, *Continuation of Mirror*

Qian Ti Hands Over the State of Wuyue to Emperor Zhao Guang Yi

Part One, Annals of Taizong, Part Four of Annals, Vol. 4, *History of the Song Dynasty*

House of Qian, Kings of Wuyue, Part Three of Houses of Kings, Vol. 480, *History of the Song Dynasty*

House of Zhou, Kings of Hunan, House of Gao, Kings of Jingnan, House of Liu, Kings of Zhangquan, House of Chen, Part Six of Houses of Kings, Vol. 483, *History of the Song Dynasty*

Part Nine of the Song Dynasty, Vol. 9, *Continuation of Mirror*

The Death of Li Yu

Part One, Annals of Taizong, Part Four of Annals, Vol. 4, *History of the Song Dynasty*

House of Li, Kings of Southern Tang, Part One of Houses of Kings, Vol. 478, *History of the Song Dynasty*

Part Nine of the Song Dynasty, Vol. 9, *Continuation of Mirror*

The Expedition against the State of Northern Han

Part One, Annals of Taizong, Part Four of Annals, Vol. 4, *History of the Song Dynasty*

Biographies of Cao Bin (including his sons Cao Can, Cao Wei, Cao Cong), Pan Mei (including Li Chao), Vol. 258, *History of the Song Dynasty*

Biographies of Cao Han, Yang Xin (including his younger brother Yang Si Zan), Dang Jin, Li Han Qiong, Liu Yu, Li Huai Zhong, Mi Xin, Tian Chong Jin, Liu Ting Han, Cui Han, Vol. 260, *History of the Song Dynasty*

Biographies of Zhang Mei, Guo Shou Yi, Yin Chong Ke, Liu Ting Rang, Yuan Ji Zhong, Cui Yan Jin, Zhang Ting Han, Huangfu Ji Ming, Zhang Qiong, Vol. 259, *History of the Song Dynasty*

Biographies of Li Jin Qing (including his son Li Yan Wo), Yang Mei, He Ji Jun (including his son He Cheng Ju), Li Han Chao (including his son Li Shou En), Guo Jin (the biography of Niu Si Jin is attached), Li Qian Pu (including his son Li Yun Zheng), Yao Nei Bin, Dong Zun Hui, He Wei Zhong, Ma Ren Yu, Vol.

273, *History of the Song Dynasty*

House of Liu, Kings of Northern Han, Part Five of Houses of Kings, Vol. 482, *History of the Song Dynasty*

Part Nine of the Song Dynasty, Vol. 9, *Continuation of Mirror*

Part Ten of the Song Dynasty, Vol. 10, *Continuation of Mirror*

Emperor Zhao Guang Yi's Expedition against the State of Liao and His efforts to Take Back the Territory of Youzhou and Jizhou

Part One, Annals of Taizong, Part Four of Annals, Vol. 4, *History of the Song Dynasty*

Part Two, Annals of Jingzong, Part Nine of Annals, Vol. 9, *History of Liao*

Biographies of Zhao Ting Mei, King of Wei, Zhao De Zhao, King Of Yan, and Zhao De Fang, King of Qin (including Zhao Zi Cheng, the Descendent of Zhao De Fang), Part One of the Royal Clan, Vol. 244, *History of the Song Dynasty*

Part Ten of the Song Dynasty, Vol. 10, *Continuation of Mirror*

The Death of Zhao De Zhao, the Elder Son of the Late Emperor Zhao Kuang Yin

Part One, Annals of Taizong, Part Four of Annals, Vol. 4, *History of the Song Dynasty*

Biographies of Zhao Ting Mei, King of Wei, Zhao De Zhao, King Of Yan, and Zhao De Fang, King of Qin (including Zhao Zi Cheng, the Descendent of Zhao De Fang), Part One of the Royal Clan, Vol. 244, *History of the Song Dynasty*

Part Ten of the Song Dynasty, Vol. 10, *Continuation of Mirror*

The Death of Zhao Ting Mei, Emperor Zhao Guang Yi's Younger Brother

Part One, Annals of Taizong, Part Four of Annals, Vol. 4, *History of the Song Dynasty*

Biographies of Zhao Ting Mei, King of Wei, Zhao De Zhao, King Of Yan, and Zhao De Fang, King of Qin (including Zhao Zi Cheng, the Descendent of Zhao De Fang), Part One of the Royal Clan, Vol. 244, *History of the Song Dynasty*

Biographies of Xue Ju Zheng (including his son Xue Wei Ji), Shen Lun (including his son Shen Ji Zhong), Lu Duo Xun (including his father Lu Yi), Song Qi (including Song Xiong), Vol. 264, *History of the Song Dynasty*

Biography of Zhao Pu (including his younger brother Zhao An Yi), Vol. 206, *History of the Song Dynasty*

Biographies of Chai Yu Xi, Zhang Xun, Yang Shou Yi, Zhao Rong, Zhou Ying, Wang Ji Ying, Wang Xian, Vol. 268, *History of the Song Dynasty*

Part Ten of the Song Dynasty, Vol. 10, *Continuation of Mirror*

Part Eleven of the Song Dynasty, Vol. 11, *Continuation of Mirror*

Emperor Zhao Guang Yi makes His Third Son Zhao Yuan Kan the Crown Prince

Part Two, Annals of Taizong, Part Five of Annals, Vol. 5, *History of the Song Dynasty*

Part One, Annals of Zhenzong, Part Six of Annals, Vol. 6, *History of the Song Dynasty*

Biographies of Zhao Yuan Zuo, King of Han, Zhao Yuan Xi, Crown Prince of Zhaocheng, Zhao Yuan Fen, King of Shang, Zhao Yuan Jie, King of Yue, Zhao Yuan Wo, King of Zhen, Zhao Yuan Cheng, King of Chu, Zhao Yuan Yan, King of Zhou, Crown Prince of Daoxian,, and Zhao Yun Rang, King of Pu, Part Two of the Royal Clan, Vol. 245, *History of the Song Dynasty*

Biographies of Lü Duan, Bi Shi An (including his sons Bi Zhong Yan and Bi Zhong You), Kou Zhun, Vol. 281, *History of the Song Dynasty*

Part Eighteen of the Song Dynasty, Vol. 18, *Continuation of Mirror*

       Emperor Zhao Guang Yi Passes Away and Zhao Yuan Kan
       Succeeds to the Throne

Part Two, Annals of Taizong, Part Five of Annals, Vol. 5, *History of the Song Dynasty*

Part One, Annals of Zhenzong, Part Six of Annals, Vol. 6, *History of the Song Dynasty*

Biographies of Lü Duan, Bi Shi An (including his sons Bi Zhong Yan and Bi Zhong You), Kou Zhun, Vol. 281, *History of the Song Dynasty*

Part Nineteen of the Song Dynasty, Vol. 19, *Continuation of Mirror*

Index